Australian One-Act Plays for Young Adults

Australian One-Act Plays for Young Adults

BRADY LLOYD

methuen | drama
LONDON • NEW YORK • OXFORD • NEW DELHI • SYDNEY

METHUEN DRAMA
Bloomsbury Publishing Plc, 50 Bedford Square, London, WC1B 3DP, UK
Bloomsbury Publishing Inc, 1359 Broadway, New York, NY 10018, USA
Bloomsbury Publishing Ireland, 29 Earlsfort Terrace, Dublin 2, D02 AY28, Ireland

BLOOMSBURY, METHUEN DRAMA and the Methuen Drama logo are trademarks of
Bloomsbury Publishing Plc

First published in Great Britain 2026

Contents

Illustrations

Brady Lloyd is an Adelaide-born playwright, performer and educator. Having lived in Australia and the UK, he has a passion for telling universal stories that celebrate the strength of the human spirit, blending hope, humour and heart. *Australian One-Act Plays for Young Adults* is Lloyd's debut publication.

Foreword

Writing Stories with Heart for Young Adults

Associate Professor Sarah Peters, Flinders University.

Brady Lloyd writes plays with immense heart, warmth and humour. Having taught high school drama for a number of years, he knows the value (and challenge!) in telling a compelling story with a variety of meaningful roles that will allow an ensemble cast to shine. Each play in this collection incorporates a balance of high-energy ensemble scenes with moments of quieter reflection, often weaving a tapestry of direct address monologues throughout, and punctuated with a well-timed dream sequence for good measure. Yet the most prominent feature in his body of work is the ability to engage with difficult themes – death, grief, longing, disaster – in a sensitive and authentic way, and to balance these narratives with humour and hope. Brady writes plays with heart, from the heart.

I have had the great privilege of reading drafts of each of Brady's plays as they were being developed. Looking over the early feedback it's clear the dramaturgical strengths of this body of work were ever present; Brady knows what he wants to say and where he wants to take his audience, and from the opening beats of performance the audience knows they're in safe hands. That clarity of intent is something many playwrights aspire to, and it is a quality that makes these plays particularly engaging. Theatre critic and playwright Elinor Fuchs asserts that a key question to ask of any play is 'what has this world demanded of me? [. . . and] how does it make this intention known?' (2004: 9). Brady's plays demand that we do not shy away from difficult conversations, and that we never underestimate the power of hope. The difficult conversations serve as a mirror, inviting us to reflect on our own relationships and actions. Have we done what was easy over what was right? Have we acted in self-interest over acting in service to others? Have we responded with fear or judgement over empathy and understanding? And ultimately, how might we lead with kindness, as so many of the protagonists in these pages learn to do? Brady writes in the note to his play *Encore* that he has always believed that ordinary people can do extraordinary things. If true character is revealed when human nature is under pressure, then Brady's work is an exploration of what that human nature looks like when struggle is coupled with hope. Hope in the form of friendship, courageous vulnerability, community and determination. This is what is demanded of us through each play in this anthology.

These plays reflect the socio-political consciousness that theatre researchers Selina Busby, Kelly Freebody and Charlene Rajendran describe as underpinning the history of youth theatre, as they simultaneously highlight the enjoyment of performance and live storytelling, just as they aspire to make a difference in the world, 'no matter how small or large' (2023: 9). Engaging with theatre, particularly through narratives that focus on relatable stories and emotional depth, can foster empathy, improve communication skills and build confidence. Professor of Creative Education Jonathan Neelands suggests that drama has 'a unique and important contribution to make to children's social and political development […] and that this is at the heart not only of school drama but drama in a democratic society' (2009: 179). Drama can be a powerful tool for social and emotional learning, helping young people navigate their own emotions and understand the perspectives of others 'through building community, enabling expression, connecting with themselves and their bodies, and building understanding' (Busby, Freebody and Rajendran, 2023: 9). From the sometimes overwhelming context of a hospital in *Encore*, to the rigid rules and regulations of a remand centre in *Birdies*, or the chaos and community of a rural town hall during crisis in *Ember*, each play in this anthology offers a rich and nuanced world for young adults to step into, learn from and grow.

Author and Professor of Theatre Jill Dolan argues that performing, and in particular performing a role that might be quite different to your own identity, can 'offer glimpses of how people might be together in a more respectful, care-full, loving human community' and that performance can enable us to contemplate a better world, one that 'can incorporate love, hope, and commonality alongside a deep understanding of difference' (2005: 64). Across this anthology are characters wrestling with their sense of difference and looking for ways to belong – whether that's distanced siblings Ally and Felicity in *Encore* who find a way to be there for each other during their sister's cancer treatment, or bride-to-be Flora in *Bloom* who summons the courage to share her doubts and fears with her best friends. There are characters who face up to their mistakes, like Vi to her son Jack in *Ember* who says things she doesn't mean in the heat of the moment but is able to acknowledge the hurt in her words and apologise, or Tanya in *Pinky* who was dismissive and derisive of her work colleague Journee but is eventually able to listen with empathy and understanding. And while often serving double duty as comedic relief, there are characters who simply cannot hide their delight in one another and, despite their often tongue-tied and awkward embarrassment, find the confidence to act on their attractions. Nothing builds confidence in a young person like having the opportunity to walk in the shoes of a character who is brave enough to wear their heart on their sleeve and tell the people they like that they like them.

Stories are how we understand ourselves and the world around us, and the stories to be found within these pages are filled with courage, care and heart.

Enjoy xo

Busby, S., Freebody, K. and Rajendran, C. 2023. *The Routledge Companion to Theatre and Young People*. Routledge.

Dolan, Jill. 2005. 'Finding Our Feet in One Another's Shoes: Multiple-Character Solo Performance'. *Utopia in Performance: Finding Hope at the Theater*. University of Michigan Press, pp. 63–88.

Fuchs, E. 2004. 'EF's Visit to a Small Planet: Some Questions to Ask a Play'. *Theater*, vol. 34, no. 2, pp. 4–9.

Neelands, J. 2009. 'Acting Together: Ensemble as a Democratic Process in Art and Life'. *RiDE: The Journal of Applied Theatre and Performance*, vol. 14, no. 2, pp. 173–189.

Acknowledgements

I had the privilege of writing these plays on Kaurna land. I acknowledge the Kaurna people as the custodians of the Adelaide Plains region. I recognise Kaurna people's connection with their land and honour and pay my respects to Kaurna elders, both past and present, and all generations of Aboriginal people, now and into the future.

A heartfelt thank you to the team at Bloomsbury Publishing, especially to Dom O'Hanlon and Mark Jones, for your guidance, patience and encouragement. Your support throughout the process has made this first-time experience genuinely joyful.

Thank you to my dear friend and mentor Associate Professor Sarah Peters, who has kindly written the foreword of this book. I am so grateful that you gave me the gentle push I needed to write the very first play.

These plays were written and first performed at Cardijn College in Adelaide, South Australia. Thank you to Cardijn College for your support in allowing me the creative freedom to write and stage these original works. Thank you to Tyler Marsland for capturing the energy of the original productions.

To the incredible drama students I was lucky enough to teach. You were the original cast members of *Encore*, *Birdies*, *Ember*, *Pinky* and *Bloom* and I couldn't be more thankful. Thank you for bringing so much heart and humour to our rehearsals and for being pivotal in first bringing these characters to life. I hope many more young people continue to find joy and camaraderie through these plays like we did.

I'd also like to acknowledge the charities we partnered with through these original productions: St Vincent de Paul, the Childhood Cancer Association and the Pink Elephants Support Network. Your ongoing work is deeply inspiring, and it was such a privilege to raise funds and awareness for your cause.

I am so lucky to be surrounded by an extraordinary support network. Thank you to the many friends who have supported me with encouragement, high fives and hugs.

It's no coincidence that many of my plays feature strong, remarkable women. To my mum, Gill, my sister, Bloss, and my late nan, Patricia: so much of what I create is inspired by you. Thank you for being such powerful role models. Thank you also to my late dad, Steve. I'm grateful for our Villi's catch-ups, our conversations and your support.

To my incredible husband Stuart. You are my biggest cheerleader in life and have encouraged me every step of this journey. Your compassion, patience and love are a constant source of strength in my life. I am so grateful for you today and every day.

Finally, thank you to *you*, for reading, performing or studying these plays. I hope they serve as a source of creativity and connection wherever they find you.

Preface

In 2019, I decided to bite the bullet and write my first play. I had been struggling to find a suitable script for my senior drama class and I was looking for a meaningful piece, with roles that could stretch and challenge my very capable students and provide opportunities for everyone in the class to shine.

I've always been drawn to stories with immense heart and a sense of humour. I love hearing about ordinary people doing extraordinary things, often in unexpected or unconventional ways. These kinds of stories have consistently influenced me and inspired my writing of the plays in this anthology.

Following that first play, I continued writing original pieces for each of my drama classes over five years, and these now form the collection in *Australian One-Act Plays for Young Adults*. In each story, I set out to incorporate powerful themes, captivating narratives, richly varied characters, and a compelling balance of humour and heart. I also wanted each piece to accommodate varying cast sizes, gender and cultural demographics and the diverse skills and abilities of a group.

As a collection, I hope these plays spark discussion around significant themes including infertility and society's expectations on women, issues in our correctional system, domestic violence, terminal illness, natural disasters and the human response to tragedy. When we first staged these plays, we also partnered with a relevant charity that aligned with the focus of the piece, to deepen our understanding and connection to these important themes.

For each play, I've included a playwright's note and a set of discussion questions. I hope these serve as a helpful addition and encourage reflection, analysis, creative exploration and critical thinking around dramaturgy, representation and theatricality.

Ultimately, I hope that the plays in *Australian One-Act Plays for Young Adults* celebrate the strength of the human spirit, blending hope, humour and heart. Thank you for engaging with these plays, either through performance or study, and I hope they offer meaningful moments of connection, reflection and creative expression.

Bloom

Playwright's note

'Often, all we need is a little bit of love'.

Bloom is a story inspired by friendship. While friendship can mean different things to different people, for many of us, our friendships enrich our lives with love and laughter, provide some light when life seems dark and strengthen our capacity to keep going when we are truly tested. Often our friendships also guide us to consider who and what we are grateful for. There's something to be said for routinely practising gratitude. Like Kiki's followers are encouraged to do, I hope *Bloom* inspires people to reach out to their nearest and dearest with messages of love.

Amongst moments of light-heartedness, there are several central themes examined in *Bloom*: the depths of human resilience in the face of adversity, the power of hope, and what it means to wholeheartedly accept and celebrate the eccentricities of the people around us.

Through Flora's passion for botany, we also explore the notion that plants and people are not too dissimilar after all. To truly flourish, both plants and people need necessary nutrients, enough sunlight, adequate space to grow and the right environment to thrive. When times are tough and our resolve wavers, much like a plant or flower, 'Often, all we need is a little bit of love'.

All proceeds from the original production of *Bloom* were donated to the St Vincent de Paul Women's Crisis Centre, a crisis intervention for women often fleeing domestic and family violence. The Women's Crisis Centre combines accommodation and wraparound services to ensure women have support, safety and peace of mind for sound decision-making within a calm, child-friendly environment. I encourage future productions to consider supporting a similar organisation or cause, amplifying the play's message and extending its reach into the wider community.

Brady Lloyd

Bloom by Brady Lloyd

Synopsis

Bloom follows the story of Flora as she is taken on a surprise autumn camping trip with her best friends, and a few extras, before marrying the man of her dreams. Though the trip is fastidiously planned by a former Girl Guide, the 'scheduled fun' is thrown askew by a mega mosquito mishap, the local handyman heart-throb, a narky sister-in-law to be and a revelation that could forever fracture a friendship.

Setting

Bloom takes place at a typical Australian campsite on a weekend away in a national park.

Characters

Eight characters (6F, 2M). Note: This play accommodates flexible and inclusive casting.

Flora, 28. A green thumb. Flora is a gentle, sensitive soul.

Beth, 28. Beth is Flora's oldest friend. Sassy, protective and loving.

Kiki, 27. Bright and enthusiastic, Kiki radiates positivity and a grateful approach to life.

Georgina, 27. A lovable perfectionist, determined to plan the perfect weekend.

Camilla-Joy, 35. Camilla-Joy is Flora's prickly, soon to be sister-in-law.

Kat, 25. Calm and thoughtful, Kat is Camilla-Joy's work colleague.

Hans, 45. Hans is a friendly and flamboyant park ranger.

Cliff, 30. The rugged, handyman heart-throb of the national park.

Scene One

Saturday, mid-morning. The first day of **Flora***'s surprise camping trip.* **Flora, Beth, Kiki, Camilla-Joy** *and* **Kat** *tentatively enter the campground, eyes closed and holding each other's hands. The site has been prepared for a celebration with bunting strung up. The girls are led by* **Georgina** *who is peaking with enthusiasm.*

Georgina This way! This way! Don't open your eyes yet. Keep them closed! I hope you will love this place as much as I do and that this will be an amazing pre-wedding celebration for our beautiful Flora. OK, open your eyes in three, two, one . . . open!

Kiki (*screaming*) Ahhh . . . mazing!

Georgina I knew you'd love it!

Kiki Georgina, babe, what are we doing here?

Georgina I'm glad you asked. Look around. I wonder if you can guess?

Camilla-Joy I don't do guessing games.

Beth Based on the tents I can see and the fact we're clearly in the middle of nowhere, I'm going to guess we are camping?

Georgina Wrong!

Kiki Oh thank God!

Georgina I promised you a weekend of fun, friendship and something entirely glamorous! So we're not camping, we're g-lamping! Ta-da! Flora, what do you think?

Flora It sounds great, George! This'll be fun! A chance to breathe in some fresh air. To get amongst nature! It's just so exciting we're all together! (*To* **Georgina**.) Thank you for organising this. I know you would have put a lot of time and effort into making this weekend happen. I really appreciate it. And I know the girls do too, right girls?

All Yeh . . . sure . . . of course.

Kiki This is divine. A little camping trip with just us girls. It's going to be fab. One question though. What's that smell, babe?

Beth Pretty sure that's nature.

Kiki (*trying to maintain her positivity*) Oh cool! Rustic!

Beth Actually, that's making me a little nauseous.

Georgina (*to* **Flora**) I'm so happy you're happy. I just thought, what could be better than getting out in the outdoors? I know you love your plants and it's so beautiful in the autumn. Thanks for letting me organise this, girls! I love organising things! Anytime I can write a list and populate a spreadsheet, I'm a happy girl.

Camilla-Joy (*sarcastically*) You really live on the edge don't you.

Kat CJ!

Beth It's what we love about our George!

Georgina   CJ is it?

Camilla-Joy   Only my friends call me that. You can call me Camilla-Joy.

Georgina   Camilla-Joy, got it. (*To* **Kat**.) And what was your name?

Kat   Kat. It's nice to meet you girls. (*To* **Kiki**.) You look familiar. Have we met before?

Kiki   I don't know. Maybe!

Georgina   How do you two know each other?

Kat   Work. I'm on the front desk and CJ is in tax.

Camilla-Joy   I'm a senior accountant at a successful firm in the city.

Georgina   Wow. That is so . . .

Kiki   Intellectual. You do look smart. Some people just do. Go off, Queen!

Camilla-Joy   How about you point us in the direction of our rooms?

Georgina (*tentatively*)   Oh. Well, I didn't realise you'd both be coming, as there was no RSVP from you, Camilla-Joy. And I didn't even know that you were invited, Kat. Which is absolutely fine . . . but it means that you'll have to share a tent and it's just down that way.

Camilla-Joy   How fabulous.

Camilla-Joy *and* **Kat** *leave to find their tent.*

Georgina (*awkwardly*)   They seem nice.

Kiki   So, Camilla-Joy is your new sister-in-law to be, Flo?

Flora   Yep.

Beth   And she's the *nice* one of the family apparently.

Kiki   She is definitely giving boss lady energy. I'm sure we can all get to know her and we can all find some sort of meaningful connection.

Flora   Let's hope so! So, now that we're here girls, surely you can tell me what the plan is for this weekend?

Georgina   Well, I'm glad you asked! Just be aware, things might get a little crazy!

Kiki (*teasing, lovingly*)   Like 'Georgina-crazy' or 'crazy-crazy'?

Georgina   To kick things off . . . I made lanyards! (*Squeals.*)

Kiki/Beth   She made lanyards!

Beth   It is your hen's weekend after all!

Beth, **Kiki** *and* **Georgina** *begin to dance and sing repeatedly.*

All   Flora's getting married! Flora's getting married!

Flora   Hey, what did we talk about? This weekend is not a hen's weekend. It's simply a weekend away for a girl and her best friends!

Kiki (*shimmying*)   Before she goes and gets . . .

All   Married!

Beth (*suddenly unwell*)   Oh God.

Flora   You OK?

Beth   Yeh, I'm fine. We were in a rush after work last night and Freddy picked up some takeaway and it's really not agreeing with me today.

Flora   Food poisoning is the worst!

Georgina (*moving to retrieve her pack*)   Well, I have a range of tablets and medicines in the first aid kit if that'd be helpful?

Beth   No, no. It'll pass, honest. George, why don't you give us the run-down for today. I know you're itching to go through the schedule!

Georgina   Guilty! OK, I have planned a few fun things to really make the most of the one night we have together!

Flora   You didn't need to plan anything!

Kiki   We want to make a fuss of you, babe!

Flora   As long as it's nothing big. You didn't have to go to any effort!

Georgina   It's no effort!

Kiki   We are your soon-to-be bridesmaids! We had to do something! Just be open minded.

Georgina   And the activities will be so fun! It's all planned out!

Beth   Scheduled fun, Georgina's superpower!

Georgina   Oi! (*Changing her tone in an attempt to sound 'chill'.*) We can just chill if you want. We don't have to stick to the schedule or the activities on the spreadsheet. We could just take it as it comes. I'm totally chilled!

Kiki   You're totally not, babe! But we still love you! OK, ladies, get in for a photo to kick off this trip. (*They all bunch up for a selfie.*) Say 'We love Flora' on three. Ready? One, two . . .

Hans *enters suddenly, holding a watering can.*

Hans (*loudly, startling the girls*)   Hello! (*All the girls scream in shock.*)

Flora   Hi! How are you?

Beth   *Who* are you?

Hans   My name is Hans!

Kiki   What a fantastic name! And your accent is giving me international energy! Are you from somewhere exotic?

Hans   Germany.

Kiki   Oh, ja! Guten tag! So, are you here for the weekend too, Hans?

Hans   I'm here every weekend!

Kiki   Wow! You must really like it here, babe!

Beth   Pretty sure he works here, Kiks.

Kiki   Oh!

Flora   Well, we're just here for a girls' weekend.

Beth   It's actually her 'it's not a hen's, hen's weekend', Hans!

Georgina   But we won't be any trouble. No nonsense at all! Absolutely none! Limited noise and limited excitement!

Beth (*sarcastically*)   Party!

Georgina   Are you the park ranger, Hans?

Hans   Correct! I run this place! Look after everything including my beautiful plants. (*Holding up a sad looking plant.*) Although, most of them are struggling!

Beth   You should get Flora onto it. We call her the crazy plant whisperer.

Kiki   She loves gardens. Like, more than humans.

Georgina   With a name like Flora, it was meant to be! She's an award-winning horticulturalist!

Flora   OK, girls. Hans, if you do need any help, just let me know. I'd be happy to take a look at any plants you're worried about.

Hans   Thank you, my dear. I might take you up on that. But for now, I'm off. If you need anything, just sing out my name. (*They all smile and nod appreciatively.*) Well, go on. Try it!

Flora   Try it?

Hans   Sing out my name: Hans. On three. *Ein, zwei, drei* . . . sing!

Encouraged, **Kiki** *sings at the top of her lungs, channelling her inner pop star. She sustains the note for an impossibly long time.*

Kiki   Haaaaaaaaans!

Hans   Very nice! *Auf wiedersehen, frauleins!*

Flora   Wow. That was . . . wow!

Kiki (*thinking* **Flora** *is talking about her singing*)   Thank you! Ooh, *danke*!

Georgina   He seemed friendly!

Beth   That's one word for it.

Georgina   Right! Let the weekend begin! Are we excited? It's time to unpack then we can get stuck into activities! (*Scanning the site for* **Camilla-Joy** *and* **Kat**.) I'd really like everyone to be here though. I wonder if the girls are on their way back?

Beth   Maybe they got a better offer!

Georgina   Beth!

Beth   Just saying!

Camilla-Joy *and* **Kat** *enter.*

Camilla-Joy   Saying what?

Kiki   Georgina is about to give the weekend induction speech, babe. Sit, sit!

Beth   I'd get comfortable if I was you!

Georgina   Right, Flo. Come and sit up here (**Flora** *moves to sit with* **Georgina** *and the girls move to be around her.*) The girls and I would like to kick this weekend off and get a little crazy with . . . a poem!

Camilla-Joy (*rolling her eyes*)   Oh my God.

Kat (*earnestly*)   This'll be good!

Georgina   We all wrote a verse of a poem just for you! Girls, are we ready?

All of the girls get out their piece of paper. Each of them stand up to read their part of the poem to **Flora**. **Georgina** *has clearly given instructions and directs the poetry recital.*

Georgina   To our dear friend Flora, you're truly sublime,
To kick off the weekend, we wrote you a rhyme! Woo!

Beth   I've known you so long and know all of your quirks,
We've travelled through life, in trackies and birks.
Through the good times, laughter, trouble and strife,
Through it all, I know we'll be besties for life.

Kat   I've only just met you,
But I've heard lots of things.
Wishing you love,
And the fun marriage brings!

Camilla-Joy   Roses are red,
Violets are blue.
You're marrying my brother,
Sucks to be you.

Kiki   Well, Flora, I did consider singing you a power ballad for my bit. You know, something Celine or Whitney inspired, but Georgina thought it might be a good idea to stick with a spoken poem. (**Kiki** *gives* **Georgina** *a wink.*) So here goes!

Collecting herself dramatically, she takes a breath then reads her poem.

There's a sun in the sky and grass on the ground,
Lucky you've got the hottest bridesmaids around!
We'll get manicures and pedicures and spray tans OK,
So we're nothing but slay on your big wedding day!
So charge up your phone and get ready to post,
Wedding spam coming for the one we love the most!

Kiki *points to* **Flora** *then blows her a kiss.*

Georgina
> She's a beautiful soul, on the in and outside,
> And we can't wait to see her as a beautiful bride.
> As you're planting new seeds in your garden of life,
> Let's celebrate Flora before she's a wife!
> So breathe in the air and soak up the sun,
> Get ready to have the most amazing fun!
> We've got lots of things planned, soon it will all make sense,
> Some might say this camping trip will be . . . intense!

Flora *applauds the girls and blows them kisses.*

Right, girls. Time to get ourselves settled in our tents then back here in fifteen minutes for activity one. Let's go!

Georgina *double claps and all of the girls move off to their tents to settle in.*

Figure 1 Flora tending to her plants. Photo courtesy of Tyler Marsland.

Scene Two

Georgina (*to the audience*)   I love camping. I do. I just love it. It's so . . . thrilling. I mean, what's not to love? The smoky smell of a campfire crackling away. The layers of clothing you have to wear at night to keep yourself toasty warm. The awkward wrangling of a tent before you get the pegs positioned permanently in place, the tent your perfect protection from a potentially problematic or precarious predicament. (*Exhaling to calm herself.*)

Sorry I got a bit carried away. Camping can do that to me. It always has. It's really quite exhilarating for me to be honest. And it has the potential to be exhilarating for everyone! That's why I booked this trip. Look, some might love a five-star resort with pools and buffet breakfasts and air conditioning and massages but I just feel a simple camping trip somewhere remote is so much more wholesome. And while the girls might be a touch hesitant at first, I know they'll love it. I've made sure of it! I did all the shopping for the food and prepared all our meals. And I got plenty of bug spray to keep the mosquitoes away as I'm highly allergic so I need to be extra-cautious as I don't want to get bitten!

I got to the grounds early to set everything up and string up the bunting which I've hand made over the last few months with Flora's favourite colours to really jazz up the area a bit. I have activities planned and back up activities just in case. It's all ready to go to make sure Flora has the perfect send-off before she starts her life as a married woman to Tim.

Tim is really nice. He's not my type really, but he's really nice. No, I'm much more into the rugged, outdoorsy type of man. You know the type that has callouses on his hands and walks around fixing things. I'm yet to meet him but I know he exists somewhere out there! But this trip is not about me, it's all about Flora and I. Am. Excited! Woo! (**Georgina** *double claps and exits.*)

Scene Three

Saturday, early afternoon. **Flora** *is typing on her phone.* **Camilla-Joy** *and* **Kat** *enter and go over to her.*

Camilla-Joy   Hey, bridezilla!

Flora   Hey!

Camilla-Joy   You know I'm just joking, don't you?

Flora   Yeh of course.

Camilla-Joy   Or am I?

Flora   What?

Camilla-Joy   Kidding.

Kat   She loves to joke around. Whatcha doing?

Flora   Just trying to get a hold of Tim. But I think I might be out of luck which is a bit of a pain! Anyway, how are you?

Kat   We're good. Hey, your friend Kiki. How do you know her?

Flora   From school. Why?

Kat   I swear I've met her before. I just can't work out where.

Camilla-Joy   Cool story. (*To* **Flora**.) You seem a bit flustered.

Flora   Do I?

Camilla-Joy   Not having second thoughts about the wedding are we?

Kat   CJ, you can't ask that!

Flora   What? No. Why would you say that?

Camilla-Joy   Oh, just checking in and making sure you're OK. Bit scary, the whole wedding thing. All that stress and expectation. And everyone looking at you with their beady little eyes as you walk down the aisle wondering if you'll trip and judging how you look. I know it would freak me out. That's why I wouldn't get married in a million years. But, each to their own I guess. I'm sure you'll love it.

Flora   Yeh.

Kat   I think weddings can be really nice. There's something special about having all your loved ones in the same spot, celebrating love. I think I'd want a big wedding. Or maybe I'd want to elope.

Camilla-Joy   You know what you miss out on if you do that though?

Kat   What?

Camilla-Joy   Presents! That's the main reason people get married.

Kat   You think?

Camilla-Joy   I know! I'm really glad Tim has chosen you.

Flora   Thank you.

Camilla-Joy   I mean the amount of girls that boy has gone through. It was like one a month for a while there. A revolving door! We couldn't keep up. And oh my goodness, some have been horrendous.

Flora   Really?

Camilla-Joy   Sure, a lot of them have been practically supermodels but they didn't have two brain cells to rub together, you know. You're definitely the smartest of all the girls he's dated. I mean, you can spell your own name at least!

Flora (*laughing along awkwardly*)   I can. That's true.

Camilla-Joy   What about you? Have you had a string of boyfriends before Tim?

Flora I don't know about that but I guess everyone has to kiss a few frogs before they find their prince.

Kat I've kissed a lot of frogs.

Camilla-Joy Yes, you have. A few toads too!

Kat No more than you!

Flora Anyway girls, I did want to thank you. For coming on this trip. I know that camping's not really your thing.

Camilla-Joy What makes you think that?

Flora Oh, I didn't mean to presume anything. I just thought that . . .

Camilla-Joy That?

Flora (*stumbling*) Ah, that . . .

Camilla-Joy You're right. It's not my thing. But I'm sure we can survive a night. In a tent. In the middle of nowhere. Can't we, Kat?

Kat I grew up going on camping trips so find sleeping in a tent kind of comforting. I actually really like it.

Camilla-Joy (*sarcastically*) OK then.

Flora Well, I appreciate you coming along. Thank you.

Camilla-Joy You owe me. (*Beat.*) Kidding!

Beth *enters.*

Beth Hey! We all good, ladies?

Flora All good. You OK? You don't look well.

Beth My stomach is really not happy. I will never eat junk food again! Anyway, what's going on?

Camilla-Joy Flora just couldn't get in touch with terrible Tim so she was a bit upset. Anyway, we should sort out our tent. You ready?

Kat Ready.

Camilla-Joy (*shrilly*) If you hear a scream, come and save me, OK?

Camilla-Joy *and* **Kat** *leave.*

Beth (*mimicking* **Camilla-Joy**) Come and save me, OK?

Flora Be nice!

Beth Remember what I always say. The bratty sister-in-law gives you trouble, you tell me and your sassy gal Beth will sort her out.

Flora She's fine. Just a bit . . . She's fine.

Beth   Don't let her get to you. And make sure you're not getting in your own head about things either. What have we talked about? Strip the rest away, Flo. It's just you and Tim. Dear Tim. (*Poking fun at* **Flora**.) Hunky, spunky, funky Tim. Such a shame I didn't meet one of his brothers before I got married to Freddy.

Flora   Freddy is awesome!

Beth   Yeh, he's not so bad. You know, we've been married three years in October.

Flora   That is amazing.

Beth   It's pretty good huh. So, be honest with me, Flora. How are you really?

Flora   Yeh. I'm OK. I'm really excited about this weekend. It's just been a lot of chat about the wedding and all of the feelings that come with that, you know? It's a lot.

Beth   I get it. And it all makes sense. Remember, I'm always here. Always will be. Try and enjoy this weekend. You deserve it.

Flora *and* **Beth** *hug as* **Kiki** *enters with several bags.*

Kiki   Ah, hello! You forgetting someone, my beautiful bodacious babes?

Beth   Here she is! Ready to rough it and have a night in the wilderness, Kiks?

Kiki   Yes! I happen to be very excited. Call me Kiki the Crazy Camper Chick. Sure, I may have never camped before but this year's mantra was 'say yes and be grateful for new experiences'. So, I'm saying a big yes to getting in touch with my surroundings and, like, yes to totally grounding myself in mother nature and the environment and stuff. Hashtag gratitude. Hashtag tenting. Hashtag nature and birds and plants and roughing it.

Beth   You're really roughing it, girl. Got enough bags there?

Kiki   These are just the essentials.

Beth   The essentials?

Kiki   The rest of the bags are in the car. Where's George? I want to see if she needs me to help her put up a tent or start a fire or something rough and ready. I'm well up for it.

Beth   Kiks, I've always admired your positivity!

Kiki *'s phone buzzes.*

Kiki   Oh geez. Sorry, girls, give me a sec. (*She takes a photo and goes to post online.*) Just posting some content.

Flora   OK, social media mogul!

Kiki   I know right? I've been told I need to post regularly to maintain followers. Seems to be working well so far so we'll go with it!

Beth   Explain what you just said please!

Georgina *enters.*

Georgina   Right, ladies, currently we're running to schedule which is just fabulous! Where is Camilla-Joy? And Kat? I'd like to begin the first activity in a few minutes time. (*Seeing they're all grinning at her and changing her tone.*) I mean, if everyone else is keen. I'm totally up for whatever. We can stick to the plan or go rogue if we feel like it! As I said, I'm chill!

Cliff *walks through the campsite with a tool belt and handyman kit.* **Georgina** *is immediately taken with him.*

Cliff   Hi, ladies!

Georgina (*hopping up to stand in front of him*)   Hello . . . man.

Cliff   My name is Cliff. I look after all the park maintenance.

Georgina (*she looks around to the girls and they encourage her to speak*)   My name is Georgina.

Cliff   Pleased to meet you. (*They shake hands.*) Sorry if my hands are a little rough. It's all the callouses.

Georgina *sharply inhales, impressed. There is an awkward pause while* **Georgina** *stares lovingly at* **Cliff.** **Beth** *and the girls immediately clock this and take great enjoyment in* **Georgina**'s *interaction.*

Beth   It's nice to meet you, Cliff. Are you single?

Flora (*trying to redirect the conversation after* **Beth**'s *brazen question*)   So how's your day been, Cliff?

Cliff   Woke up with breath in my lungs and a working ticker so I can't complain!

Flora   Can't complain indeed!

Beth   How's your ticker, George?

Georgina   Ticking. Definitely ticking!

Kiki   I am loving your energy, Cliff! Snaps for Cliff everyone!

Kiki *snaps her fingers, encouraging the other girls to do the same.*

Cliff   Thank you! So, what brings you here, ladies?

Georgina   Love.

Cliff   Sorry?

Georgina   I mean, marriage.

Cliff   Huh?

Georgina   Love and marriage! Ah, our friend is in love so she's getting married (**Flora** *waves.*) So we're here to celebrate that.

Figure 2 Georgina impressing Cliff, as Kiki, Flora and Beth watch on.
Photo courtesy of Tyler Marsland.

Cliff   Excellent.

Georgina   How about you? What brings you here, Cliff?

Cliff   Ah, I work here.

Georgina   Right. Of course you do.

Cliff   Before I go, I wanted to ask. Who put your tents up?

Georgina (*shoots her hand up*)   That would be me!

Cliff   Well, well, well. I'm impressed. Your tent pegs are expertly hammered in. You're clearly an experienced camper.

Georgina (*dramatically*)   I am. Thank you, Cliff.

Cliff   You're welcome. Well, best be off. Enjoy your stay, ladies. And nice to meet you, Georgina!

He exits.

Flora   You OK, George?

Georgina   Yes.

Beth (*mocking, with a deep voice*)   Nice to meet you. Sorry about my callouses!

Kiki And my handyman ruggedness.

Flora Nice tent pegs, little lady!

Georgina Oh shush, you guys!

Flora One thing's for sure. I've never seen such a 'happy camper'!

Beth This trip just got fun!

Kiki So fun!

Georgina Guys, shush!

Camilla-Joy We're here! Party can start!

Georgina Right! Good! Time for the first game! It's a short one but a fun one! Are we all excited? (*Nods to* **Kiki** *to start.*)

Kiki We have some questions that we've asked your hubby-to-be Tim, and he's sent us his answers. (**Kiki** *holds up a pile of papers and hands these out to everyone.*) Now you have to guess what he's said! Ready?

Flora Ready!

Kiki I've got the first few quick-fire ones. Here we go. One, who made the first move?

Flora Tim, definitely.

Kiki Correct! Two, if Flo was a plant, what would she be?

Flora Some sort of flower?

Kiki Keep going.

Georgina A sunflower?

Kiki No.

Beth Ooh, I know. A bougainvillea!

Flora Look who's talking!

Kiki Tim has answered: "the most beautiful rose in the most beautiful garden!"

All react with a sigh. **Camilla-Joy** *rolls her eyes.*

Beth My turn. Right, who is the better cook?

Flora Tim! (**Beth** *nods that she has it correct.*)

Georgina True or false. Tim snores louder than you do?

Flora True! Very true.

Georgina Next!

Kat   OK, I'm next. What's the thing Tim loves the most about you?

Flora   Um, my love for Bunnings?

Kat   No, come on. His answer is really sweet.

Flora   This is hard! I honestly don't know.

Kat (*reading*)   He said your courage, kindness to others and complete honesty.

Flora *reacts awkwardly to this last answer. Only* **Beth** *notices.*

Camilla-Joy   Boring! OK, me now! Next question. What are three of Flora's worst traits?

Georgina   I don't remember sending that one to Tim.

Kiki   I'm not sure that's the vibe we're going for, babe.

Kat   Maybe not the best question to ask!

Camilla-Joy   I added it in. This game needed a little spice, you know. Come on, go!

Flora   Ah, I don't know. Maybe being grumpy in the mornings?

Camilla-Joy   Close. He said that one, you can be a bit of a nag, that two, he wishes you enjoyed watching sports with him, and that three, sometimes, he can't quite work out what you're thinking. Mysterious Flora, huh! Keeping him on his toes?

Kat (*quieter to* **Camilla-Joy**)   Did he really say those things?

Camilla-Joy   Close enough.

Beth   Well, they're not that bad. Mine would be way worse.

Kiki   Totally. And watching sports? Ew! Snooze fest, am I right? OK, George, last question!

Georgina   Last question! What is Tim most nervous about on the wedding day?

Flora   Ahh. He's never really said he's nervous about anything to be honest.

Camilla-Joy   That she'll actually show up? (*The girls all react disapprovingly, frustrated at* **Camilla-Joy**.) Kidding!

Flora   You know, this game was really fun but I'm getting a bit of a headache.

Beth   You OK?

Flora   Yeh, I'm fine. Honestly. I might head back to my tent for a quick lay-down and meet you back here soon.

She leaves and all look to **Camilla-Joy**.

Camilla-Joy   What?

All girls get up and head off to continue unpacking and sorting out the site.

Scene Four

Flora (*to the audience*)   I remember the first time I felt that feeling. You might know the one? Doubt.

It's a funny thing, doubt. At times, it can smack you right in the face like a freight train you never saw coming. But it can be more cunning than that too. Like a knot in your stomach. Or a tightening of your chest. Or a voice that somehow has a way of nagging at you and seems to get louder and louder with every passing minute. And it's hard to silence. Sure, you can get your hands dirty in the garden or play some music or get stuck into something that takes your mind off things for a second. But that's temporary. You then sit down to catch your breath or lay your head on the pillow at night and it's just you and that feeling that won't seem to go away. Doubt.

I mean sure, you can doubt your outfit that day or why you agreed to the overtime at work. But, then there's the big stuff. When you doubt why you thought you were worthy of something special or your decision to settle for someone you knew wasn't right. I've definitely been there. And it's really hard. And even if you do have the ring on the finger or the wedding planned or presents from the engagement party taking up space in the spare room, there's that feeling of doubt taking up space in your mind.

And even if that feeling goes away, there's always the worry that it will come back. And then what do you do?

Scene Five

Saturday, mid-afternoon. **Georgina**, **Hans**, **Cliff**, **Beth**, **Kiki**, **Camilla-Joy** *and* **Kat** *carry and set up art easels in the campsite clearing, ready for the next activity.*

Georgina (*to* **Cliff** *and* **Hans**)   Thank you so much for helping me bring these in from the car. It's really gentlemanly of you. (*Directing the rest of the girls.*) Girls, we'll finish setting up just over here I think.

Hans   You're very welcome!

Cliff   Are you girls doing some painting?

Georgina (*sincerely, impressed with* **Cliff**)   How did you guess, Cliff?

Beth (*jokingly*)   Nothing gets past you, Cliff!

Hans   I've seen this sort of thing before. What do you ladies call it. A . . .

Georgina   A 'paint and sip'. Essentially, we pick something to paint and have a few bubbles and chats as we let our creative juices flow!

Hatching a plan, **Kiki** *and* **Beth** *move to stand either side of* **Cliff**.

Kiki   It's a shame we don't have a model to paint.

Georgina   I've got a potted plant in the car I thought we could use. It's a fascinating species of Spathiphyllum. I thought Flora would love it if we painted that!

Kiki   It's one thing to paint nature but another thing to paint a real life person.

Beth   You're so right, Kiks. Don't suppose you know of someone who could step in at the last minute and be our model?

Kiki (*hinting towards* **Cliff**)   I don't know. Maybe Georgina could ask someone. That's if she can think of anyone. George?

Hans   OK, OK. I get what is going on here. It's plain to see.

Georgina   What's that?

Hans   The answer is yes.

Georgina   Yes?

Hans   Yes. I will be your model. I have quite a lot of industry experience back in the day so I think you'll be pleasantly surprised! Watch this!

Hans *does three or four exaggerated and overly cheesy modelling poses.*

Georgina   Wow.

Hans   Just confirming though. This is a clothes-*on* modelling gig isn't it?

All   Yes!

Georgina   Definitely clothes on! Definitely!

Beth   The only thing is . . . we were hoping for *two* models. Hans, do you know anyone else we could use?

Hans   Well, Cliff here can help. It'd be our pleasure, wouldn't it, Cliff, old boy. Now tell us where you want us!

Beth   Ooh! Let's use the props on the boys!

Georgina *leads them off to stand in place. They place props and costume items on both* **Hans** *and* **Cliff** *who seem to love it.*

Kiki   Good idea!

Flora *enters.*

Kiki   Just in time, babe! Flo, you ready to get your artist on?

Flora   Sure am! Let's do it. (*Spotting* **Hans** *and* **Cliff**.) Oh and we have models?

Kiki   And bubbles! (**Kiki** *hands out drinks to the girls.* **Beth** *declines.*)

Georgina   Right, everyone. Find an easel! Your paints and canvases are all ready for you. Time to paint something special!

Beth   Is that what you're calling him now? (**Georgina** *shushes* **Beth** *with her eyes.*)

Kiki   You work those costumes, boys! Yass! OK now freeze! (*The girls continue to paint the 'models'.*)

Scene Six

Camilla-Joy (*to the audience*)   So, we were invited to this weekend to celebrate Flora marrying my brother. Gross. So far, the weekend is so lame. The girls are all super-boring.

Kat   Really? I feel like they're really nice.

Camilla-Joy (*rolling her eyes*)   Anyway, Georgina, who is this goody-two-shoes Girl Guide you do not want to get stuck talking to, has planned all these events including a 'paint and sip'. I mean, talk about unoriginal! No one likes 'paint and sips'!

Kat   Everyone likes paint and sips! I actually haven't painted anything since school so I'm looking forward to having a go.

Camilla-Joy   Bottom line is: I'm not sure Flora is right for my brother. There's just something about her I don't trust.

Kat   CJ!

Camlla-Joy   What? I can't quite place my finger on it. But I said I'd give her a go so that's what I'm doing (**Kat** *smiles at her.* **Camilla-Joy** *rolls her eyes again.*) Well, get me a paintbrush. Let's do a little painting and a lot of sipping!

Scene Seven

Kiki *takes out her phone and hands it to an audience member. She positions them to film her, using the camera as a conduit to address the audience.*

Kiki   Hey, Kiki crew. It's me, Kiki. Welcome to 'It's great to be grateful with Kiki'. I just wanted to jump on and say hello and give you your daily dose! Lots of you have been asking where I am at the moment. You'll never guess! Go on, guess! (*Beat.*) OK, I'll tell you! I am on holiday with my girlfriends. Camping. Like, in tents and everything. Are you shocked? I thought you'd be shocked. It's a little off brand for Kiki but a lot of fun so far! So cute!

Today's quote as we own our attitude of gratitude . . . (**Kiki** *clicks three times, repeating a ritual she has done before.*) 'Let us be grateful to the people who bring us joy; they are the gardeners who make our hearts bloom'.

That beautiful quote was inspired by one of my best friends, Flora, who happens to be a gardener of plants and stuff but also a gardener in how she tends to the souls of the people around her, making her friends and her family feel loved. Feel nourished. Feel happy.

So I want you to do something for me now. Think of a person who makes you feel happy. Who you feel grateful for. I want you to picture them right now. Picture the person who makes you feel happy. And now for your daily challenge. You ready? Before you place your head on your pillow tonight, I want you to let them know. Whoever it is that you feel grateful for, send them a text. Or some other sort of message. Or even a cheeky photo of you smiling your big, beautiful smile. Now your loved one might be like my friend Flora, who isn't one for social media and probably won't see this video, so just remember, you can always give them a call too. Very retro!

Life can be tough sometimes. You never know when you won't be able to let that special person know that they're special. So, while you can, do it. (*Flicking back into influencer mode.*) Until tomorrow when I'll bring you another day of 'It's great to be grateful with Kiki'. Love ya! (*She blows a kiss to her audience and retrieves her phone.*)

Scene Eight

Saturday, mid-afternoon. The girls are in the midst of their 'paint and sip'. **Cliff** *and* **Hans** *continue to pose.*

Georgina   But it's such a good story. Go on. Tell it again!

Flora   It's not *that* exciting!

Georgina   Yes it is! It gives all of us some hope that there are good guys out there! Come on, tell it!

All   Tell it! Tell it! Tell it!

Flora   OK, OK! Well, I met Tim at a dinner party that Kiki hosted.

Kiki   Yes you did! I had just done this Chilean cooking class to try and impress my gym instructor at the time, Mateo. Anyway, go on!

Flora   Anyway, Tim was a late ring in. I think one of your other friends couldn't make it.

Kiki   Doug, the excavator.

Flora   So Tim came along. And he was pretty cute. He had a kind face. Not threatening at all. Anyway, he brought these flowers for the host (*nods at* **Kiki**) which is a beautiful thought but the flowers were half dead. At one point, I saw that he'd put the flowers in an empty vase. So I quickly popped some water in there. He saw me and was a bit embarrassed I think. I teased him a little, he made a few jokes and we got chatting.

Kiki   He suddenly became fascinated with all things gardening and plants!

Flora   He did! And that was it.

Beth   And that was it! Right, I've got to sit down. Ooh, tell them about your first date!

Flora   Really?

Camilla-Joy   You don't have to.

Kat   Yeh, come on.

Flora   Well it was actually a trip to Bunnings.

Camilla-Joy   Lame.

Kiki   I think it's smart. Men love Bunnings. And tools and gadgets and things. I mean, I once went on a date with a man who talked for 55 minutes about his front lawn.

Beth   It's a thing. They're obsessed.

Kiki   This guy couldn't find a picture of his family but flicked straight to the lawn album on his phone. Unbelievable. I mean, who loves lawn that much?

Cliff   I love my lawn. Like, a lot.

Kiki   Well, there you go!

Georgina   Well, there you go!

Kat   Anyway, you went to Bunnings.

Flora   We went to Bunnings. And just so we're clear, women like Bunnings too. It's not just a man thing!

Kiki   Yes, Queen. Empowerment!

Flora   So Tim got in touch the day after the party and said he wanted to find a perfect lemon tree to pot and would I help him. I said yes and we booked a lunch date and then a Bunnings trip. We found this beautiful tree, potted it up and that was it.

Beth   You gotta tell the best bit!

Flora   Well, on our first anniversary, Tim gifted me the tree. He said he had wanted to choose a lemon tree that day because he had read that lemon trees were a symbol of love and prosperity. He said that if you owned one, it was supposed to represent that you would be blessed in life. He said that he felt all of those things the night he met me.

Kiki   It's like a movie storyline or something! And the note.

Flora   Attached to the lemon tree he gave me on our anniversary was a note from Tim asking if I'd like to find a place together.

Georgina   So sweet!

Beth   It's honestly so beautiful it makes you want to vomit. Which, given how I'm feeling today, might actually happen.

Georgina   The best bit is, that lemon tree now sits happily on their front porch.

Flora   It does!

Kiki   It was fate. But I take all the credit! If it wasn't for me and my party, and those dead flowers, who knows where you'd be?

Cliff   How much longer, ladies? I think my leg might be falling asleep!

Hans   Patience, boy, patience. You can't rush art! Soak up the attention!

Cliff   Well, the roof next door won't fix itself!

Kiki   You have been there a while, boys. Let me play you some music to inspire some new poses. Any requests?

Beth   Georgina just asked if you have the Magic Mike playlist handy?

Georgina (*shocked*)   I never said that! Kiki! I would never request anything like that!

Kiki   I've got you, girl. Here we go! Right I want to see your runway walks, boys. Get your model on! Live your best Naomi Campbell fantasy!

Hans and **Cliff** *strut down an imaginary catwalk to the music.* **Georgina** *is especially impressed. Some of the girls join in. Overly excited at seeing* **Cliff**'s *moves,* **Georgina** *can't take any more and finally stops the music.*

Georgina   Right, everyone, let's just settle things right down. (*Encouraging herself more than anyone else.*) Take some breaths and do what we can to calm down! I'm assuming everyone is done with their paintings? OK good. Now it's time for the big reveal!

Kiki   Cliff and Hans, I think you've earned the right to be the judges of this competition. Right! Everyone in a line!

All the girls make a line, ready to reveal their paintings.

 Count us down, Hans. Eins, Vei, Drei . . .

Cliff/Hans   Reveal!

The girls reveal their paintings and react to each other's pieces.

Camilla-Joy   So, who wins?

Kat (*to* **Camilla-Joy**)   Definitely not you!

Cliff (*referencing* **Georgina**'s *very complimentary painting of him*)   Well, I really like the look of some paintings. (*Referencing* **Camilla-Joy**'s *very dark interpretation.*) And I don't understand some of the others. So I think the winner has to be . . . Georgina! (*All cheer except* **Camilla-Joy**.)

Camilla-Joy   Rigged!

Georgina *holds up her painting proudly as she and* **Cliff** *stare lovingly at each other.*

Beth   Well, this is one of those times that a picture is definitely worth a thousand words.

Kiki   I really loved your picture, Flora. I think you were robbed!

Flora   You think?

Beth   I think Kiki is being nice! I'd stick to gardening if I was you! George, it's free time now isn't it?

Georgina *is still wrapped up in* **Cliff** *and barely hears* **Beth**'s *question. The girls begin to pack up the easels and paintings.*

Georgina   OK, guys, see ya!

Thank you for awarding me first prize, Cliff! I never expected to win an art competition this weekend and I really appreciate your feedback.

Cliff   Well, I appreciate your smile.

Georgina   Well, thank you.

Cliff   You want to go grab a soft drink?

Georgina   I have some cold lemonade in the esky.

Cliff   Maybe we could make our own lemonade one day. You any good at planting lemon trees? (*He holds out his hand and they leave together.*)

Scene Nine

Saturday, later in the afternoon. **Flora** *has found a handful of plants that need some love and is tending to them at a picnic table with her gardening gloves on.* **Kiki** *enters, bringing more bags in. She has changed outfits, dressed up for a night out.*

Kiki   Hey.

Flora   Hey.

Kiki   Whatcha doing?

Flora   I thought I'd help Hans out and have a look at a few of these plants before dinner. They're not doing too well.

Kiki   That one looks grim.

Flora   It does.

Kiki   You think you can bring it back?

Flora   Well, here's hoping. But I don't know.

Kiki   If anyone can do it, it's you.

Flora   Thanks, Kiks. (*Suddenly noticing* **Kiki**'s *outfit.*) Um, Kiks, what are you wearing?

Kiki   You like it? (**Kiki** *does a twirl.*) Wanted to make an effort for dinner. And I don't know, we might hit a few clubs or bars afterwards so I wanted to be ready. I can dance for hours in these heels!

Flora   I don't think we'll be hitting any clubs.

Kiki   You not in the mood?

Flora   No. It's just, there aren't any.

Kiki   Oh.

Flora   We're a two-hour drive from the nearest servo, Kiks, let alone a club.

Kiki   I guess a cheeky Maccas run on the way home is out of the question too then? (**Flora** *nods.*) Ooh, we can Uber eats it! (**Flora** *shakes her head.*) Oh right.

My bad. Well, never mind. I'll be best dressed around the campfire tonight. That's a plus!

Flora   You will. You look glamorous as always.

Kiki   Thank you. As do you. (**Flora** *holds up her hands.*) Gardening gloves suit you!

I have no idea about plants. Like, none. I want to be earthy and organic but I'm just not. Well, not at the moment. Always room to grow! (*She winks, acknowledging her pun.*) So, what are you going to do to help bring these back?

Flora   Well, it depends to be honest.

Kiki   On what? Teach me, guru!

Flora   Well, almost all plants need five things to survive. To flourish. Sunlight, air, water, nutrients and space to grow. This one here for instance has been watered far too much.

Kiki   Too much? I thought that would just make them happier.

Flora   Plants that grow in soil that is too wet can suffer from a lack of oxygen which can lead to the death of roots or yellowing of leaves or leaf burn or stunted growth or just a general loss of strength. It almost smothers the plant. It's just not good for them and can do as much damage as no water at all.

Kiki   Right. Is it not just easier to chuck them out and buy some new ones?

Flora   I guess but a little bit of the right TLC and they'll come back. They just need the right conditions and someone to love them.

Kiki   Like people I guess.

Flora   People?

Kiki   Yeh. I mean, that's all people need really. Some love and the right environment to thrive.

Flora   True.

Kiki   And even if someone is struggling or looks like they're on the way out like this little plant here, there's always a chance they'll regenerate if their surroundings are improved. If they're replanted somewhere better. And if they're given someone or something they can be grateful for.

Flora   Yeh, I guess so.

Kiki   That got deep. I liked it. (**Kiki** *winks at* **Flora**.)

Flora   You know, I think people underestimate how clever you really are.

Kiki   You think?

Flora   I think. You're always such a great example of what it means to find the positive in a situation. To have gratitude. If only you could make a fortune off that right!

Kiki   Right! (*Beat.*) So, if we're not going dancing, I might switch out these shoes. But I'm keeping the outfit! Love ya, Flo Flo. (**Kiki** *does two air kisses.*) And hey. I'm really proud of you.

Scene Ten

Beth *enters. In the background,* **Flora** *continues to tend to the plants.*

Beth (*to the audience*)   Flo and I have been friends since just after school. I mean, all of us have. You might not picture it now as we're all pretty different, but somehow it works. George is the Girl Guide, organiser of the group. Kiki is fabulously positive and a bit of a princess, self-proclaimed. I'm apparently a little hippy and a lot sassy, and Flora is your earthy, deep thinker. We're all tight but I guess Flora and I are especially close. Even if I have to share her with Tim now.

Tim is pretty great. He's smart and has a sense of humour and he showers regularly. You'd think that was a given but with some boys, you never know! Unfortunately for Flo, there have been a few hiccups before Tim. Like some real 'fall in a heap, my life might be ending' moments. I honestly don't know how she made it through some of the things that have happened to her in the last few years. She's stood strong, resolute. It's weird, she says the same about me. She's always looking out for me, even when I tell her to mind her own business. There's this selflessness about Flora that I have never seen in anyone else.

I had a pretty awful car accident a month after I turned twenty-one. It was bad and pretty 'touch and go' for a little while there. Flora was with me through it all. I mean, you couldn't keep her away. She was always telling me stories and buying me trashy magazines and feeding me Snickers bars while she'd brush my hair. For hours at a time.

It's funny the things that fast track a friendship. That transform it from a sapling to something steadfast with deep, established roots. I don't think my life has ever really been flashy or successful and I certainly haven't won a Nobel Prize. Yet. But I think I've struck gold with some of my friends. Especially with Flora. And at the end of the day, I think that's worth something.

Scene Eleven

Saturday night. Everyone is sitting around a campfire, after dinner.

Georgina   So, I bought marshmallows, everyone! Who's keen?

Kiki   I am so full from dinner!

Georgina   So, no marshmallows?

Kiki   Oh twist my rubber arm then, babe. Go on!

She and the group proceed to roast marshmallows around the campfire.

Flora   That dinner was amazing, George.

Georgina   Thank you. Can I get you anything else, Hans?

Hans   Not at all my dear. That was just scrumptious.

Cliff   Thanks for inviting us to eat with you all.

Georgina   It's my pleasure. Our pleasure.

Kat   I just love a campfire cook-up. Can't beat it!

Camilla-Joy   Yeh, it was pretty good I guess. (**Kat** *gives her an encouraging look.*) Thank you. (*Clearing her throat dramatically towards* **Georgina**.) Um, Georgina. I have a problem I've been meaning to ask you about.

Georgina   What is it?

Camilla-Joy   I may have forgotten my sleeping bag and pillow!

Georgina   Oh.

Camilla-Joy   You got a spare I could use?

Georgina   Ah, no I don't.

Camilla-Joy   Are you sure? (**Camilla-Joy** *stares at her until she caves.*)

Georgina   I could always lend you mine. I'm sure I could do without it for a night.

Beth   George, you don't have to . . .

Camilla-Joy   Thanks. That would be really great. Do you mind if I just grab it out of your tent now and throw it in mine?

Georgina   Sure. Just please remember to zip up my tent. I'm really allergic to bites and don't want any mosquitoes in there.

Camilla-Joy   Yep. I'll try and remember. (*She leaves.*)

Beth   There's only one thing left to do now!

Georgina   Yes! I was just thinking the same thing!

Beth *and* **Georgina** *say the following at the same time.*

Beth   Bedtime!

Georgina   Campfire songs!

Oh, I mean. Bedtime is a great idea too.

Beth   Let's do both. A song then bed!

Georgina   Yes! This is an old favourite we used to sing on our Girl Guide camps.

She accompanies herself, singing the first part of 'Kumbaya'.

Kiki (*interrupting* **Georgina**)   As amazing as that was, George, do you know anything else?

Georgina   I actually did have a little something special prepared for you, Flora. I know it's one of your favourites and I think it's really fitting to play to you this weekend.

She sings a heartfelt ballad for **Flora**, *a tribute to their friendship and the bond shared by the girls.*

Flora   George, that was beautiful.

Kiki   You could be a viral campfire singing sensation, Georgina!

Beth   I love it when you sing.

Kiki   Same. (*Hinting.*) But I also love it when you dance! When we all dance!

So, I'm thinking we re-create a moment from the Year 9 Cresco High School Disco. Surely you all remember the choreography we made up, girls? Kat, you join in too. And boys, if you can keep up, then feel free to get involved. Let's go!

Beth *plays a song and all of the girls dance around the campfire, having fun to an old school classic and remembering the dance they choreographed and performed as high schoolers. There is a particular section where* **Georgina** *has an Irish dancing solo. At the end of the song,* **Camilla-Joy** *enters in a robe, towel around her head and a face mask on. She holds the torch to her face. Startled, the girls scream.*

Camilla-Joy   What? I love that song. Aren't I allowed to join in?

Beth   What's with the torch? You scared the living daylights out of us!

Camilla-Joy   Sorry!

Kiki   That's OK. Come join us.

Camilla-Joy   Georgia, do you think you'll play some more guitar?

Georgina (*uplifted by* **Camilla-Joy**'s *question*)   Yeh, I can!

Camilla-Joy   Right. Off to bed for me then. And I hope you don't mind but I just borrowed your bug spray. I just don't want them anywhere near me overnight.

Georgina   Oh OK.

Camilla-Joy   One more sleep closer to marrying my brother, Flora. Make sure you wear socks to bed!

Flora   Why is that?

Camilla-Joy   Don't want you getting cold feet! Night, everyone.

Beth   You know what? That might be our cue too

Everyone says goodnight and heads off to bed. **Beth** *stops* **Flora** *before they go.*

You OK?

Figure 3 Camilla-Joy interrupting the fun. Photo courtesy of Tyler Marsland.

Flora   I'm OK. It's just . . . nothing. Let's head to bed.

Beth   You sure?

Flora   Yep. Goodnight!

Scene Twelve

This optional dream scene offers an opportunity to explore **Flora***'s internal fears and doubts surrounding her upcoming wedding to Tim. Through a stylised blend of physical theatre, costume and dance, tension is built, and elements of* **Flora***'s past are explored.*

Scene Thirteen

Sunday early morning. **Cliff** *is tidying up after the night.* **Georgina** *comes out of her tent in disarray, her hair messed up, and with a mass of mosquito bites on her face and arms. Seeing* **Cliff***, she tries to hide herself.* **Kiki** *enters.*

Cliff (*to* **Georgina**)   Well, hello! It's mighty nice to see your face.

Kiki   Thank you, Cliff. I was really pursuing a camping chic vibe with this outfit so I'm really glad someone has noticed. Thank you.

Cliff (*gently*)   I was actually talking to Georgina. I wanted to ask her something.

Kiki   Oh. Um, yeh I know. I was just being funny (*Laughs.*) Gotcha! Anyway . . .

Cliff   Hello.

Georgina (*embarrassed and still trying to hide herself*)   Hello, Cliff.

Cliff   What seems to be the matter?

Georgina   Oh nothing. (**Georgina** *blows hair out of face.*)

Cliff   You sure?

Georgina   Well, OK. If you must know. (*She turns to him, almost like a dramatic reveal.*) I'm covered in bites!

(*On a rampage now.*) Someone, not mentioning any names, Camilla-Joy, left my tent wide open before bed and when I came back to the tent, ready to try and get a few hours of shut eye, it was full of mosquitoes and I had already informed everyone I was allergic to mosquitos in my initial invitational email which was clearly not read by Camilla-Joy because she didn't think to even RSVP, let alone zip up my tent to prevent me from being ravaged by the minute mosquito monstrosities!

Kiki (*to* **Cliff**)   She's normally a lot perkier than this. (*To* **Georgina**.) Did someone just get out of the wrong side of the bed?

Georgina   That could be true, if I *had* a bed. But Camilla-Joy forgot her mattress so, being the kind person I am, I let her use mine which is extremely comfortable. And I think she enjoyed my extremely comfortable mattress because all I could hear last night was her snoring!

Kiki   It was loud wasn't it! The noise seemed to just travel.

Georgina   Oh, and to make matters worse, according to Camilla-Joy, the 'paint and sip' wasn't 'fun' enough. I heard them talking in their tent! I had fun! I had lots of fun!

Kiki   I had fun too! I loved it. So creative and fab!

Georgina   You're so positive, Kiki, and you're very supportive which we love. But not everyone is as grateful unfortunately!

Ouch, my poor hands! I've been tossing and turning and scratching all night. I look like a banshee dragged through the bush backwards!

Anyway, I'm sorry, Cliff. I didn't mean for you to cop all of that. You've been nothing but kind and considerate and handsome. (*Catching herself.*) I mean helpful! Kind and considerate and helpful! So, what was it you wanted to ask me?

Cliff   I was going to ask if you wanted to tie the knot?

Kiki   Oh my goodness! This is a moment! This is a moment!

Georgina   Excuse me?

Cliff   Tie the knot! (*He holds up a piece of rope.*) I am fixing up a pergola a few K away and need an especially good knot. I thought you'd be my go-to girl because of your Girl Guide experience.

Kiki   How romantic!

Georgina   Look, Cliff, I'd love to help you but I'm afraid my hands just aren't working at their full capacity at the moment.

Cliff   I have a special cure for mozzie bites if you're up for it?

Georgina   Oh. Of course, if you think it'll help.

Cliff   Hold out your hands.

Georgina *immediately holds out her hands.* **Cliff** *proceeds to spit into his hands, rub them furiously together then rub his hands on her hands.* **Kiki** *is encouraging but also horrified.* **Georgina** *sighs loudly in relief as the itchiness eases. The 'treatment' lasts for quite some time.*

Georgina   Oh, Cliff. You're so dexterous! That feels better already. Thank you!

Cliff   You're welcome.

Beth *and* **Flora** *enter with cups of tea, having gone for a morning walk. They witness* **Cliff** *rubbing* **Georgina** *'s hands and her enthusiastic responses.*

Flora   We're not interrupting are we?

Kiki   Oh no. Cliff and George were just . . . Cliff was just . . .

Georgina   Working his magical hands!

Beth   Magical hands?

Georgina   It's not what you think it is!

Beth   That's a shame.

Georgina   Beth!

Beth   Oh relax!

Kiki   You two do look cute together. Hashtag couple goals, hashtag get it girl.

Flora   Have you seen the others?

Georgina   No, I think they're still sleeping.

Cliff   Well, I'm off.

Beth   Yeh, I can smell ya!

Georgina   Thank you, Cliff. I'll never forget how you heroically rubbed your spit all over my hands to cure my bites.

Cliff *tips his hat to her and continues around the campsite before leaving.*

Flora   You want to explain that sentence, George?

Georgina   Um, well. Let's not talk about it. (*Looking to* **Kiki** *for support.*)

Kiki   George had an awful night's sleep but Cliff has really lent a helping *hand* this morning to make things better. (**Beth** *dry wretches.*) You OK girl?

Beth   Fine. Ignore me please.

Georgina   Anyway, how are you, bride to be? One day closer to being married!

Flora   Yeh.

Kiki   It's just so exciting! I bet it's all you can think about!

Flora   Yeh, it's a lot. That's for sure. But anyway, let's talk about something else.

Georgina   You're allowed to be happy, Flo.

Flora   I know. It's just . . . it's nothing.

Georgina   What's up then? (**Flora** *looks to* **Beth** *for guidance.*)

Beth   You can tell them. If you're comfortable.

Flora   OK. There's just a lot that has been going on lately. Lots of things and they've kind of been getting in my head.

Kiki   Is it about your surname? Because women do not need to change their name these days. A friend from yoga, Crystal, refused to change her name when she married Adam Ball. Crystal Ball! Can you imagine?

Beth   Surprised she didn't see that one coming!

Flora   It's not that.

Georgina   Is it his family? Because if Camilla-Joy is anything to go by, (*whispering*) I get it.

Flora   No, it's honestly not. It's just . . .

Beth (*encouraging* **Flora**)   A problem shared is a problem halved.

Flora   OK. You guys remember William don't you?

Kiki   Your ex-fiancé.

Flora   Yeh.

Georgina   He seemed nice enough.

Kiki   But you mentioned you guys just grew apart.

Flora   I guess we did. In a way.

Beth   There's a little more to it though, isn't there, Flo?

Flora   Yeh. Things didn't end well with William. In fact, in the end, I needed to get out. To get out quick because things had become . . . not good.

Kiki   Not good?

Flora   Violent.

Georgina   Violent?

Flora   A few things had happened and William had started to drink more and more and was becoming more and more frustrated with things, With his job. His life. With me. We'd only been engaged for a few months but it felt like in only those short months, our worlds had completely shifted.

At first, it was just a lot of silent moments. Where there had previously been laughter and love, there was silence. Tense, palpable silence. This silence seemed to push us further and further apart and pretty soon, there was this awkward, ugly distance between us. If only I'd known what was to come.

When there wasn't silence, there was yelling. His touch changed next. Where he'd normally touch my shoulder as he brushed past me in the morning while we were getting ready, he started to just circle around me, keeping his distance. Where he'd once kiss my cheek before work, he started to just leave. I'd shudder as the door slammed shut morning after morning. Then, he started to go through my phone. He wanted to know where I was going and when I'd be home. He either wanted nothing to do with me or to know every detail about what I was doing and why. It was completely smothering.

I was consumed with worry and fear and doubt about our future and the man I was planning to marry. I built up the courage and decided I needed to have a conversation. Not an argument, just a conversation. I thought we could work it out. I was hopeful we would . . . I thought that maybe he'd agree and it would prompt a beautiful, cathartic conversation that would end in us hugging and working it out and making plans for the future. That's not how it went though. That night was the first time he hit me.

Kiki   Flo. Oh my goodness.

Georgina   I'm so sorry.

Kiki   What did you do?

Flora   Nothing at first. I was in shock. I couldn't believe it. This man that I'd known for years had turned into a man I swore I'd never be with. I knew I needed to get out. It was just working out how.

Everything we had, we had together. It took me four months. Four months of making nice and avoiding anything that would lead us into dangerous territory. Put me at risk. But I did it. I packed my stuff and went to Beth's and she let me stay for what felt like ages until I could get myself together again and find another place. I've not spoken to him since that day.

Georgina   I can't believe we didn't know.

Flora   I'm sorry I never said anything.

Georgina   Can we make one thing clear, Flo? You have nothing to apologise for. I can't imagine the struggle you were in and the processing you were doing.

Kiki   I'm just so glad Beth was there. We would have been there too. Just as long as you know that.

Flora   I do.

Beth   You are so brave.

Flora   I don't know about that . . .

Beth   So brave.

Kiki   You are.

Georgina   Flora, this isn't happening again with Tim is it?

Flora   Oh absolutely not.

Georgina   Thank goodness.

Beth   You have seemed a bit distracted on this trip though.

Flora   Yeh, I have. I guess I'm just getting in my own head about things. Feeling doubt. The thought of getting married is so exciting and to Tim who I love. It's a dream. But those other, unhelpful thoughts that creep in have been hard. The idea that I'm engaged to a man for the second time. That, out of nowhere, things went horribly downhill with William and I'm scared, I guess, that it could happen again. Even though I know Tim is a completely different man. He's so gentle and kind and loving and . . . I know all of those things rationally but . . . sometimes it's just hard.

And I keep second guessing myself. I know the things that happened with William were not my fault. But I'm just scared. I can't help but feel worried. That perhaps it's actually me. The common denominator in both is me.

Beth   You are not responsible for the situation with William. You are brave and courageous and strong for getting yourself out of that situation. And you cannot let that get in the way of you being happy now. Truly happy.

Flora   I just need to tell Tim.

Kiki   He doesn't know?

Flora   No, not the whole story. I have to tell him. I will, when we get back. I guess that's what's been on my mind this whole weekend.

Beth   Just remember. We're here for you. We always will be.

Kiki   Always.

Georgina   Always.

Beth   And he'll understand. It'll probably bring you closer. Talking about things can do that.

Flora   Thank you, girls. I'm so lucky to have you.

Kiki   We love you, Flo Flo.

The girls hug.

Beth   And you're right. You are lucky to have us.

Camilla-Joy *and* **Kat** *enter.*

Camilla-Joy   Morning!

Kat   Hi girls. How did you all sleep?

Flora   Pretty good thanks. You?

Kat   Good.

Camilla-Joy   Not so good. That mattress you lent me, Georgia. It's really uncomfortable. You should really buy a new one.

Georgina (*through gritted teeth*)   Oh, I'm sorry to hear that, Camilla-Joy.

Camilla-Joy   I forgive you.

Georgina   Oh. Thank you.

Camilla-Joy   Also, this is awkward to say, Flora, but I heard what you were saying before. About your ex, William.

Flora   Oh.

Camilla-Joy   I could hear everything you told the girls. These tents don't block out any noise.

Georgina   You got that right.

Camilla-Joy   So what now?

Flora (*flustered*)   Look, I'm going to tell Tim. I wasn't trying to withhold information or anything. He does deserve to know, everything. I was just trying to work out how to tell him. But I will. Please trust me on that, I will. I didn't mean to keep anything from him. You probably think I'm dishonest and deceitful and . . .

Camilla-Joy   I actually think you're really brave.

Flora   You what?

Camilla-Joy   I think you're brave. And courageous. And I admire what you've had to go through to be where you are today. That takes guts.

Flora   Thank you.

Camilla-Joy   Of all Tim's girlfriends, you're definitely not the worst.

Flora   Thank you. I feel really . . . touched.

Camilla-Joy   And I'm grateful. That you're becoming part of our family. One thing I know about Tim is that he will be fine when you tell him. And if he's not, you march him straight to me. And hey, you tell him when you're ready to tell him.

Flora   Thank you, Camilla-Joy.

Camilla-Joy   Call me CJ. Now, I am not a hugger but I'll allow it this one time.

She and **Flora** *hug.*

Figure 4 Kat reveals Kiki's secret stardom to the group. Photo courtesy of Tyler Marsland.

Scene Fourteen

Later that morning. Everyone is packed and ready to leave.

Flora   I can't believe this weekend is done. It's been so much fun. George, thank you for making it all happen.

Georgina   You're welcome.

Flora   And before we wrap this all up, I have something small for you all. I really hope you like it.

Flora *gives each person a decorated pot filled with what appears to be just soil.*

Beth   This is just beautiful, Flo.

Kiki   What is it, babe?

Flora   Well, it's not much now. But it will be. I've planted daffodil bulbs in each of your pots. So they should be beautiful yellow flowers in early spring.

Georgina   That is so lovely. Thank you.

Flora   I did just want to also say that I really appreciate your support this weekend, and always. I'm feeling so much stronger about things and I wanted to let you know that I'm going to talk to Tim later today.

Beth   I think that's a really good idea.

Kiki   Same.

Cliff *and* **Hans** *enter.*

Georgina   Oh good timing. Cliff, would you come over here, hun.

Beth   Hun?

Georgina   Before we all go, I wanted to make a little announcement. Cliff and I have decided to schedule our first date. We're officially a thing! (*All of the girls react, thrilled for* **Georgina**.)

Hans   *Wunderbar*! Congratulations, old boy! What a match!

Cliff   You had me at hello . . . and straight tent pegs.

Georgina   Cliff, you're like a dream. Honest you are!

Beth *dry wretches.*

Georgina   Beth!

Beth   Sorry. This is not a reaction to you both. I'm really happy for you. I'm just still feeling . . . (**Beth** *dry wretches again, louder this time.*)

Kiki   Gosh, babe, it's like you're pregnant or something.

Beth   Well . . .

Flora   What?

Beth   Since we're making announcements, I did a test a week ago and Freddy and I are expecting. (*All of the girls react, thrilled for* **Beth**.)

Flora   Oh my goodness. Beth! You've been trying for so long now.

Beth   Over a year. I still can't believe it.

Kiki   This is so exciting!

Camilla-Joy   Now I get why you've been so moody, Beth! I actually have an announcement to make as well. While it's not a baby or a new relationship, it is something that's pretty important so why not tell everyone now. Everyone be quiet and listen carefully.

Georgina   The floor is yours!

Camilla-Joy   I have decided, after eleven months and some really good results, to change gyms. I'm going to end my membership and take up aqua aerobics.

Flora   Wow.

Camilla-Joy   I know.

Kiki   You go, girl. Make those decisions!

Kat   You could also tell them the business news.

Camilla-Joy   Oh yeh! And Kat and I are going into business together.

Flora   Congratulations! Doing what?

Camilla-Joy   We are launching a startup company, hosting children's birthday parties. I thought with Kat's organisational skills and my bubbly and Camilla 'joyous' personality, it's sure to make us lots of money. I'll give you a discount when your little brat is old enough, Beth.

Beth   Thanks! Ah, your turn, Kiki. You got any news to blow us all away with?

Kiki   I guess.

Beth   Well, spit it out.

Kiki   So you guys know how I love my social media and I'm always on about being grateful.

All   Yes!

Kiki   I kind of put the two together and I've kind of blown up online. Like majorly. It's kind of my full income now and I keep getting gifted things just for posting videos about gratitude. It's actually really cool.

Kat   Oh my goodness, that's where I know you from. You're Kiki from 'It's great to be grateful with Kiki'. You're a big deal!

Flora   So how many followers are we talking? A few thousand?

Kat   Try a few hundred thousand. She's huge!

Kiki   I don't know about that but I did just get gifted an all-expenses paid trip to the Maldives so I was hoping we could all go together soon. Before Beth can't fly anymore.

Flora   Um, yes!

Georgina   Absolutely!

Camilla-Joy   Count me in!

All of the girls politely smile at **Camilla-Joy***'s comment.*

Flora   Kiki, you are amazing. You really are.

Georgina   We're going to have to up our social media game and start following you!

Beth   You little star!

Flora   Well, go on, give us some gratitude attitude to end our trip with.

Kiki   No!

All   Come on!

Kiki   OK. Let me think. This one is for everyone but especially for you, Flora. (*Referencing the pot she is still holding.*) Daffodils are a symbol of new beginnings, of rebirth. I think as people, we go through lots of different things. We feel immense happiness, we struggle with our sense of self and moments of doubt, and we experience all of the other feelings that come with being human.

I think we have to remember to treat ourselves with kindness, the way we'd treat the ones we love. We're not that different to plants or to flowers really. Depending on the season, we can be dormant, in a state of rejuvenation or thriving. Often, all we need is a little bit of love.

These beautiful daffodils, yet to fully grow, are a good reminder of that. There's one thing left for this beautiful flower to do. And Flora, there's one thing left for you to do.

Flora   What's that?

Kiki   Bloom.

End of show.

Bloom Discussion Questions

1. Referenced in the play's title, how is the parallel between plants and people used to explore the idea of growth and catharsis?
2. How does Flora's camping trip bring characters together in unexpected ways and serve as a catalyst for character and plot development in *Bloom*?
3. Significant challenge often reveals strengths we didn't know we possessed. How is this statement true in *Bloom*?
4. How is tension built and sustained throughout *Bloom*?
5. How are different relationships represented in *Bloom*? How do these relationships develop throughout the script and provide instances of comfort, conflict and humour for the characters involved and the audience?
6. Identify and discuss the presence of the following themes: friendship, gratitude, resilience, identity, love and accepting others. What aesthetic strategies are used to represent these themes in the play?
7. Consider the character of Flora. How might her recent experiences impact her sense of self and inform her behaviour throughout *Bloom*?
8. Research the significant issue of domestic violence across Australia and the world. How does domestic violence impact individuals and communities? What are the broader social consequences? What supports are available for victims of domestic violence?

Pinky

Playwright's note

'You got a pinky, you got hope'.

I was inspired to write *Pinky* after witnessing many of my friends become parents or make attempts to do so over the last years. While falling pregnant is relatively straightforward for some, what I've observed is that the journey of parenthood is often a scary one. There's so much to consider: the weight of expectation, the onus of responsibility and the fear of the unknown among other things. And that's if everything goes to plan.

While I have seen that parenthood and having a baby can be incomparably beautiful and life affirming, for many the journey to becoming a parent is one filled with obstacles, some of which make the journey unsurmountable. In *Pinky*, I wanted to reflect a number of different voices. The voice of an expectant parent, the voice of someone who has decided parenthood is not for them, the voice of a person who is constantly navigating their ever-changing parental role and the voice of a parent or would-be parent, displaced by grief. While I hope this piece navigates these stories with the delicacy they deserve, there is also a lot of fun to be had in *Pinky*. What better place than an annual baby expo to explore some diverse characters and their often hilarious stories!

Through all the fun, there are a number of central themes explored in *Pinky*. The play examines the many nuances of love, the importance of friendship, the power of persistence and the idea that the notion of family can be something we create for ourselves. This story is ultimately one of hope though. An acknowledgement that through immense challenge, a shred of hope can often be the one thing to gently nudge us along in life and that, if we look hard enough, we can always find some semblance of hope. After all, as Hannah says, 'You got a pinky, you got hope'.

All proceeds from the original production of *Pinky* were donated to the Pink Elephants Support Network, an organisation dedicated to supporting women and families through the grief of early pregnancy loss. I encourage future productions to consider supporting a similar organisation or cause, connecting the story to meaningful real-world causes.

Brady Lloyd

Pinky by Brady Lloyd

Synopsis

Pinky is a heartwarming and humorous exploration of the unpredictable journey to parenthood. Set against the backdrop of an annual baby expo, the story introduces a collection of diverse individuals, including a kooky wellness expert, a well-meaning work experience kid, a self-proclaimed Casanova and a heavily pregnant mother very ready to pop. As the day unfolds, the expo guests take part in a series of quirky baby-inspired workshops. Through shared laughter, unexpected conversations and moments of vulnerability, they begin to open up and discover a sense of connection they never thought possible.

Setting

Pinky takes place at 'Baby, Baby', a wellness-inspired baby expo in 2020. Six people have won the chance to attend a pre-event and experience the expo before it opens to the public.

Characters

Fourteen characters (8F, 6M). Note: This play accommodates flexible and inclusive casting.

Expo staff:

Tanya, *36. Tanya is the uptight, no-nonsense expo coordinator.*

Journee, *36. Kind and kooky, Journee facilitates the expo wellness programmes.*

Niall, *18. A well-meaning work experience kid, Niall wants to impress.*

Johnny, *18 Johnny is unwillingly dragged to the expo by his Auntie Tanya.*

Hugh, *30. A self-proclaimed Casanova, Hugh oozes confidence and flair.*

Jim, *32. Jim is Hugh's lovable best friend and the expo security guard.*

Kim, *30. Kim is the sarcastic niece of the expo founder.*

Invited guests:

Martha, *36. Warm and loving. Martha is pregnant with her fourth child.*

Michael, *40. Michael is an endearing goofball who adores his wife, Martha.*

Hannah, *28. Hannah is a nervous mum-to-be, focused on a perfect pregnancy.*

Lexi, *25. Sassy and strong, Lexi is Hannah's sister-in-law.*

Tiff, *20. Tiff is a young woman who finds unexpected connections at the expo.*

Wendy, *58. Quirky and a little old-fashioned, Wendy is Tiff's mum.*

Bruce, *50. The classic Aussie bloke, Bruce is an accidental guest at the expo.*

Scene One

The sound of a baby crying. As this fades, we hear **Martha** *sobbing noisily behind her pusher, alone. She is heavily pregnant.*

Michael (*rushing in*)   Darling, are you OK? There you are! What's wrong?

Martha (*in a state*)   What's wrong? What's wrong?

Michael   Martha?

Martha   I'm not sure I'm ready to have this baby, Michael!

Michael   You're not sure?

Martha   I don't think I am ready, love. I don't think my body is ready, you know.

Michael   I think you're ready, sweets. You're enormous!

Martha (*starts a new round of sobbing*)   Michael!

Michael   Enormous, but beautiful. Baby number four and you couldn't look bigger! (*Correcting himself.*) Better! You couldn't look better!

Martha (*starting to recover*)   You really think so?

Michael   Absolutely. (*Offering* **Martha** *a handkerchief.*) Here you go, sweets. Now let's get you something to eat before things kick off. That always helps. I packed some of your favourite muesli bars. (*They retrieve the muesli bars and start eating.*)

Hannah *and* **Lexi** *enter.*

Hannah   So, Lexi, there are lots of things we need to look at today. You studied the spreadsheet that I sent you, didn't you?

Lexi   Yes, Han.

Hannah   Excellent. So let's just go over it all, OK? I want to look at prams and buy some bottles, the ones that come with a steriliser kit. And breast pads, and nappies and bulk packs of wipes. I've heard they have great specials on wraps and swaddles too so that would be good to check out. Most of all, I'm really interested in all the wellness stuff they are going to run. Have I missed anything?

Lexi   You lost me at breast pads.

Hannah   Lex!

Lexi   We've got all day. No need to rush. You should try and enjoy today!

Hannah   You're right.

Lexi (*to herself*)   One of us should enjoy it at least.

Hannah   OK, game face on. We want to make sure we get as much information as we possibly can today. I have to use it as a real opportunity to upskill you know? Take it all in. Be the sponge! You know, I still can't believe we got these exclusive tickets giving us full access to this expo before the general public. I mean, that's a sign, right?

Lexi   Han, what did we talk about on the way in?

Hannah   I know, I know. It's just, I really want today to go well. For it to be perfect. For everything about this pregnancy to be perfect. And the more I know, the less chance there is . . .

Lexi   It's going to be fine. I know it.

Hannah   Thank you for coming. When Billy said he needed to work, I started to worry and wasn't sure if . . . Sister-in-law to the rescue!

Lexi   There's not many people I'd come to a baby expo thing for. I hope you feel special.

Hannah   I do. Now, it's almost nine. According to our schedule for the day, there's an official welcome in just a sec. This is all so exciting. I can't believe we're here!

Lexi   Neither can I!

Tanya *and* **Journee** *enter.*

Tanya   Ladies, welcome! And a gentleman too! Lovely to see a man here! My name is Tanya and I am the event coordinator of the most loved baby expo in the country, 'Baby Baby'. You are all winners of our exclusive pre-opening sneak peek and therefore today you become a part of the 'Baby Baby' family for life! We hope you will enjoy being with us today.

At 'Baby Baby' we have a real focus on wellness. Yes, we have wonderful deals on every product you could ever dream of, but we're really more interested in looking after mumma and bubba wellbeing! In light of this, I'd like to now introduce our wellness expert who will look after you today. She's a little alternative but she's very passionate!

Journee   Good morning and *namaste*. (**Journee** *bows and prompts everyone to also bow. They do, awkwardly.*) I want to acknowledge the sun and the moon, the winds and the waters and the life that is in all of us. From our minds, to our hearts, to our bellies!

Lexi   Not this belly!

Hannah   Shhh, Lex!

Journee   Join me in a morning stretch. Reach up and stretch your fingers like this. Now morning shimmy and let your voice ring out. (*She shimmies with her hands above her head and then unleashes a high-pitched warble. Everyone copies awkwardly, far more self-conscious.*) And rest. (*Everyone quietens.*) Today, you will bathe in buoyant brooks of blessedness and experience the trickling tiny tides of truthful tranquillity. My name is Journee and I will do exactly that. I will assist you on the most important journey. Motherhood. It is a great privilege to bring a child into the world and a great privilege to help you do it. Who is ready?

Hannah   I'm ready!

Journee   Yes you are!

Tanya   Thank you, Journee. (*With a touch of judgement.*) Very inspiring. Journee and I have been in the baby business together for years now, haven't we? Hard to believe really! Anyway, today is all about sampling what we have to offer here at 'Baby, Baby'. Make sure you get along to all of the workshops we're running!

Journee   Especially my yoga wellness sampler coming up. It's an absolute must!

Tanya   It's certainly a unique experience! Now, without further ado . . .

Wendy *and* **Tiff** *enter.*

Wendy   Oh my goodness! Hello, everyone. We're finally here. Couldn't find a park and bugalugs here didn't want to walk. (*To* **Tiff**.) Come on Tiff! (*To* **Tanya**.) I'm sorry we're late.

Tanya   Not a problem. There's always one. Come in!

Wendy   Hi, everyone. Name's Wendy and this is my daughter Tiff.

Tanya   Well, you haven't missed a thing! We were just welcoming everyone to today's sneak peek! What brings you here this morning?

Wendy (*looks at* **Tiff** *then speaks up*)   Ah, that'd be me. Just dragged Tiff along for some moral support. Well, introduce yourself.

Tiff   I don't really think we need to do that here, mum.

Wendy   Can't hurt. Go on.

Tiff   OK. I'm Tiff.

Journee   *Namaste*, Tiff.

Tiff (*awkwardly*)   *Namaste.*

Tanya   I think it's time for a spot of bubbly to kick off the morning!

Lexi   Now we're talking!

Journee   Don't worry, ladies, there's plenty glasses of non-alcoholic.

Lexi   Boo!

Journee   Boys! Bring in the champers!

Niall *and* **Johnny** *enter.* **Niall** *is excited and eager to please, dressed up for the day. Disinterested,* **Johnny** *could not care less. He is in ripped jeans and street wear.* **Niall** *carries a tray of champagne flutes.* **Johnny** *has his hands in his pockets, chewing gum.*

Niall   Did someone say champers? (**Johnny** *rolls his eyes.*)

Tanya   Everyone, this is Niall and he is doing some work experience with us. He's very keen and is at your beck and call today. Need anything, just sing out!

Niall   Your wish is my command, ladies. (*Sees* **Michael**.) And man.

Tanya   And this is Johnny. (**Johnny** *waves.*) Johnny is my nephew and I've dragged him here today to give his eyes a rest from all the video games he is constantly glued to! Say hello, Johnny.

Johnny   Hello, Johnny. (**Tanya** *rolls her eyes lovingly.*)

Niall   Please let us know if there is anything we can do to make your day at 'Baby, Baby' brilliant brilliant! (**Tanya** *looks at* **Johnny**, *prompting him to say something.*)

Johnny   What he said.

Suddenly, lights dim and exaggerated music plays. The only male staff member **Hugh** *struts on. He is the self-proclaimed Casanova of the baby expo scene and considers himself a real ladies man.*

Tanya   Why does he insist on the lights and the music and the entrance?!

Journee   It's very theatrical!

Hugh   Everyone can relax now. Hugh is here and the party can starty!

Tanya   Yes, hello, Hugh. (**Tanya** *gives the nod to* **Niall** *who begins to move around giving out the champers.* **Lexi** *takes two.* **Journee** *is impressed.*) Journee, focus!

Hugh   Can I get a woohoo if you're excited? (*The crowd woohoo.*) Can I get a woohoo if you want to learn about baby . . . stuff?! (*The crowd woohoo.*) Can I get a woohoo if you're single? (*Only* **Lexi** *woohoos with both champagnes in the air.* **Hugh** *gives her a wink.*) Good to know. Right, everyone, Hugh is my name and car seats are my game. Any questions, you just drive yourself over to me, strap in and Hugh will help you out!

Tans, have you seen Jimbo yet today?

Tanya   No, but I'm sure he's around here somewhere. Do you mind doing a quick look-around to find him?

Hugh   Sure. (*Shouting.*) Jimbo!

Tanya   Guessing you haven't seen Kim either?

Hugh   Nope.

Jim *enters.*

Jim   Did someone call for me?

Hugh   Here he is. Ladies and gents, this is our one and only Jimbo. He's a very important man. Teller of terrible jokes, owner of the most luscious locks you'll find this side of the city and best mate to your dear man Hugh!

Jim   You're too kind, my friend.

Hugh   You pull up OK after last night?

Jim   Better than you!

Tanya   And Jim is our very professional, very experienced, security officer!

Jim   Protecting mums and bubs from nappy thieves and baby burglars since 2018!

Tanya   Right. A couple of minutes to mingle and finish your refreshments then it's our first class! Welcome to 'Baby, Baby'!

Scene Two

Everyone mills around, finishing their drinks and going over the day's schedule.

Journee *and* **Hugh** *have left to prepare for the morning ahead.* **Niall** *and* **Johnny** *offer a drink to* **Tiff**.

Niall   Good morning, mam. Drink?

Tiff   No thank you.

Niall   What's wrong?

Tiff   Let's start with you calling me mam. I'm about thirty-years younger than any mam I've ever met.

Niall   Sorry, I didn't mean to offend you. I was just trying to be polite.

Johnny   Everything OK over here? You trying your luck, mate?

Niall   Trying my what?

Johnny   Flirting. You know, trying to get the girl.

Niall   Absolutely not.

Johnny   Come on, mate. You don't have to be so uptight. Loosen that bow tie a little. You're allowed to chat up a pretty girl. Get in there. Capture the flag!

Niall   I was not capturing anything!

Johnny   I bet you gave it a shot. (*To* **Tiff**.) He did, didn't he, babe?

Tiff (*sarcastically*)   Actually, that's exactly what was happening, babe. He just said 'Good morning, mam' and I fell in love. Like, bam. Head over heels in love. We were just about to ride off into the sunset together too. (*Moving towards* **Johnny**.) I just can't believe that, here, at this baby expo, I have finally found my soul mate. The man I'll spend the rest of my life with. He's won me over in a matter of minutes. He's 'captured the flag' so to speak.

Johnny   Really?

Tiff   He has about as much chance of chatting me up as you do of growing a moustache. Or showering apparently.

Niall (*geekily*)   Burn!

Johnny   You look familiar.

Tiff   OK.

Niall (*to* **Tiff**)   I'm sorry about all this. (*To* **Johnny**.) I really think you should be a little more respectful you know. We are 'on the clock' so to speak. Remember you are supposed to be a professional.

Tiff   Professionally irritating.

Wendy *enters.*

Wendy   Tiff, there you are. What are you doing? Chatting to boys!

Tiff   Mum, I wasn't.

Wendy   We've talked about this.

Tiff   Mum! They came up to me.

Niall   It's true, mam, we did.

Wendy   Whatever you say, Tiffany. You ready for the first class?

Tiff   Not really.

Wendy   A little positivity wouldn't go astray. Wouldn't hurt you to look on the bright side for once, Tiffany. And God forbid, you might learn something today.

Tiff   Mum, just give me a second.

Wendy   To do what, Tiffany?

Tiff   Just one second. (**Wendy** *tuts and moves away to prepare for the class.*)

Niall   Are you OK?

Tiff   What?

Niall   You just seem upset.

Tiff   I'm fine.

Niall   I'm sorry if we upset you with the drinks and *his* general personality.

Johnny   Oi!

Tiff   It's fine. I just have a lot on my plate at the moment. And the last thing I want is to come to this stupid baby expo and hear about stupid baby stuff with stupid baby-obsessed people. It's not where I need to be right now.

Johnny   Why are you here then? (**Tiff** *pauses, uneasy.*)

Niall   Weren't you listening before! Tiff's mum is pregnant. She's here for moral support. Isn't that right, Tiff?

Tiff   Yep. Anyway, better get myself ready for a day of moral support. See ya, boys.

Johnny (*stopping her*)   That's where I know you from! You were in my older brother's year at school.

Tiff   I don't think so. Must be someone else.

Johnny   No, I'm sure it was you. Weren't you dux of the school?

Tiff   So what?

Johnny   My brother hosted all the parties in his final year. You must have been at one of them at least?

Niall   OK, Johnny, no need to interrogate the poor girl.

Johnny (*to* **Niall**)   I'll explain to you later what a party is.

Niall   I know what a party is and I've attended many parties in my time. I'll have you know, I quite enjoy dancing *at* parties. Speaking of. Have you been rehearsing for later today?

Johnny   Do we actually have to do that?

Niall   Of course! Lucky for you, I took dance as an elective in Year 8 and Year 9 so I'm quite agile and I'll gladly help you with some of the choreography. (*To* **Tiff**.) Let's catch up later, Tiff. (*To* **Johnny**.) Follow me. We have to get set up for morning tea!

Niall *and* **Johnny** *leave.* **Tiff** *remains in deep thought before joining the* group.

Scene Three

Journee *makes a grand entrance wearing brightly coloured eighties workout wear, ready to take the class. She bangs a gong to start.*

Journee   The time is now, beautiful people, for a beautiful yoga class. Hey, Google, begin playlist 'Meditation, Massage and Manifestation Top Hits'. (*Music begins.* **Journee** *notions for them to all come in.*) Everyone, come and cluster, come and cluster.

Michael   Oh, Journee, I've got a joke for you. What did the yoga instructor say when his alarm went off?

Martha   Michael, really?

Michael   *Namaste* in bed! Get it?

Martha   Oh Michael, love. Save your jokes for your poker nights.

Lexi (*to* **Hannah**)   You OK?

Hannah   I don't know about this. Billy said that I shouldn't do anything I'm not comfortable with, you know.

Lexi   Hannah, you've done plenty of yoga before. You're almost as hippy dippy as our new friend Journee, so relax. You'll be fine. I missed my dance class this morning so this is going to be great.

Journee   Those that are feeling more confident to the front please.

Lexi   You don't mind do you? (**Hannah** *shakes her head.*) Catch you after. (**Lexi** *moves to the front and proceeds to stretch higher and longer than* **Journee** *and try to outdo her in every way throughout the class.*)

Hannah   Journee, how safe is this class for those that are pregnant? I don't want to do anything that might be dangerous.

Journee   Darling, there is no danger here. You're part of the 'Baby, Baby' family now remember. I'll look after you and provide an option for beginners and (*looking at* **Lexi**) alternatives for our more confident participants. If you have the capacity to move, then you will be fine.

Michael   That probably rules you out then, sweets.

Martha   You're not wrong, love.

Michael   And me too, to be fair. Tennis elbow, you know.

Journee   Some gentle stretches to begin everyone. Nice and calm. Come on, Wendy, I know you've got some flexibility somewhere in there. You may be old but you were young once!

Martha (*flinching at a kick*)   The baby's kicking today.

Hannah   Oh, wow. Does that happen often? That must feel magical.

Martha   You could say that! Want a feel? (**Martha** *places* **Hannah**'s *hands on her stomach and holds them there. As she does, the baby kicks and* **Martha** *yells out, scaring* **Hannah**.)

Hannah   I can't wait till my little princess kicks.

Michael   Oh you're having a girl?

Hannah   Well, I don't know for sure. But I hope so. I couldn't imagine having a boy. They can be so . . . gross, you know.

Martha   I do know! I've got three gross boys at home and one gross boy on the way!

Hannah   So you'll have four boys?

Martha (*lovingly*)   Five if you count the gross one I married!

Michael   Our very own basketball team!

Journee   Beautiful bodies bare your soul . . . and breathe . . .

Martha   Michael's a big NBA fan. Thinks he's quite the Michael Jordan himself.

Michael   I was quite a skilled point guard in my prime. Could dribble the ball quicker than most.

Martha   Now, you just dribble asleep in front of the TV.

Michael   True. Having kids is tiring.

Martha   This your first, love?

Hannah   You could say that.

Martha (*feels the baby kick*)   Oh, did you feel that one?

Hannah   Yeh, I did. Wow.

Martha   This one kicks harder than all his brothers combined!

Journee   And breathe . . . and stretch . . . and breathe . . . and stretch . . .

Hannah   Four boys. I can't even imagine!

Martha   It has its moments. But it can be a blessing.

Michael   Yeh, when they're all asleep.

Martha   It's messy but we manage. Oh and don't even get me started on the state of our toilet floors! Wee everywhere.

Michael   Everywhere!

Hannah (*horrified*)   That sounds . . . I'm just imagining it. Wow.

Journee   And breathe . . . and reach . . . and breathe . . . and reach . . . now take in a large breath and hold.

Everyone doing yoga inhales and holds their breath.

Hannah   I'm feeling quite short of breath suddenly.

Martha   Yes, I know the feeling. Gets worse the bigger you get. And don't get me started on the weak bladder! The other day, I practically wet myself. Right in the middle of Kmart! You've got that to look forward to!

Everyone doing yoga exhales loudly.

Hannah   Excellent! (*Getting more flustered.*) Is it hot in here? I think it's hot in here.

Hugh (*arrives in fluro workout wear, joining* **Journee** *at the front*)   Did someone say it was hot in here? Do you mind if I turn up the temperature just a touch more? (*Showing off his outfit.*) Ladies, what do we think?

Journee   Nice of you to join us, Hugh. Your entrances always sparkle with drama! Too bad we're nearly finished!

Hugh   You can call me the finale then! You don't mind do you? (*Enjoying the attention.*) Ladies, I'd like to talk about one of my favourite muscles in the human body. The pelvic floor. Here's an exercise you might want to try out to keep yourself strong as an ox as you prepare for labour

He proceeds to thrust enthusiastically. **Journee** *is trying to stay calm but it is clear her yoga class has gone off the rails. She begins a breathing exercise.*

Lexi   It is too early to see that!

Wendy   Excuse me! What sort of yoga class is this?

Tiff   Mum, don't make a fuss.

Hannah   It *is* free at least!

Lexi   It would want to be!

Wendy   He should be paying us!

Tanya (*storming on*)   Now Hugh, what have I told you about gatecrashing Journee's yoga class! It's kooky enough as it is let alone you coming in to make it even stranger!

Journee   Breathe in positivity and breathe out negativity . . .

Hugh   I know, Tans. It's just, it seems a shame to not show these pins off to all our clucky clients you know?

Tanya   No, I don't know. How about you stick to your car seats?

Hugh   That I can do!

Tanya (*guiding him to apologise*)   And is there anything you'd like to say to these people before you go Hugh?

Hugh (*beat*)   You're welcome! (*He winks.* **Jim** *enters.*) My main man Jimbo. How are you, mate?

Jim   Good, man. You got a sec? (*To everyone.*) Sorry for the interruption.

Hugh   Ladies and gentleman, not a word ever comes out of this man's mouth that isn't inspirational. That isn't insightful. That isn't unbelievably intelligent and unimaginably astute. So, give it to us Jimbo, my main man. What gold nugget of wisdom can you offer us?

Jim (*reading from a tattered note he has written*)   Ah, a red Toyota Corolla number plate UQT 854 has left their lights on.

Hugh   What did I tell you, ladies and gentleman! Solid gold.

Scene Four

Hannah, **Tanya** *and* **Lexi** *enter.*

Hannah   So, what other recommendations do you have for today? I don't want to miss anything, you know? Make the most of this opportunity. I'm also taking lots of notes since my husband Billy can't be here. He's at work. Which doesn't mean that he'll be an absent father or anything. It's just that on this particular Friday, he wasn't able to get the time off. Which we discussed and I was fine with but, I'm not going to lie, is presenting some challenges today. But we keep on keeping on. So, my apologies. You go.

Tanya   Sorry, what was the question?

Lexi   Han, remember that today we are just going to go with the flow. Relax and enjoy.

Hannah   Yeh of course. This is me relaxed. I'm so relaxed I could . . . I could . . . I don't know. What do relaxed people do?

Lexi   She's a work in progress.

Tanya   Well, no worries. We have some time now before a few different workshops are starting. There is a very 'relaxing' hand massage session that Journee is assisting with.

Lexi   You and Journee. What's the story there?

Tanya   What do you mean?

Lexi   I mean, I sense some friction. You're business partners and all but does she drive you a little bit nuts, being so alternative?

Tanya   Of course not. We've worked together for years now.

Lexi   There's more to it than that.

Tanya   Let's just say a few years ago, Journee had a life epiphany. It seemed to change her whole personality. She became extremely spiritual and 'alternative' as you call it. A bit of an adjustment for us all, I guess.

Kim *enters with a coffee in hand and headphones in.*

Tanya   Well, well, well. What time do you call this?

Kim   What?

Tanya   Ladies, this is Kim. Kim, this is Hannah and Lexi. Kim runs one of our stalls. Children's birthday parties (*under her breath*) if you can believe it. (**Kim** *rolls her eyes.*) Kim, did you want to tell these ladies a little about what you do?

Kim   Not really, no.

Tanya   Kim!

Kim   Sure. (*Putting on a sickly sweet accent, dripping with sarcasm.*) Hello. My name is Kim and I run children's birthday parties. They're overpriced and tacky and marketed at mummies that have too much money and are obsessed with outdoing the birthday parties that *their* mummy friends put on for *their* little brats. (**Kim** *takes out a party blower and blows on it sarcastically.*)

Lexi (*matching her sass*)   So you're really passionate about what you do then?

Hannah   Lexi!

Kim   I'm so passionate I could scream.

Tanya   Kim happens to be the niece of the 'Baby, Baby' founder Melanie Matthews. So, she's still here doing her thing. Whatever that thing is.

Lexi   Lucky you!

Hannah   Do you have a brochure, Kim?

Kim   Does it look like I have a brochure, Heather?

Hannah   It's Hannah.

Kim   Of course it is.

Tanya   Well, I need to go set up so I'll leave you be. Kim, try to be nice. For once.

Kim   Before you go, Tanya, I need to book my holidays for this month.

Tanya   Your holidays? You just had three weeks off.

Kim   And I need another three weeks off starting next week. That won't be an issue will it? I don't want to have to get on the phone to Auntie Melanie, you know?

Tanya   Let's discuss it at the end of your shift today.

Kim   Oh, and I'm probably taking tomorrow off. Lots of appointments you know. (*Frustrated,* **Tanya** *leaves.*) So, if you've asked all of your annoying questions and taken up enough of my time, feel free to go now.

Lexi (*sarcastically*)   Thank you for your customer service. It's really made my day.

Kim   I'm so glad.

Lexi   I'm sure you are. Hopefully we'll bump into each other a bit later on. See ya, Kelly.

Kim   It's Kim.

Lexi   Of course it is. (**Kim** *is impressed by* **Lexi***'s boldness.*)

Hugh *and* **Jim** *return after a break.* **Hugh** *pushes on his portable baby car seat stall, helped by* **Jim***.*

Hugh   Ladies, hello. (*Motioning for* **Hannah** *and* **Lexi** *to come over.*) If you can tear yourself away from the charisma that is Kim, come on over.

Kim *sticks her finger up at* **Hugh***, settles in with a magazine and starts to read.* **Hugh** *sees an opportunity to flirt.*

Hugh (*to* **Hannah**)   Interested?

Hannah   Not sure.

Hugh   What about the car seats then? (**Hannah** *politely smiles.*)

Hannah   Do you have any information brochures, so I can show my *husband* tonight?

Hugh   That I don't. It's all up here. (*Tapping his head.*) But I do have a website. You should check it out. Can't remember what the address is now but jump on Google. I'm sure I'll pop up.

Hannah   Well, thank you so much. Now, I need to go and use the ladies before the massages start.

Lexi   Sounds good.

Hannah (*sincerely*) Bye, Kim. It was nice to meet you. (**Kim** *looks up from her magazine and gives* **Hannah** *a perplexed look before going back to her magazine. To* **Lexi**.) You ready?

Lexi I might just ask a few questions about this car seat. Just in case I ever need to know, you know?

Hannah (*clocking that* **Lexi** *might be interested in* **Hugh**) Suit yourself. See you later on. Don't be late though. If you need me, call me. Or text me. I'll have my phone on loud as always.

Lexi Will do. See you soon.

Realising that **Lexi** *is about to come over,* **Hugh** *drops down and starts doing push-ups.*

Lexi Hi.

Hugh Oh hello, honey bun. Was just getting a few more push-ups in, you know. Aim for 500 a day. At least.

Lexi (*unenthusiastically*) Great.

Hugh Lexi, wasn't it? You interested in some car seat service are you?

Lexi Absolutely not.

Hugh Sorry?

Lexi There's no way I'll ever have something like that in my sports car, thank you very much.

Hugh You might have to if you have 'little Lexis' running around one day.

Lexi Not a chance. I'm not having kids.

Hugh Really?

Lexi What's so surprising about that?

Hugh Well, you are at a baby expo, speaking to someone who sells baby seats which are made for babies. So you could understand why I made the leap.

Lexi Oh, I'm only here because my workaholic brother couldn't be here for his sweet, but super-stressed-out, wife. So, sister-in-law steps in. I needed a break from the schedule so here I am!

Hugh Well, I think that's very . . .

Lexi (*to* **Jim**) Hello. Do you speak?

Jim Yeh.

Lexi Great.

Jim Great.

Lexi I'm Lexi.

Jim   Hi, Lexi.

Lexi   Hugh, do you think I could speak to you for a second. Just the two of us. (*She motions for him to come over.*)

Hugh (*jokingly*)   Does baby poo smell?

Lexi   What? Ew. Just come here.

Hugh   Your wish is my command. Won't be a second, Jimbo. Duty calls. Watch and learn. (**Hugh** *goes over to* **Lexi**.) What can I do for you, sweetheart? I get off at five if you want to catch up for a drink.

Lexi   Tempting but I'm good. Listen, your friend Jim.

Hugh   Yeh?

Lexi   What's his deal?

Hugh   What do you mean?

Lexi   Is he . . . single?

Hugh   What?

Lexi   Is he single?

Hugh   Ah, I don't know. I think so. I never asked.

Lexi   OK. Well, could you?

Hugh   Wait a minute. You like Jimbo?

Lexi   What's not to like?

Hugh   Huh?

Lexi   There's something intriguing about a man with a certain silent broodiness about him. And don't get me started on that hair. (*Unknowingly,* **Jim** *flicks his hair,* Baywatch *style.*) Anyway, find out for me would you? And be cool about it. If you know how to do that.

Hugh   Cool? I'm the king of cool. I'm the master of cool. Cool is my middle name. I'm like cucumber cool, which is very cool.

Lexi   Whatever you say. (*To* **Jim**.) Bye, Jim.

Jim   See ya round . . . like a donut.

Lexi (*giggling at* **Jim**'*s joke*)   Hope so! I love donuts. (**Lexi** *leaves.*)

Hugh   Jimbo, I didn't know you had moves!

Jim   What?

Hugh   Moves! She's keen as mustard, mate!

Jim   Keen on what?

Hugh   On you!

Jim   You really think?

Hugh   Come on, we have some talking to do. Activate wingman Hugh.

Scene Five

After lunch. The guests sit, ready to partake in the next workshop, a unique hand massage experience. Sitting, in order: **Lexi** *(massaged by* **Johnny***),* **Hannah** *(massaged by* **Niall***),* **Martha** *(massaged by* **Journee***),* **Tiff** *(massaged by* **Tanya***),* **Wendy** *(does not participate but sits down to rest her feet).*

Martha   This is dangerous. A full belly after lunch then a massage. Excuse me if I start snoring.

Hannah   This kid is surprisingly good. I'm really starting to feel relaxed.

Lexi *(to* **Hannah** *quietly)*   Mine keeps forgetting to do the actual massaging so I have to shake him back to life.

Johnny *keeps staring lovingly at* **Lexi** *and forgetting to massage her hand*s.

Journee   Ladies, there's research to suggest that we hold terrific amounts of tension in our hands. So we must take time to release this tension and let it go, like a wave returning to the ocean or a bird taking flight or a dog licking your face.

Johnny   Next we'll be singing, Kumbaya, together.

Tanya   Journee is right. This is especially effective during labour. When that baby is causing you all sorts of pain and there is twisting and screaming and ripping, a simple hand massage will alleviate stress and bring about calm. Redirect your mind.

Martha   That's the plan then! The thought of going through another labour doesn't make me that excited if I'm honest. All that sweating. And the blood! All that blood!

Hannah   Did you have a bad experience, Martha?

Johnny   You're not all about to share labour stories are you? I didn't sign up for that!

Lexi   Hear, hear, kid!

Niall   I actually find it all quite fascinating. The circle of life and everything.

Johnny   Of course you do.

Martha   This is amazing! I've got to teach Michael how to do this. I'm sure we have some massage oils at home!

Johnny   Gross.

Tanya   We do offer a short course so book him in. Might be a great Chrissie present with some benefits for you too! And we offer discounts to those who are part of the 'Baby, Baby' family. *(To* **Tiff.***)* How's the pressure?

Tiff   Fine, I guess. I've never had my hands massaged before. It's kind of weird.

Wendy   Just enjoy it, Tiff. You could do with a release of some tension!

Tanya   Are you sure you wouldn't like someone to work with you, Wendy? This is especially good for pregnant women.

Journee   Of all ages.

Wendy   No, no. I'd rather Tiff have a go. Plus, I'm not a big fan of people touching my hands, no offence.

Tanya   None taken. We do offer a fungal foot treatment. Johnny, maybe you could assist Wendy with that?

Wendy   Oh that sounds interesting.

Johnny (*disgusted*)   Sorry, that ain't happening. No offence. Feet are weird.

Niall   I'd be happy to assist. I've never worked with foot fungus before.

Martha   Journee, you are working wonders.

Journee   I'm so glad. Allow my hands to massage your hands and my spirit to massage your spirit. Feel the magnificence and majestic magic of massage.

Tiff   She loves herself some alliteration.

Tanya   That she does.

Journee   You're on a journey with Journee, Martha. Relish the ride.

Martha (*referencing her name badge*)   It's such an interesting name, Journee. I like unusual names. And I love it if the spelling is changed, just to jazz things up a little you know.

Tiff   Have you thought of a name for your little one?

Hannah   If it's a surprise, you don't have to share.

Martha   Darling, this will be my fourth boy. Nothing's a surprise anymore. We were thinking a name that's timeless. Something that won't date but that really makes a statement, you know. Something really edgy. We were thinking 'Knife'.

Hannah   Knife?

Lexi   That certainly makes a statement.

Johnny   I went to school with a spoon.

Martha   Really?

Johnny   No.

Martha   Well, our other three boys all start with 'Kn'. We like the sound of it. Thought it was really original. So we have Knickson, a Knox and a Kned, all with the silent 'K' just to keep it classy, you know.

Tiff   What if it's a girl?

Martha   I can dream but I doubt very much it'll be a girl. I'm destined to be surrounded by boys it seems. But I have heard some fascinating girl names recently. Absidee, spelled A-B-C-D-E or Ladasha, spelt L-A-dash-A. Oh, and a friend of mine had a great idea. She merged some names. She was keen on Amanda and her wife wanted Samantha so they joined the two and named their daughter Amantha. Oh, and a girlfriend from TAFE did the same thing with her two favourite singers, Beyoncé and Shakira. Named her little girl Shakonce.

Hannah   Shakonce?

Tiff   It's unique I guess.

Martha   Look, I agree and I think there's something to be said for being inspired by music. But my favourite song is Daryll Braithwaite's 'Horses' and I'm just not sure 'Horse' is appropriate to name a little girl.

Johnny (*sarcastically*)   You think?

Tanya   Johnny! How about you do a little less talking and a little more massage! What about you, Wendy? Have you thought of any names?

Wendy (*to Tiff*)   We have had a bit of a think, haven't we. But haven't landed on anything yet.

Journee (*to Wendy*)   Oh come on. You must have some names swirling around in your mind?

Wendy   Well, I guess there are a couple of front runners. Tell them, Tiff.

Tiff   No, it's fine.

Martha   Come on, love.

Tiff (*dreamily*)   Well, I kind of liked Danae if it were a girl and Stuart if it were a boy.

Tanya   Very nice.

Wendy   They're beautiful names.

Tiff (*bringing herself back to reality*)   But, we haven't given it that much thought have we, mum? Mum has been really clear about not wanting to get ahead of ourselves. Just take it a day at a time and see how things go. I mean, something could go wrong, you know. It often does. At any moment, there could suddenly be no baby. So, best not to think too far ahead.

Wendy   Tiff, not really the place to be talking like that. In a room with expectant mothers.

Tiff   Oh, sorry. I didn't meant to . . .

Hannah   It's true though.

Martha   What do you mean, love?

Hannah   Well, the reality is something could go wrong. Things do go wrong. So you can't ever be too sure.

Lexi   Han.

Hannah   Well, she's right.

Martha   It'll all be OK, I'm sure.

Hannah   Yeh.

Martha   The first one is always stressful, love. Trust me.

Hannah   Yeh. Except it's not my first one.

Martha   It's not?

Hannah   No.

Lexi   Hannah, you don't have to if you don't want to.

Hannah   I know. (*To the group.*) I don't really talk about it much but maybe I should.

Martha (*gently*)   Take your time. It's a safe space. We're all here for you.

Hannah (*taking a deep breath then beginning*)   So, my husband's name is Billy. We're childhood sweethearts.

Lexi (*smiling*)   They're so in love, it makes me sick.

Hannah   Lexi's had to put up with me for a long time now. Anyway, Billy and I met just before Year Twelve exams started. He always said that I'm the one responsible for him flunking out in Chemistry because our first date was the night before his exam, which I didn't know at the time!

Johnny   Bit of chemistry study of the practical kind! Nice!

Tanya   Can it, Jonathon.

Hannah   Anyway, we've always, weirdly, talked about kids and how many we'd want. A big family was always the plan. We'd been trying since we got married about three years before and, finally, we did it. About a year ago now. I actually couldn't believe it when it happened because it didn't happen straight away. It was stressful, you know. Thinking it wouldn't be possible. That maybe being a mum might not be in my life's plan or something like that.

I started to really worry. Which, as you guys know from meeting me for only half a day, is very on brand.

Lexi *pulls her hand away from* **Johnny** *who is massaging her hand and places it on* **Hannah**'s *for support. The hand massages have largely stopped by now with all eyes on* **Hannah**.

Hannah   Anyway, it happened. We were pregnant with little Pinky.

Journee   Pinky?

Hannah   I didn't know if I was having a boy or a girl at that stage but when we had our first doctor's appointment, she said that the baby was the size of the fingernail on my pinky. I couldn't believe it. So small but I felt it inside of me. Like I was growing this beautiful thing that was going to change my life.

A few nights later, Billy and I were in bed about to turn off the light and he reached over and put his hand on my belly, kissed me right here (**Hannah** *touches her stomach.*) and said 'Goodnight, Pinky'. And that was it. Pinky it was. For a little while. As quickly as we had it, it was gone. I miscarried four weeks later at thirteen weeks.

Martha   Oh, love. I'm so sorry.

Hannah   The pain was unbearable. Like it was tearing me up from the inside out. But the funny thing is, it's not what we focused on after we'd had some time to process it all. Things had changed. There was this little flicker of hope now. Like a realisation that it didn't happen this time but it *could* happen. After all these years, it was possible.

It's so weird to think of it now but I'd look down at my pinky finger and amongst all of the devastation and the fear and feeling just . . . sad, I'd still feel hope. That if not now, that I would get pregnant one day, you know? There's hope. And sometimes, you only need a little bit of hope to make it through the day.

To keep us going when we started trying again, Billy used to say, 'You got a pinky, you got hope'. We still say it in our family now. Or just the gesture.

She and **Lexi** *put their pinky up, clearly an action they've done many times before.*

Figure 5 Hannah sharing her story. Photo courtesy of Tyler Marsland.

Johnny   How much longer do we have to do this massage for?

Tanya   Jonathon! Way to ruin a moment!

Johnny   What?

Tanya   Perhaps you boys could go and fetch some refreshments for these ladies. I think we could all do with a drink.

Johnny   I like the sound of that!

Niall   Don't worry, Tanya, I'll oversee things. Come on, Johnny.

Johnny   Yes, boss.

Martha (*getting up to stretch, leaning on the back of a chair*)   You know, I think you're very brave talking about all of this, love. I think in a way we're always pushed to keep these things to ourselves. Hidden inside, which can be really difficult sometimes.

Wendy   That's true.

Martha   I had a similar experience after my first boy Knickson. A miscarriage. Early but still. At the time, it was common practice to keep things secret when you fell pregnant. Just in case something were to happen.

Tiff   Did that make it harder?

Martha   Absolutely it did. And because I hadn't told anyone, I had no one to tell when things fell apart.

Tiff   How did you cope? Keeping it all to yourself and not talking to anyone or anything?

Martha   To be honest, I don't really know. I remember only a week or so after it happened. I was at Woolies one day with Knickson doing a food shop. He was crying and I was trying to hold him and manoeuvre this trolley and I tripped and stubbed my toe on the trolley wheel. I think half the skin of my toe came off. God, it hurt. I don't know if my toe has ever recovered! Well, I just lost it. I started to cry and I couldn't stop.

It was a build-up of everything I'd been feeling in the last week and it completely took over, like I was possessed or something. I couldn't stop crying. I was sobbing and I think lots of people were staring. It was quite the scene.

I remember this older lady came over to me in the middle of it all. She was so kind and seemed to almost know what was going on. I remember she smiled at me and said that it was going to be OK. Then, somehow she was holding Knickson and hugging me and just let me weep into her chest. We stood there for what felt like hours until I was all cried out. I never did catch her name. Gosh, it makes me all teary thinking about it now.

Journee   Here, have a tissue. Actually, take the whole packet!

Martha   Thank you, Journee. I think what I've learned over the years is that mums and mums-to-be and women in general should be talking. Supporting each other.

Giving each other the finger (*she holds up her pinky finger*) and filling each other with hope that things will be OK.

Wendy (*to* **Tiff**)   It's true.

Martha   And sharing the good stuff, but sharing the bad stuff too. So that when things fall apart, you don't have to rely on kind, random strangers in shopping centres to hug you and tell you it'll be OK.

Hannah   You can rely on kind, random strangers at baby expos instead!

Tanya   As I've said, you're part of the 'Baby, Baby' family now!

Martha (*to the women around her, especially* **Hannah**)   This has been nice. Thank you, ladies.

Jim *enters.*

Journee   Speaking of nice, we have a special surprise coming up very soon.

Tanya   Special might be the right word!

Journee   Well, it promises to be an absolute riot! I, for one, am excited! I can feel my heart starting to beat.

Wendy   What is it?

Journee   All will be revealed soon enough! I think it's worth us all freshening up beforehand. What do we think?

The women chat excitedly as they leave to freshen up. **Lexi** *leaves her bag behind. Only* **Jim** *remains.*

Jim (*sniffing himself*)   Was it something I said?

Hugh *enters.*

Hugh   Jimbo, where did everyone go?

Jim   Beats me.

Hugh   You OK, mate?

Jim   Huh?

Hugh   You've seemed a bit quiet ever since we started talking about Lexi and her enormous crush on you.

Jim   Stop it would you. I don't even . . . forget it.

Hugh   What were you going to say?

Jim   Well, it's just. I don't even know how to talk to women. What to say.

Hugh   Lucky you're talking to the doctor of love himself. Yours truly. So, the trick with wooing a lady is to show interest in what they're interested in. They like cats, you talk about cats. They like sushi, you like sushi! They like salsa dancing, you are a salsa dancing El Divo. You get me?

Jim   I guess so.

Hugh   The chickadee is falling hard for you, Jimbo! Stress less.

Lexi *re-enters to collect her bag.*

Hugh   Well, hello hello. Speak of the devil.

Lexi   Hello. I forgot my handbag. (**Hugh** *motions for* **Jim** *to say something so* **Jim** *grabs* **Lexi***'s bag for her.*) Hi, Jim.

Jim (*abruptly*)   I like handbags.

Lexi   You do?

Jim   Yeh. They're so . . . bag like. And you can hold them in your hand.

Lexi   That you can. (**Hugh** *encourages him to keep trying.*)

Jim   I also like other bags. Paper bags. Plastic bags. Ooh, some bags have wheels! I wheely like those bags! But yeh, just a big fan of bags!

Lexi   Yeh. I'll just grab *my* bag now if that's OK.

Jim   Oh sure. (**Jim** *gives her bag back.*)

Lexi   Thanks, Jim. Catch you later. Maybe for another chat about bags.

She exits.

Hugh   Wow.

Jim   Shut up!

Hugh   I mean, I thought you'd be awkward but, man, that was something else. Who knew you liked bags so much!

Jim   You told me to be interested in stuff she was interested in!

Hugh   Interested! Not weirdly obsessed!

Jim   Oh, man.

Hugh   You know the weird thing?

Jim   What?

Hugh   I think she was wheely into it. Come here, you big teddy bear. (**Hugh** *grabs* **Jim** *and shakes him around.*) Mate, we gotta get cracking. We're on in ten. I think it's gonna go off today!

Jim   Look, mate, I'm really not up for it.

Hugh   Too bad, you agreed. The ladies will love it and we always sell a heap more car seats afterwards. Plus, I reckon once Lexi sees Jimbo's moves, she won't be able to help herself. It'll be *bags* of fun, trust me!

Bruce (*entering, dressed in flannelette*)   G'day, fellas!

Hugh Hi, mate. You all good?

Bruce Yeh, all good. But where are all the boats and fishing equipment? I need to restock my tackle.

Jim Sorry?

Bruce I'm here for the Boating, Camping, Fishing Expo. Keen to look at a new tinny as well. Instead, I had to walk through a whole heap of baby crap which is not what I had in mind today!

Hugh Mate, this is a baby expo. The Boating, Camping, Fishing Expo is next weekend.

Bruce Oh, man, that sucks! I drove three hours to get here! Alright, may as well head off. Thanks, boys.

Hugh Any chance you can move?

Bruce Huh?

Hugh Dance? Any chance you know how to dance?

Bruce I'm not too bad. At least, that's what my missus says after a Saturday night at the footy club! I'm Bruce by the way!

Hugh Nice to meet you, Bruce. Follow me. Come on, Jimbo! Lexi awaits!

Scene Six

Hannah *and* **Tiff** *are waiting for the next session.*

Hannah (*reviewing her schedule*)   Well, it says here that things are supposed to start any minute now. (**Tiff** *smiles at her.*) Your mum on her way?

Tiff Just in the loo.

Hannah Any clues on what the next session might be? It says here (*reading*), 'A surprise session which promises to get you thinking, feeling and laughing'. That sounds good, doesn't it?

Tiff Yeh.

Hannah (*putting her schedule away, wanting to connect*)   Are you enjoying the day, Tiff?

Tiff I guess so.

Hannah How did you get dragged into coming anyway? Your dad not free?

Tiff Ah, my dad's not really in the picture anymore.

Hannah Oh. I'm sorry to hear that.

Tiff It's OK. It wasn't recent. It's kind of complicated.

Hannah   I see. Well, it's so good of you to be here with your mum. I imagine it's a bit strange for you, hearing all this pregnancy stuff when you're so far away from that stage of life.

Tiff   I guess it's important information to know at some point.

Hannah   True, true. It's just so good that you're there to support her, you know. Pregnancy is so difficult and they say it's just the bit before actually having the baby, which is even harder. I'm lucky to have Billy. I can't imagine how it would be for your mum. Single parent and all of the difficulties that come with that.

Tiff   She has lots of friends and family support too so I think she'll be fine.

Hannah   Oh no doubt. But it's not the same though is it? The sleepless nights, the getting up on your own, working out feeding schedules and eating routines and God forbid something happens and you're on your own with no one to call on for help.

Tiff   I'm sure it won't be a problem. Plenty of people raise a baby on their own these days.

Hannah   It's true. But it's not easy I guess. Well, better her than you, hey!

Tiff   Yeh. One day . . .

Hannah   Oh, you want kids one day?

Tiff   Maybe.

Wendy enters, shaking her hands after washing them.

Wendy   They were out of hand towel. What did I miss?

Hannah   Tiff was just telling me that she might like to have kids one day.

Wendy   Really?

Tiff   I wasn't really saying that. It was nothing.

Wendy   It's OK if that's what you said, Tiff.

Kim enters, scowling.

Kim   Follow me. Oi, this way.

Martha, **Michael** and **Lexi** follow **Kim** on stage. **Tanya** and **Journee** follow behind, having encouraged **Kim** to take the lead.

Kim   There is a top secret surprise thing happening now. I'm apparently in charge of telling you so . . . consider yourself told.

Hannah   Thanks, Kim.

Tanya   Yes, thank you, Kim. Now, you all good to go ahead? You have the questions, don't you?

Kim   No.

Tanya   I gave you the cards this morning, remember?

Kim   Oh, yeh. I accidentally put them in the bin.

Tanya   Never mind. I have a spare set.

Kim (*sarcastically*)   Yay.

Journee   Well, everyone. It's time to channel some intuition and get in touch with the depths of our general knowledge and understanding of the world! Feel your insides tingle with anticipation!

Michael   What's that in layman's terms, love?

Tanya   A 'Baby, Baby' quiz! Get your thinking caps on. Right, first things first. We need two groups.

Kim   Tanya, I can run things you know.

Tanya   OK, sorry.

Kim   Well, what are you waiting for? Split up!

Journee   And you can't go with the person you came with today!

Hannah, **Wendy** *and* **Martha** *go together and* **Michael**, **Lexi** *and* **Tiff** *team up.*

Kim (*reading with complete disinterest*)   So, this is the famous 'Baby, Baby' quiz. I'm excited. Are you? You will be asked a series of questions and must choose a member of your team to answer on your behalf. Journee will tally the score for one group and Tanya will do the other. Yay.

Each team nominate someone to step forward. **Hannah** *and* **Lexi** *go first.*

Kim   Question one. True or false. Babies have a natural instinct when submerged in water, slowing their heart rate and holding their breath when submerged.

Lexi   That sounds weird. They're not fish.

Hannah   I'll go true.

Lexi   False.

Kim (*reading the card*)   Drumroll please. (*Everyone does a drum roll.*) OK, enough. It's true. (*The team cheers.*) Excuse me. I still have to read the fact thingie. So it says here: 'Babies are born with a "diving reflex" known as bradycardic response, which means their body naturally adapts to their surroundings when under water. A baby's heart rate will slow and they'll instinctively hold their breath when submerged in water'.

Hannah   Fascinating.

Lexi   And yet, kind of gross.

Tanya   One point to Hannah's team!

Kim   Next! (**Tiff** *and* **Wendy** *step forward.*)   This is multiple choice. (*Reading.*) Of these three facts, which is untrue:

   A. Adults have 206 bones. When babies are born, they have 300.

   B. A baby has around 30,000 taste buds.

   C. Babies begin crying from within the womb.

Wendy   Geez, it's hard enough remembering them all, let alone deciding on which one is wrong.

Tiff   It's C. The one about babies crying. I read somewhere that newborns are actually tear-free. They cry but they don't produce real tears until about three weeks. 'Peak crying' is around forty-six weeks after gestation, or six to eight weeks for full-term babies.

Tanya   Very impressive, Tiff!

Hannah   Amazing!

Wendy   Well done, Tiff. Proud of you.

Tanya   That's one point each!

Journee   This is thrilling!

Kim (*again, sarcastically*)   So thrilling! Next!

Martha   We're the last ones left, love. I'll try and go easy on you!

Michael   You go your hardest, sweets.

Kim   The last question. Another multiple choice. (*Reading.*) From data taken in the last five years, the average age of mothers in Australia is:

   A. Between twenty-one and twenty-five.

   B. Between twenty-six and thirty.

   C. Between thirty-one and thirty-four.

   D. Older than thirty-five. (*At this,* **Journee** *places her hand on* **Wendy***'s shoulder.*)

Martha   I think it'd be the second one. No, the first. No, the third. Definitely. Yep. Between thirty-one and thirty-four.

Kim (*pointing at* **Michael**)   What do you think?

Michael   I think it might be the last one. Over thirty-five.

Kim   Drumroll please. The answer is C. (*Reading.*) Over a third of mothers in the last year were aged between thirty-one and thirty-four. Says here the average age of mothers has been rising over time.

Martha   Makes sense I guess. Having babies is hard and a little more life experience behind you probably helps. For mothers and fathers.

Tanya   Do you think it's easier being a bit older, Michael?

Michael   I think so yep. I mean, being a father is hard. Going through a pregnancy as a man is hard too. It's not spoken about enough I don't think. This one has been especially hard on me for instance.

Martha   Excuse me, love?

Lexi   Be careful, mate.

Michael   Well, you know. I'm tired all the time. Work's been really busy and I don't know why but my feet are always sore. They just ache, you know.

Martha   *Your* feet are sore?

Journee   Slippery, slippery slope, Michael.

Tanya   Should we change the subject?

Michael   And to be honest, you've been a little grumpy lately, sweets. And sometimes you snore at night time.

Martha   I do, do I?

Michael   Look, I'll never understand what it's like for a woman when they're pregnant but I think that sometimes we forget that men do it just as tough.

Martha   Darling, come over here so I can show you how tough life can really be for you!

Kim   This just got fun.

Journee   Wait! I have a tantalising idea! Michael, if I told you there was a way you could experience just a little of what it was like for a woman with child, would you do it?

Michael   Why not!

Journee   Introducing . . . Bertha the Belly! And Michael, I think it's your size! Come here.

Michael *goes over to* **Journee** *and* **Bertha**, *a prosthetic pregnancy vest, is placed on him.*

Martha   Looks good on you, love!

Journee   So, you can wear this for the rest of the day then tell us how it feels!

Tanya   Hopefully it won't make your feet ache too much!

Wendy   How does it feel?

Michael   It feels . . . it feels . . . surprisingly good.

Hugh *runs on with excitement.*

Hugh   We're all ready when you are!

Tanya *nods for* **Journee** *to do an introduction*

Journee   So, ladies and Michael, it is now time for a simply superb surprise. Here at 'Baby, Baby' we like to encourage a little laughter and more than a meagre measure of merriment.

Tanya   Spell it out, Journee. I think everyone's lost.

Journee   We have a show planned for you! Please place your two, terrific hands together and welcome to the stage: the 'Baby Baby' boys!

*The boy band (***Hugh**, **Jim**, **Niall**, **Johnny**, **Bruce***) perform a choreographed baby-inspired pop dance routine. Fully costumed, they lip synch and dance up a storm. ***Jim** *is especially impressive and flicks his hair liberally. They also involve* **Michael** *who enjoys himself, still wearing Bertha the Belly. Once finished, they are very chuffed, beaming with pride. The women chat excitedly with each other as the boys celebrate their performance.*

Hugh   Well, turn me round and slap me silly! Boys, what a show! We zigged, we zagged, we smouldered! We nailed it! Wouldn't be surprised if Justin Bieber got in touch with us himself. Asked us for some advice you know?! Can't believe you were all able to keep up with me if I'm honest! And Bruce! What a last-minute find!

Figure 6 The boys celebrating their big performance. Photo courtesy of Tyler Marsland.

Bruce   Thanks for having me, fellas!

Michael   That was fun!

Niall   I agree. It was quite exhilarating moving my body like that! I felt quite sexy!

Johnny   Please never say sexy again.

Hugh   Leave the boy alone! He was owning it. You have a gift, little man! Speaking of gifts, we might be in the presence of greatness here, men. (*To* **Jim**.) My main brotheroo with the moves! Jimbo, you'd give Michael Jackson a run for his money! You popped and locked and flicked that gorgeous hair like your life depended on it!

Jim   This hair is made for flicking! But seriously, man, I didn't make a fool of myself did I?

Hugh   Quite the opposite, you big stud muffin!

Niall   Do we think an encore performance is a good idea? I'd be available for rehearsals if everyone was keen to schedule something soon.

Hugh   Might be a plan!

Johnny   Are we done?

Hugh   Of course not!

Niall   Well, what now?

Hugh   Now, we wait for applause and adoration from our fans! In three, two, one . . .

On cue, the women move towards the boys, clapping and cheering.

Martha   Boys, that was fabulous!

Hugh   Bingo!

Martha   Michael, wow. Just wow. You really got up there and shook your tooshie!

Michael   Did you like it, sweets?

Martha   Like it? I loved it! And so did this one. (*Pointing to her belly.*) Lots of kicks! You've found a new talent I think, love!

Niall   What did you think, Tiff?

Tiff   Ah, it was good. You were good. You were all very confident. You seemed like you were having a lot of fun up there. That's the most important thing, they say!

Wendy   I thought it was just precious! And I love the song. Very catchy and very relevant! (*To* **Bruce**.) And I loved what that man in the flannelette did. Very rugged!

Lexi   Hello, Jim.

Jim   Hi, Lexi.

Lexi   Nice moves.

Jim   Thank you.

Lexi   I like a man that can dance.

Jim   Me too.

Lexi   You do?

Jim   I mean I . . . Well . . .

Lexi   I know what you mean. Listen, I've been looking for my very own personal security guard for a while now. Hoping you might know someone?

Jim   Well, lots of my mates are security guards. I'm sure one of them is probably out of work at the moment and would be free.

Lexi   Right. Well, here's my number. Give me call if someone you know happens to be 'free'.

Tanya   Very good, boys!

Journee   Gentlemen, that was thrillingly theatrical. I am impressed, enlightened and in love with your enigmatic energy!

Tanya   Just for once, stop talking in riddles so these people can actually understand what you're trying to say.

Journee (*hurt*)   Excuse me?

Tanya   Honestly, drop the act!

Journee (*taking a breath and composing herself*)   Everyone, we'd love to invite you to please move outside where afternoon tea is served. (*Instructing the boys.*) Niall and Johnny will look after drinks and Hugh will direct you to the assortment of nibbles which have been prepared. Please help yourself. We will meet back in an hour for this afternoon's session. See you soon. (*She smiles and signals for everyone to leave.*) Tanya, a quick word? Are we OK?

Tanya   Of course. Why do you ask?

Journee (*calmy*)   I'm really getting a sense that you may be feeling frustrated. I want to clear the air. Provide an opportunity for you to speak your truth. Release whatever frustration you may be feeling.

Tanya   It's fine. I'll be fine. (*With some level of sarcasm.*) Perhaps I just need to go do a meditation.

Journee   There are significant benefits in practising meditation regularly.

Tanya   Journee!

Journee   Tanya!

Tanya   Once upon a time you joked about people that meditated.

Journee   Things change.

Tanya   Do they though? Do you think you could drop the Journee wellness facade for just one minute?

Journee   Tanya, this isn't a facade. This is me.

Tanya   This didn't used to be you. The only thing hippy dippy about the Journee I knew was her name, which you never liked. And now, the name suits you. I just don't understand how a person wakes up one day and is completely different.

Journee   And if I am different, is there anything so wrong with that?

Tanya   No, it's just that . . .

Journee   If I want to focus on wellness and healing and the positives in life, isn't that OK? If I find peace in meditating and I like to be creative with the language I use and spend time dreaming up dreams and learning to be more grateful, is there anything wrong with that?

Tanya   That's not what I'm saying.

Journee   And if I need to wake up each morning and make a conscious decision to choose not to focus on the fact that I can't have children, isn't that OK?

To choose not to focus on the fact that I have worked so hard for years in an industry centred on mothers and babies and pregnancy and childbirth only to realise one day that I would never be lucky enough to have children of my own? That I would never fulfil the one thing I dreamed of most?

Is it so wrong, Tanya, that I choose to focus on these things rather than the fact that sometimes I feel such a sense of overwhelming worthlessness simply because I will never bear children?

Tanya   Journee, I didn't know.

Journee   You never asked.

Tanya   I don't mean to sound insensitive but I thought you had come to terms with not having children years ago now. The whole wellness gratitude thing has only been recent.

Journee   Something had to change. I wasn't coping and needed to focus on something else. I had to get help and it's helped. I love the work we do with all of my heart but to keep doing it, I needed to find a new perspective. A new purpose. And I have.

Tanya   But you just feel like a completely different person.

Journee   In some ways, I am. I had to be. But I'm happy. Actually really happy. And I have this sense of calm that has finally brought me peace. And I need you to accept me and the hippy dippy, happy parts of me.

Tanya   I can do that. And I'm sorry I haven't been there for you like I should have been.

Journee   I honestly think it was something I had to go through myself. To go on my own journey if it's not too ridiculous to say that

Tanya   It's not. Not at all. (*They hug.*)

Scene Seven

The women enter, minus **Tanya** *and* **Journee**. *They are ready to participate in the next session: Music Mindfulness.*

Hannah   Ah, Kim, we're running a bit late and the music session was supposed to start a little while ago. Was Journee running that one?

Kim   Nah, she asked me to.

Hannah   OK. When did you want to do that then?

Kim   Never.

Hannah   Right.

Wendy   Maybe Tiff could run it. She can sing.

Tiff   Mum, no.

Kim   You know what, I think that's a great idea. Here you go. Journee wrote it all down. You'll be great. (**Kim** *goes and sits herself away from the group.*)

Tiff   I really think that it would be best if you ran the session since you work here and all, and I have no idea what I'm doing.

Martha   Go on love. I think you'll be great. You'll be committed, and that's more than we can say for our dear Kim over there. No offence, love. (**Kim** *shrugs her shoulders, agreeing.*) I like to think we're all quite close by now so you've nothing to worry about. You're in the presence of friends here.

Tiff   OK. (*She looks over the notes.*) Well, it welcomes everyone back from lunch. (*Looking at everyone.*) So, welcome! Then it says that this session is about music mindfulness and using music to soothe our stress, relax our body and connect with our baby. So, the first step is a siren warm-up. Does anyone want to demonstrate what that is?

Wendy   Oh you know how to do that. Like you do in the shower every night. She sounds like a bloody ambulance. Have to continually shush her so I can hear the news! Show 'em love.

Tiff   I don't know . . .

Hannah   Just do your best, Tiff.

Martha   Take your time, love.

Tiff   Fine. You just take a deep breath and make an 'ooh' sound. Then move the sound upwards until you reach the top of your vocal range then come back down to the bottom. (**Martha** *tries this poorly.*) No, it's not really like that.

Martha   Well, show us love. (**Tiff** *does a siren.*) Oh right. That's not what I did at all. Everyone try it. (*They all attempt a siren. They sound average.*)

Tiff   Now it says to do a siren repeating the following phrase 'Brimming with blissful baby bodies we are beautiful'. Is that right, Kim? (**Kim** *gives her a look and a shrug.*) Sounds like something Journee would write. Ready, everyone? On three. One, two, three. (*The women siren this phrase together.*) Apparently if we do this exercise daily, you're able to connect with your baby on a deeper level.

Lexi   Can't relate.

Wendy   Neither!

Tiff   Mum . . .

Wendy   What? (*Realising.*) I mean, I'm just not a great singer. I sound like a cat being thrown against a wall. With force!

Tiff   OK. Now, here is the music we've been given to sing. (**Hannah** *passes out the sheet music.*) Hopefully people can read music. (*The women share mixed reactions.*)

Journee and **Tanya** *enter.*

Tanya   Hi, everyone. How are we going?

Journee   Hopefully you are feeling connected to each other and your precious baby through music.

Tanya   Where's Kim?

Kim (*gets up*)   Here! We've done all the ambulance noises and stuff. It's sounding great. Lot of hard work happening here.

Tanya   Is that right? Well, please go ahead. I'd love to hear the product of all your 'hard work'.

Journee   I'm excited.

Tanya   Maybe I'll sing along too, just in case you need some direction this afternoon.

The women all sing a piece of music together in harmony and sound beautiful. The sound is almost heavenly. **Tanya** *is shocked. So is* **Kim**.

Journee   Oh my goodness. It's as if angels walk on the earth! That was beautiful!

Tanya   How did you . . . I thought that . . .

Kim   Told ya, didn't I!

Tanya   Are you all singers?

Wendy (*motioning to* **Tiff**)   She is and I used to be.

Martha   I just got inspired I think! Maybe I'm learning a new talent too!

Hannah   Only in the shower but Lexi's amazing. She can do it all. Sing, dance, and anything else.

Journee   Really? Quite a talent.

Hannah   In fact, she's missing her dance class today to come to this expo with me.

Lexi   I sure am!

Tanya   Well, at least all of this information on pregnancy and wellness will come in handy if you have children, Lexi.

Lexi   Oh I don't want kids.

Tanya   You don't?

Lexi   Absolutely not.

Hannah   Really, Lex? I knew it wasn't in your short-term plan but I didn't think it was never in your plan at all. Are you sure there's no chance of you having kids, if you were able to of course?

Lexi   No chance. Actually take no chance and minus it by a million then you'll have about as much chance as there is of me wanting to have children. No offence to women wanting children but it's just not for me.

I know it might be weird to say, being at a baby expo and all, but I think there's this unfair pressure on women to have to have children. And if a woman doesn't have them by a certain age or, heaven forbid, doesn't want them at all, she gets funny looks or funny comments. It's not right. I don't want kids and I think that's perfectly normal. I have other plans.

Martha   That sounds exciting!

Tiff   What are your plans?

Lexi   I want to perform.

Martha   Like in a pub or something?

Lexi   No. I want to dance on the big stages around the world.

Martha   Our local pub has an enormous stage. Just to the left of the toilets in the beer garden.

Lexi   No. Think the biggest superstar you know then make it bigger. That's my dream.

Wendy   I love the sound of it! A woman going after what she wants! You go, girl!

Lexi   If I close my eyes, I can see it all come together. See myself on the stage in front of thousands of people. Tens of thousands. Cheering my name. Cheering for me!

As though her dream is coming to life, a chant begins.

All   Lexi! Lexi! Lexi! Lexi!

As lights change, **Lexi**'s *dream sequence begins and continues to play out. The chants crescendo and suddenly stop as enormous applause is heard.* **Lexi** *stands and opens her eyes as music begins. She provides narration and dances, showcasing her incredible moves, as a group of back-up dancers perform choreography around her. Later, the boys run on and become a part of* **Lexi**'s *dream as superfans with personalised posters. The dream scene includes group choreography, smoke, flashing lights and everything* **Lexi** *imagines in her visions of stardom. The following narration occurs throughout this sequence:*

Lexi   The music starts. The crowds are ready for a show.
My back-up dancers surround me. They are the best in the business and they have been rehearsing for months for this moment.
Everyone is here to see me! To see Lexi!
The crowd goes wild.
My dancers lift me into the air.
Everyone can't believe that they're witnessing a star in the making!

Figure 7 Lexi in the limelight, living her dream. Photo courtesy of Tyler Marsland.

Scene Eight

Niall *and* **Johnny** *enter.*

Niall   Come on, we have a few more jobs to do before the shift ends.

Johnny   Man, I'm done. I said I'd help out for a day and I've done that so I say we sneak out for a quick drink. We'll be back before any of the pregnant birds even realise we're gone.

Niall   Absolutely not. We have a job to do! Plus I said to Tiff that we'd catch up before the end of the day and I am always true to my word.

Johnny   Mate, I don't think she really cares about catching up with you.

Niall   That's a bit rude.

Johnny   Safe to say, she's got other things on her mind.

Niall   What do you mean?

Johnny   My brother just messaged me. There's a bit more to Tiff than she lets on. (**Niall** *looks confused but intrigued.*) She was dux of the school like I said but she might not have lived up to all the hype since then.

Niall   Huh?

Johnny   If I tell you, we go for a drink.

Niall   I don't know. Maybe a Diet Coke.

Johnny   Come here.

He shows **Niall** *his phone and his brother's message. Everyone starts to enter for the final farewell.*

Tanya   Well, everyone. We'd like to thank you all for coming today. I hope that you've been able to see just a snapshot of everything on offer here at 'Baby, Baby'.

Journee   Thank you from the depths of our soul for the way you've engaged with our wellness programs. We hope that there was something you connected with and that you can join Tanya and I in the future for your own benefit and that of your beautiful babies. You are all part of our 'Baby, Baby' family now.

Tanya   Our expo begins next week so please tell your friends and family as we'd love to see as many people as we can. (**Martha** *flinches as her baby kicks.*)

Michael   You OK, sweets?

Martha   Yes, love. Just feeling quite a bit of movement. I think all the singing has woken him up.

Michael   It's not . . . *time* yet is it?

Martha   No, I don't think so. Just the later stages where all the fun happens you know! I'll be fine. (*To* **Journee**.) Sorry, go on.

Journee   We have a gift bag for all of our pregnant mummas to take home today. It's full of goodies and hopefully you'll enjoy!

Tanya   Niall, would you please give these out?

Nial   Of course.

Johnny   Actually, Auntie Tanya, I'd be happy to do that.

Tanya (*surprised*)   OK, thank you, Johnny.

Johnny   So, just to our pregnant ladies right? Here's one for you, Martha. And you Hannah. (*Pausing for dramatic effect.*) And here you go, Tiff. One for you. (*Holding out the bag to* **Tiff**. *She doesn't take it.*)

Wendy   I think you mean me. I'll take that.

Johnny   I think I mean Tiff.

Tanya   Jonathon, don't be rude! Give Wendy the bag.

Wendy   It's fine. Everything is fine. I think everyone's just a little tired. I know I am. I think my pregnant feet are a bit swollen after such a big day!

Tiff   Mum, it's fine. We may as well be honest.

Wendy   Darling, it's OK.

Tiff   It's not. I'm not. He's right. It's me, not mum. I'm twelve weeks pregnant. OK? I'm twenty years old with no savings, no partner, no house but a baby coming in a matter of months! Surprise!

Martha (*kindly*)   Why didn't you say earlier, love?

Tiff   I didn't want to be judged.

Hannah   No one here is judging you.

Tiff   Maybe not, but people are judgemental. Especially about things like this. I told one friend just because I needed someone other than mum to say something comforting. To say it was all going to be OK. Next minute, people in my year at school are texting me and there's rumours and I just can't deal with it. It's bad enough processing this whole thing myself, let alone hearing what everyone else thinks about it.

Johnny   Hey, I'm really sorry. I didn't mean to cause trouble. I wasn't thinking . . .

Tiff   It doesn't really matter. People knowing doesn't change my situation.

Wendy   We didn't mean to be dishonest. It's just been a difficult last few months.

Journee   Go gentle on yourself, darling girl. There's a lot of processing still to happen I imagine.

Tiff   I still can't believe it! I mean, I know so many women have fertility issues and have trouble falling pregnant or can't fall pregnant at all and I don't want to be disrespectful or ungrateful but this just wasn't the plan.

The plan was study and travel and moving out sometime this year and now that plan is not the plan. The plan is this. (*She gestures to her stomach.*) To have a baby. And the strange thing is, I always wanted to be a mum. To have children. I just didn't think it would happen like this and I'm just so aware of everyone thinking that twenty is too young and not mature enough and . . . It's so overwhelming. I mean, I don't even have a partner! How am I going to raise a baby, alone?

Wendy   You're not alone.

Tiff   I know, mum, and I am so thankful to you. But aside from you, my friends don't understand. I don't expect them to. And we don't have any other family.

Hannah   *We* understand though.

Tanya   We do. (**Journee** *and* **Martha** *nod along.*)

Hannah   And maybe you'll meet other people who will be your supports. They might become like family. Maybe you've already met them, at a random baby expo. Tanya and Journee have said all day that we're now part of the 'Baby, Baby' family. Maybe it's *that* family that will be the supports you need to bring your beautiful baby into the world. They say it takes a village. Let us be part of that village.

Tiff   That's really kind but you're all so busy as it is. I don't want to burden you with that.

Journee   Burden us? Rubbish!

Tanya   Just you try and stop us!

Tiff   Thank you.

Hannah   Come here!

They all embrace **Tiff***, aside from* **Martha** *who is suddenly hunched over.*

Come over here, Martha!

Martha*'s waters break suddenly.*

Martha   Ah, everyone might need to come over here!

Michael   Either you have wet yourself again, sweets, or your / water just broke!

Martha   / water just broke. Yep, I think it's that, love!

Michael   Holy moly and then some! What do we do!

Niall   Mop it up?

Wendy (*to* **Michael**)   You've had three babies before. Surely you know!

Michael   They were in hospital, not in the middle of a bloody baby expo!

Hearing this, **Kim** *exits.*

Lexi   I'll call an ambulance. (*Checking her phone.*) Ah, my phone is flat.

Jim   Here, take mine.

Lexi   Thanks, Jim.

She leaves to call an ambulance.

Bruce   I might have a first-aid kit and some tarps in my fishing box in the car?

Tiff   It might be too late for that!

Journee   Right, let's all work together. Tanya, you give some instructions.

Tanya   I don't know what to do!

Hugh   Right, let's lay her down.

Jim   Here, I'll help. Hang on to me. Easy now.

Tiff   Niall, can you guys get some ice chips and a flannel?

Niall   On it. Come on

He and **Johnny** *leave to get ice chips and a flannel.* **Kim** *arrives with blankets.*

Kim   I've got some blankets. Now, everyone, stay calm. We'll be fine.

Everyone is visibly taken aback by **Kim**'s *sudden leadership.*

What?

Martha *is laid down and people gather around to support her.*

Hannah   Just focus on your breathing, Martha. Deeply in, deeply out. Like Journee taught us earlier today.

Martha   I'm really worried. This isn't how it's all supposed to go.

Hannah   You're going to be OK. Your body has done this before.

Wendy   Several times!

Journee   We're all here, darling. Just breathe.

Michael   I'm breathing!

Journee   I meant Martha but you're doing great too, Michael.

Michael   Thank you.

Lexi   Ambulance is on their way. Here's your phone back, Jim. With my number in it.

Jim   Awesome. (*They make eyes and cosy up.*)

Niall   Here are the ice chips.

Johnny   And the flannel.

Tiff   Good work.

Figure 8 The group gathers for Martha's big moment. Photo courtesy of Tyler Marsland.

Martha   I really hope this goes OK.

Hannah   It's going to go great. You know why? (*Making eye contact with* **Tiff** *at the same time.*) Because you have a whole village of support around you. We're all here and we're all behind you!

Martha   Plus I got a pinky finger. (**Martha** *holds up her pinky finger and gives it a wiggle.*)

Hannah   You got a pinky? You got hope.

Martha   I think this baby is in a rush to meet you all. I think I need to start pushing.

Michael   Are you sure, sweets?

Martha   Yep. Here we go. Count me down!

Journee   Everyone . . .

All   Three, two, one . . .

Blackout. A baby's cry is heard. End of show.

During bows, **Martha** *enters with her baby wrapped in a pink blanket. She has had a girl!*

Pinky Discussion Questions

1. How is the extended metaphor of the 'pinky' used to explore the idea of hope?

2. How does the baby expo bring characters together in unexpected ways and serve as a catalyst for character and plot development in *Pinky*?

3. Stepping into parenthood can be both thrilling and terrifying. How is this statement true in *Pinky*?

4. How is tension built and sustained throughout *Pinky*?

5. How are different relationships presented in *Pinky*? How do these relationships develop throughout the script and provide instances of comfort, conflict and humour for the characters involved and the audience?

6. Identify and discuss the presence of the following themes: love, grief, hope, change, connection and the strength of the human spirit. What aesthetic strategies are used to represent these themes in the play?

7. Consider the character of Hannah. How might her past experiences inform her behaviour throughout *Pinky*?

8. Research one of the following topics: societal expectations of women, infertility and reproductive health, non-traditional families, childfree by choice, mental health in parenthood. How does this issue affect individuals and families? What are the broader social or cultural implications? In what ways does *Pinky* reflect or engage with this topic?

Ember

Playwright's note

'If I've learned anything from life, it's that our experiences, our memories of love and of loss and everything in between, swirl around in our chest just like embers. Embers that, at any moment, can burst into flames and remind us how much we love somebody, how much we miss those we've lost or how precious life is'.

I love telling stories of ordinary people experiencing extraordinary things. It is often fascinating and quite inspiring to explore the ways in which people call upon the very depths of their resources of resilience, strength and courage in the face of brutal adversity with the single hope that things will one day be OK.

Personally, my family had experienced significant loss in the years before writing *Ember*. As a result, I found that grief seemed to be a theme woven throughout the fabric of the play, sometimes in subtle moments but always with a heaviness that only grief can embody. More prominent, however, are themes of love, survival, resilience and the strength of the human spirit during times of trial.

Ember is inspired by the strength of community during the 2020 Australian bushfires. I wanted to explore how ordinary people summon their deepest reserves of courage, kindness, and sometimes even humour, to endure the seemingly unendurable. For the original production of *Ember*, we collected non-perishable food items for a local shelter supporting those in need. This initiative echoed the play's themes of connection and community. I encourage future productions to support similar causes, extending *Ember*'s message beyond the stage.

Ember is set in the fictional town of 'Kardla' which means 'fire' in Kaurna language. I acknowledge the Kaurna people as the custodians of the Adelaide Plains region, the land where this play was written and first performed. I recognise Kaurna people's connection with their land and honour and pay my respects to Kaurna elders, both past and present, and all generations of Aboriginal people, now and into the future.

Brady Lloyd

Ember by Brady Lloyd

Synopsis

Ember is set in the Kardla Town Hall, a make-shift temporary shelter for members of the town, while the bushfires blaze. Among others, we meet town matriarch Margery and her squeeze Bill, two travelling journalists from the Big Smoke and the flamboyant star of the local amateur theatre scene Cynthia Taylor (pronounced Te-Law). Also taking refuge is Jack, who is harbouring a painful secret, too dark to even tell his worried mother Violet.

Setting

Ember is set in a small, fictional town called Kardla in country South Australia during the January 2020 bushfires. 'Kardla' is the Kaurna language word for fire.

Characters

Ten characters (5F, 5M). Note: This play accommodates flexible and inclusive casting.

Violet Mills, *41. Maternal and protective of her children.*

Jack Mills, *17. Violet's son, known for being responsible and trustworthy.*

Margery Mead, *58. A kind and caring matriarch of Kardla.*

Bill Hopkins, *62. A long-standing, lovable Kardla resident with a crush on Margery.*

Cynthia Taylor, *41. The flamboyant, self-anointed star of the Kardla theatre scene.*

Eleanor Tott, *28. A reporter from the Big Smoke, in town to cover the bushfires.*

Timothy Chattleton, *25. Eleanor's eager colleague.*

Charlie Winifred, *61. Bill's best mate. A grump with a good heart and a quick wit.*

Gerry Halliday, *35. An eccentric local café owner.*

Belle Brown, *22. Gerry's obedient apprentice.*

Scene One

In darkness, we hear a soundscape montage of news reports of the Australian bushfires of 2020. Then, silence. Lights slowly come up.

Thursday, 9 January 2020. Early morning. People are sleeping in the Kardla Town Hall, spread out. The hall is filled with donations already gathered, a noticeboard covered in community notices, some tables and chairs and makeshift beds. The people of Kardla have been evacuated from their houses and are seeking safety together.

Having had a nightmare, **Vi** *wakes with a start, screaming.* **Jack**, **Margery**, **Bill**, **Cynthia**, **Eleanor**, **Timothy** *and* **Charlie** *awaken too.*

Charlie   Not again!

Vi   I'm sorry. I'm sorry, everyone. Go back to sleep.

Charlie   Bit hard now!

Margery   Charlie, shush. No need to apologise, love. Take some breaths and back to sleep for you. For all of us.

Charlie   If only it were that easy!

Bill   She didn't mean to, Charlie.

Charlie   I understand that but still. The whole town of Kardla's in this mess. Screaming the place down will hardly help.

Cynthia   Is that right, Charlie? It makes a nice change from your trumpeting.

Charlie   My what?

Cynthia   Your trumpeting. From your bottom. It was like the symphony orchestra in your trousers once you fell asleep last night. And you woke me up several times. Between you and that terrible sleeping mat!

Vi   I am sorry, really.

Charlie   I can't help what happens when I'm asleep!

Cynthia   Exactly. If only it were just the noise. The smell that followed was a whole other issue. Wouldn't want an exposed flame anywhere! You'd start another fire! That honestly was the worst sleep of my life!

Charlie   Oh don't be so dramatic!

Cynthia   Remember who you're talking to, Charlie boy. I am after all an /actress.

Charlie   / Actress. Yes we've heard. We all know. We don't need to hear about it anymore.

Cynthia   Well, don't you forget it! I've been in more professional shows than you've had cooked dinners.

Charlie   A hundred years ago maybe!

Bill   Right, let's all calm down shall we? Focus on the fact that we're all here.

Jack   Not everyone. (*Beat.*)

Margery   Right you are, Jack. Not everyone. So let's count ourselves lucky shall we? And while we're here, let's make an effort to get along. It won't be forever. The latest online update is supposed to be up soon. Then we'll know more about when we can go back to our homes.

Charlie   Or what's left of them.

Cynthia (*to* **Charlie**)   Now who's being dramatic!

Margery   Well, let's wait and see. And who knows, there might be good news right around the corner. Especially for some of us. (**Margery** *looks at* **Vi** *and* **Jack** *with a nod.*) We're owed some good news I think. (*Getting up and beginning to get organised for the day.*) May as well get the morning started. It's almost seven. I think Gerry's already up getting breakfast ready. (*She begins moving before awkwardly bumping into* **Bill**.) Morning, Bill!

Bill (*blushing*)   Margery! Right, who's up for a cuppa?

Everyone murmurs yes and thanks as **Bill** *wanders over to* **Timothy** *and* **Eleanor**. **Timothy** *is awake but* **Eleanor** *is still sleeping.*

Bill Can I get you two something then? (**Eleanor** *stirs.*) Hello? Cup of tea?

Eleanor   What? I told you last night when we arrived, I don't drink tea.

Bill   Well, Eleanor, what do you drink then, love? Perhaps I can fix it for you this morning.

Eleanor   Do you have oat milk?

Bill   Ah, no I'm afraid. We have regular milk though.

Eleanor   Fine. Just a half strength hot chai latte with four sweeteners.

Bill (*confused*)   I'll see if we have any of that out the back shall I? And you, Timothy?

Timothy   Just a tea for me will be great. Thanks, Mr Hopkins.

Bill (*making another effort*)   What brings you to our humble town of Kardla anyway?

Timothy   Well, our boss wants us to come and scope out some tourism opportunities. He thought we'd work well together so he sent us both.

Bill   Well, you'll find plenty of tourist gems around here.

Eleanor   Not anymore, I'm guessing. (*Beat.*)

Bill   Well, you're both very welcome here. If you need anything, please just let us know. I better get moving and look for your cha-cha coffee. I'll be back in a jiff.

He nods and exits to go make tea in the kitchen. **Timothy** *looks to* **Eleanor** *after her rudeness.*

Eleanor (*calling after him*)   It's chai! (*To* **Timothy**.) What?

Timothy   Nothing, Eleanor. It's just, we only arrived last night. And these people are putting us up.

Eleanor   Only because the hotel we were supposed to stay in is in a fire danger zone. Forgive me if I'm not brimming with gratitude! The sooner we can get back to the city, the better.

Timothy   What's with you and being in the country?

Eleanor   Nothing. I'm just a city girl, through and through.

Timothy   I'm not so sure. The country air looks good on you. You might even feel less stressed after spending some time out here. Catch up on some sleep.

Eleanor (*sarcastically*)   Yeh maybe.

Timothy   Speaking of sleep, did you know that koalas sleep on average twenty hours a day?

Eleanor   How interesting.

Timothy   I know our circumstances aren't ideal but I think it's important we're really nice to everyone while we're here.

Eleanor   I am nice! I am very nice. I am a lovely person. Some people have even called me bubbly. I'll be in the shower if anyone needs me. Oh and go and see what's for breakfast would you? I don't want to miss out if there's anything eatable.

She exits towards the bathroom as **Timothy** *heads to the kitchen.*

Vi   You OK, love? How did you sleep?

Jack   Fine I guess. You?

Vi   I'm glad it's morning. Today's going to be a good day. We're going to find your sister. I can feel it.

Jack   What if we don't? It's been a day now.

Vi   No need to even think like that, darling. We will. We have to. Have you checked for any updates online?

Jack   Yeh. Nothing yet. I'll keep checking. Mum, I feel like this is all my fault. I . . .

Vi   Nonsense, it is not.

Jack   But, mum . . .

Vi   Jack, I will not hear another word. Now, are you hungry? I think breakfast will probably be ready soon. Why don't you go find out?

Jack   OK. You coming?

Vi   I might eat a bit later, love. But you go.

Jack   Love ya, mum. (**Jack** *kisses her on the cheek and leaves for the kitchen.*)

Gerry *and* **Belle** *enter.*

Gerry   Alright, you sorry-looking bunch. Morning! All your dreams are about to come true. Breakfast is ready. Now, it might not be as good as something you'd get at my café and it's definitely not my famous scrambled eggs but I didn't have a whole lot to work with. I think you'll still be impressed. Even you, Charlie!

Charlie   Yeh yeh.

Belle   Boss, do we have butter?

Gerry   Excuse me?

Belle   Do we have butter? It's just that Bill asked. For his toast.

Gerry   I reckon there's some butter between your bloody ears, love! Yes, we have butter! Now go and make yourself busy. Breakfast won't make itself. Make sure no one touches the muffins. I want to serve them later this morning.

Belle   Yes, boss.

She exits.

Gerry   Apprentices huh!

Margery   Go easy on her, Gerry. She's only young.

Gerry   Young and mouldable!

He leaves to go back to the kitchen. *Everyone aside from* **Margery** *and* **Vi** *have left for breakfast by now.*

Margery (*to* **Vi**)   Give us a hug, love.

Vi   Marge, do you know when they'll be updating things online? Jack said he checked before but nothing yet. I'm worried sick about Izzy.

Margery   I bet you are. Bill said the update would probably come through soon.

Vi   I hope so. You know, I just still can't understand how it happened. How she disappeared. (*Going over the details yet again, this time to* **Margery**.) Jack says that he took Izzy to the local to buy her some drinks for lunch. She was desperate for some strawberry milk. Apparently, she'd been whining about it all morning and I think he was a bit fed up listening to her. So, he's in there buying the drinks and picking up some snacks and he said that she just . . . wandered off. Disappeared. Jack panics and starts looking for her but can't find her anywhere, so he jumps in the car and starts to drive around. Only, she's gone. An hour later, they declared Kardla a bushfire zone and two hours later, we're here. Without Izzy.

Margery   It's a small town. Someone would have picked her up. Got her to safety. We just haven't heard yet.

Vi   God I hope so.

Margery   And you know you can trust Jack. I mean, he's so responsible.

Vi   I know that. It's just . . . it's been a whole day. Why wouldn't we have heard something? What if she's not OK, Marge?

Margery   Now, try not to think like that.

Vi   Hurt or trapped somewhere or . . . worse. I can't even imagine.

Margery   Try not to get ahead of yourself, love.

Vi   I can't lose her, Marge. I won't cope. How could any mother cope?

Margery (*beat*)   Losing a child is not an experience any mother should have.

Vi   Oh my God. Tommy. I'm so sorry.

Margery   It's OK.

Vi   No, it's not. Here I am going on and on about losing a child. I didn't even think.

Margery   Honestly, it's fine.

Vi   This must all be bringing things back for you. It must be awful.

Margery   It certainly isn't easy.

Vi   Please ignore me. Forget I said anything.

Margery   Tommy would be turning thirty tomorrow.

Vi   Wow.

Margery   Thirty years old. My boy, thirty. Who knows what he'd be doing or where in the world he'd be living. Probably somewhere busy. Tommy never liked being alone. He always loved being surrounded by people. Maybe because he was an only child.

Vi   How did Tommy . . . I've never actually asked. How did it happen? If you want to talk about it.

Margery   You don't want to hear about that now, love. Especially with Izzy.

Vi   I do. I want to hear. If you want to tell me. (*Beat.*) Tell me about Tommy.

Margery (*remembering*)   Well, Tommy was a special kind of boy. He would do anything for anyone. And since his father, my Michael, passed away when he was only four, he thought he was the man of the house, so to speak. Even though he was a real mummy's boy.

Vi   A bit like Jack.

Margery   A lot like Jack. He would do anything I asked of him and always looked after me. Bring me a cup of tea each night after dinner, make sure I had flowers for my birthday. He was good at school and quite popular with his peers and just loved helping other people. That was his undoing in a way.

The Black Saturday fires hit our town. 2009 it was. He was only nineteen. But he had been volunteering for the CFA for a few years, like most of the boys in his class, and he didn't think twice. He just went and helped out. He was fit and, boy, was he clever. Just like my Michael. But the fires were just too vicious.

An ember attack they said it was. He'd been caught in an ember attack at one of the local houses and hadn't made it out. I remember this man, this firefighter, telling me the news. I still remember his deep, sad green eyes. Those eyes told me what had happened to Tommy before his mouth even uttered the words. Tommy hadn't made it. Eventually, he said they'd tried to resuscitate him but they just couldn't.

Vi   Oh, Marge. I don't know what to say.

Margery   Me neither most of the time. It's been eleven years now but it still feels like yesterday. Losing a husband is one thing but losing a child is another altogether.

Feels like *I've* been stuck in an ember attack of sorts since that day too. Making it hard to even get up, let alone breathe without thinking of Tommy. Sometimes I feel like I wake up and another unexpected fire has started in my chest. That's what love is, I guess. Why we grieve so deeply. Anyone that's ever lost somebody has these embers swirling around inside of them. Embers that, at any moment, might burst into flames and remind us how much we love somebody. The memories you shared together, the pictures you look at again and again and all of the reminders you have that the person you loved is gone. I used to be tormented by them but now these little ember attacks remind me how much I loved Tommy. How lucky I was to have him in my life.

You know, Tommy's favourite song as a boy was the Nat King Cole classic *Smile*. I used to sing him to sleep with that song. You know it?

Vi   I do.

Margery   We played it at his funeral too. It's beautiful. And it has a beautiful message. So that's what I'll keep doing. What we all have to keep doing when things turn pear-shaped. Smile. Thank you for listening. It's not often I talk about Tommy these days. It's just too difficult. I miss being a mum though. I always wished I'd had more kids. Always wanted another two or three.

Vi   You did?

Margery   Yes. We tried but it wasn't to be.

Vi   We talked about a third after Izzy too but things were not good so it wasn't really an option.

Margery   Not good?

Vi   No. Jack's father had quite the temper. He was always very intense. Passionate at first. I guess that's one of the things that drew me to him. But, as the years went on, it became hard. Less passionate and more fiery. Then, angry. Then, violent. Bad traffic or a speeding ticket or an odd look from a stranger and that would be it. He would be out of control at the flick of a switch. Even if I told a joke he didn't like. And what's not to like about my jokes?

Figure 9 Vi and Margery open up to one another. Photo courtesy of Tyler Marsland.

I feel like I spent most of my kids' childhood trying to protect them to be honest. To make sure he didn't hurt them in any way.

Margery   And did he?

Vi   No.

Margery   Did he ever hurt you?

Vi   Only a handful of times.

Margery   Oh, Vi.

Vi   You know I swore I'd leave him one day. I told him again and again that he couldn't hurt me like that. It wasn't right. But he always apologised the next day. And kept apologising until I just gave up. And stayed.

I thought about leaving hundreds of times. Thousands. I knew exactly what I'd say to him. But I just never did. I could never do it. The words just wouldn't come.

Margery   So how did it end?

Vi   In the end, he left. He just got up and left. I'd cooked dinner one night. The kids were in bed. He came out of the bedroom with a navy sports bag. He looked at me and said, 'Vi, I'm done. I can't fake the family thing anymore. I don't love you. So I'm leaving'.

Can you believe it? All the things he did to us and the crap he put us through and *he* decided that *he* needed to leave!

Margery   Oh, Vi.

Vi   He didn't even say goodbye to the kids.

Margery   Did he ever call?

Vi   He did. Once or twice.

Margery   How did the kids cope?

Vi   They didn't at first. They were devastated. Izzy especially. She always loved her dad. And I always thought he was the best version of himself around her.

Jack not so much. They weren't close. Jack could never stand the yelling. The raised voice. I think Jack took a lot longer to process it all. It made him so shy as a little boy. He'd hardly speak. He always worried about saying the wrong thing and what people would think of him.

Margery   Well, you wouldn't know it now. He's so confident now.

Vi   In some ways. But I think he carries it with him. Remembers a lot of the arguments and the yelling, you know? There's a heaviness in his heart. He was always so scared he'd be like his father as an adult.

Margery   And is he?

Vi   In some ways. The good ways. And he's the spitting image of his dad, down to the curly hair and all. But mostly, Jack is his own person.

Margery   Kids are resilient, aren't they.

Vi   More than adults I think.

Margery   What about you? You must be pretty resilient yourself.

Vi   When you're a mother, you don't have a choice do you?

Margery   Spot on. I think sometimes, we can only do our best.

Vi   True. Marge, I'm so sorry about Tommy.

Margery   Thank you, love. But remember, Tommy's story is Tommy's story. And it's heart breaking. But it's not Izzy's story. So let's keep up hope. She's going to be OK. I know it.

Vi   You think?

Margery   Call it mother's intuition.

Scene Two

Mid morning. **Vi**, **Margery**, **Bill**, **Cynthia**, **Gerry**, **Belle** *and* **Timothy** *are in the hall, passing the time.*

Gerry (*to* **Belle**)   Right, these muffins need coffees to go with them! I'm going to do a coffee run!

Belle   To where, boss?

Gerry   To the urn.

Belle   The urn is right there.

Gerry   Yes, but if I call it a coffee run, it sounds far more enticing and exciting. Who doesn't want a coffee when one does a coffee run? Trust me. Attention, everyone!

He claps his hands and everyone mills around him. **Jack** *enters.* **Eleanor** *enters, eating a muffin with a towel around her head.* **Gerry** *directs* **Belle** *to give the muffins out.*

Gerry   Time for coffee. I'm doing a run. Who wants one?

Bill   I'll have a cup of English breakfast. White with one sugar is how I take it.

Gerry   Of course you do.

Margery   I'll have the same as Bill.

Gerry   You two are quite the pigeon pair. Should shack up one of these days!

Belle   Boss!

Gerry   What? Old people are allowed to get it on too!

Belle   Cheaper bills I guess.

Charlie   Aren't you gonna write this down, Gerry?

Gerry   No, I have the memory of an elephant.

Charlie   I've never liked elephants.

Gerry   Charlie, your order?

Charlie   Black tea.

Vi   Just a green tea for me thank you, Gerry.

Jack   Same thanks.

Cynthia   I'll have a chamomile tea thank you, Gerry. No sugar. I'm sweet enough!

Charlie   Sickly.

Cynthia   Despite hardly sleeping a wink last night! I need to find a better mattress for tonight. (*Shooting a look at* **Charlie**.) And some ear plugs!

Charlie   I wouldn't mind some ear plugs too. To block you out!

Cynthia   Very funny!

Charlie (*hatching a plan*)   You know, I think there's an air mattress around here somewhere. I'll have a look if you'd like?

Cynthia   Really? Thanks, Charlie. That would be fab!

Gerry (*to* **Eleanor** *and* **Timothy**)   How about you two? Drink?

Timothy   Just a cup of . . .

Eleanor   We're fine thank you. Nothing for us.

Gerry   Well, if you change your mind, just sing out. My apprentice Belle here can grab it for you. Can't you, Belle?

Belle   Yes, boss.

Gerry   Righto. Thanks everyone So, just to repeat the order. So that was a long black for Charlie, a green tea with sugar for Bill and Margery, an English breakfast without milk for Vi and Jack, and a cardamon tea for Cynthia. Done.

Belle   Ah, boss. I don't think that was right.

Gerry   Not right? Yes, it was right. The only thing that's not right is your head I think! Come on. These drinks won't make themselves.

Gerry *and* **Belle** *go to the urn and start making drinks. While this is happening and people are eating,* **Jack** *checks his phone.*

Jack   Everyone, there's been an update.

Everyone gathers around **Jack** *to listen. The notification lists* **Bill**'s *street as being in a high danger zone, at risk of being taken over with flames. To not worry* **Bill**, **Jack** *does not read this information aloud. While people are coming together,* **Margery** *gets quite close to* **Bill**.

Bill (*flustered*)   Margery, you smell nice.

Margery   Oh, do I? Thank you Bill.

Bill   You smell like a mandarin.

Margery   Oh. OK.

Bill   I like mandarins. They've my favourite fruit. Very citrusy. (*At this,* **Margery** *smiles.*)

Charlie   Are we listening to an update or watching an episode of 'The Bachelor, Seniors Edition'?

Jack   Right. (*Reading.*) 'Incident number: N014. Towns affected: Bleach Hill, Kardla, Greater Mordon Valley. The following update is in relation to the Bleach Hill blaze issued at 0900 hours, February 18. Fire front has moved in a north-easterly direction towards Black Hill. Current advice for between Armstrong Road and Stuart Street is you are . . . (*improvising this next section*) needing to be cautious and wait for more alerts'. (**Jack** *does not read what the update actually lists: 'You are now in danger. Shelter in a safe place'.*)

Margery   Bill, that's right near you!

Bill   It is.

Jack   But it just says to be cautious. It's not that close. (**Jack** *continues to read.*) 'Fire front is expected to worsen in the coming six hours as a result of wind. Call-outs are being made for further support and strike teams to commence at 1800 hours'.

Vi   Jack, is there anything about Izzy?

Jack   No. Nothing about anyone missing.

Vi   We have to get out there and look for her. We can't just stay here while she's still missing.

Margery   You can't go out there, love. It's too dangerous.

Vi   Izzy is out there!

Charlie   There's no point you being in danger too, Vi.

Vi   No point? I think finding Izzy would be the point.

Timothy   I know it's hard but you have to let the firies do their job.

Vi   Please don't tell me what I have to do. I know everyone is trying to help but none of that is going to *do* anything.

Jack   They're right, mum.

Margery   You know what? There's a delivery coming soon. I'm sure whoever drops off the packages will have some more information about what's happening. So we'll only have to wait a little while. How about we catch our breath, play a quick game of cards while we wait then work out a strategy when we know more.

Vi   OK.

Cynthia   I'll join you.

Margery (*with a grimace, making little effort to disguise her dislike for* **Cynthia**)   You really don't have to.

Cynthia   I know. But I want to. (*She follows the ladies.*)

Scene Three

Midday. People are playing cards, reading and passing the time. **Jack** *is on his phone, sitting on his own.* **Timothy** *goes to him.*

Timothy   Jack, are you OK?

Jack   Ah, yeh. Of course. As well as anyone at the moment.

Timothy   It's just that you don't look so good. Pale. Can I get you something? Some water?

Jack   No, I'm fine. It's just been a big couple of days I think. I'm just worried about everyone. And Izzy. Wishing there was some positive news.

Timothy   Same. You know, they all rave about what a great kid you are. How you're really going to make something of yourself one day.

Jack   I don't know about that.

Timothy   It's true. Everyone seems to really admire you.

Jack   There's nothing people should admire about me.

Jack's *phone goes off again and he checks it, reading more bad news about* **Bill**'s *house.*

Eleanor (*interrupting*)   So, Jack. You're the kid with the ideas. When do you think we're going to be able to head off?

Jack   Head off?

Eleanor   Yes. Leave. You seem to have a handle on it all so when are they going to reopen the roads and allow people out again?

Jack   I don't know, I'm sorry.

Eleanor   Fine. Well, I guess I'll just sit here and wait until you do.

Timothy   I bet you can think of worse people to be stuck with, can't you, Eleanor? We can finally get to know each other. I've been working for you for three years now and I hardly know anything about you.

Eleanor   Right.

Timothy   So tell me something about yourself. Anything.

Eleanor   OK. Well, I'm a private person and I really enjoy silence.

Timothy   Oh me too. The quieter the better. I think it all started in my childhood. You know, as a kid I used to . . .

Eleanor   No offence but perhaps we could just be silent right now?

Timothy   Oh sure. You know, I read this book about silence once. Interestingly, apparently being silent for long periods of time can noticeably lower stress levels.

Eleanor   Really?

Timothy   I think it would be because silence . . .

Eleanor (*to* **Jack**)   You hanging in there, kid?

Jack   Huh? Oh yeh I'm fine. I have to make a call. Excuse me.

Timothy   Is he OK? Maybe I'll go check.

Eleanor   Please. Let me.

Tired of playing cards, **Cynthia** *interrupts* **Eleanor** *before she can approach* **Jack**.

Cynthia   Hello, you two! You look a little out of place. I have something you can do while you wait to get out of here. Back to the big city. The Big Smoke!

Eleanor   What's that?

Cynthia   You could interview Kardla's biggest celebrity! She's been in three television commercials, has made numerous theatrical appearances on stage and was an extra in a feature film starring Adelaide Apps!

Eleanor   Who?

Cynthia   Adelaide Apps! She was a big deal in the nineties. Anyway, that celebrity is none other than, drumroll please, me!

Timothy   You?

Cynthia   Yes, me. I am that actress! Take this autographed photo. On the house. (*She hands them a large, signed head shot from a pile she has in her bag.*) You might have heard of me? Cynthia Taylor. (*She pronounces Taylor as Te-Law.*)

Charlie (*disparagingly*)   Your name is Cynthia Taylor.

Cynthia   Shush you. It's French and it's pronounced Te-Law. Maybe it rings a bell?

Eleanor   I don't think so.

Cynthia   So, in the height of my career, years ago now, just as things were starting to take off, I decided the bright lights and fame just wasn't for me. (**Charlie** *rolls his eyes.*)

You know, people were desperate for my autograph. For me to play the lead in whatever show was on at the time. Weren't they, Charlie? (**Charlie** *sniggers again.*) But I thought. You know what really matters? Country community theatre. So, I decided to move back home. For the sake of the arts scene in Kardla. To give back. You know?

Eleanor   Is she serious?

Around this time, **Margery** *exits to meet the volunteer organisation bringing food and blankets.*

Cynthia   So I'm sure you have a heap of questions for me! Ask away!

Timothy   Right. Well, Miss Taylor.

Cynthia   Te-Law!

Timothy   Te-Law. What can you tell us? About this community? Eleanor and I were just talking about how lovely everyone is.

Eleanor   We were?

Cynthia   What do you want to know? I'm an open book!

Charlie   With a lot of empty pages.

Eleanor   Our boss would like us to scope out some tourism opportunities in this town. I know that right now is really not the time, with all the hazardous, life-threatening, inconvenient fires and all, but maybe you could list a few things people like to do in this town and we can add it to our report.

Cynthia   Well, of course. I am President of the Kardla Dramatic Society.

Eleanor   Of course you are.

Cynthia   And our tri-annual shows are just the talk of the town. We have currently been rehearsing our production of *Jersey Boys*. Of course it's hard to get men these days to audition, especially in a country town so we've adapted our production. Called it *Jersey Gals*. Pretty much the same show. It was going to be very good. I was playing Frankie Valli. The reviews would have been excellent. (**Charlie** *sniggers more audibly this time.*)

Charlie, I've been practically harassing you to come and audition for us one day but you're always so busy!

Charlie   So busy. Washing my hair. Doing my taxes. Sticking pins in my eyes.

Cynthia   You don't know what you're missing!

Charlie   Trust me, Cynthia, no one wants to hear me sing. I'm even worse than you. I've been telling you for years, get Violet involved. She's the only one in this town who can actually sing.

Cynthia   Vi? Well, yes she's OK I guess. For someone who hasn't trained.

Timothy   You know, I did a musical when I was younger. What was it now . . . *Fiddler on the Roof.* I was Hodel, or was I Motel?

Cynthia   How wonderful. I once did a one-woman show inspired by *Fiddler on the Roof* called *One Fiddle. One Roof. One Message.* Rave reviews!

Timothy   What was the message?

Cynthia   The what?

Timothy   The message. Of the show?

Cynthia   God knows but the people at the door said I had so many people walk out during the show. Apparently they were so emotional they just couldn't watch anymore.

Charlie   I bet they couldn't!

Timothy   I'm sorry I missed it.

Eleanor   So, anything else worth doing in this town? Charlie?

Charlie   Ah, the bakery does a good sausage roll. You should get one when this all dies down.

Eleanor   I'm vegetarian.

Margery *enters.*

Margery   Right, everyone, gather round. A delivery is due to arrive in five minutes. We've got some food and blankets coming. Can I have a hand?

Figure 10 Cynthia responds dramatically. Photo courtesy of Tyler Marsland.

Cynthia   Ah, we're kind of in the middle of something here, Marge.

Margery   Is that right?

Timothy   Oh it's OK. We can pick this up another time.

Cynthia   No, it's fine. I'm sure Margery doesn't need everyone to help.

Margery   I'm sure Margery does.

Cynthia   Fine. Anytime you want to talk again, I'm all yours. Day or night. I could even do a little performance for you. I'm sure I could throw a dramatic reading together if you'd be interested.

Timothy   Sounds excellent.

Eleanor   So excellent.

Cynthia, **Charlie**, **Eleanor** and **Timothy** *join the group, bringing cans and blankets in and placing them in piles around the hall.*

Scene Four

Early afternoon. Alone, **Jack** *is on the phone.*

Jack   Hi, Sam. Thanks for the text. I've called as quick as I can. Any news on Izzy? (*He listens. It's a no.*) Will you keep asking around? And how about the house? The update said that areas between Armstrong and Frenton are in danger. That's smack bang where Mr Hopkins lives. Yeh, Bill Hopkins. Then your text said that it doesn't look good. Had to wait till I could find a quiet place away from everyone to call you. Didn't want to cause more worry, you know. You're sure it's Mr Hopkins? The whole house? OK.

Eleanor *enters, overhearing the last part of* **Jack**'s *conversation.*

Jack   Yeh I'm still at the hall. No, I don't want to be the one to tell him, especially since we don't know the damage yet. Sam, I appreciate you letting me know. I'll be fine. Honest, I will. Surely we'll find Izzy soon. Chat later.

Eleanor   Hi, Jack.

Jack   Oh, hey.

Eleanor   Everything OK?

Jack   All good.

Eleanor   I'm sorry, Jack.

Jack   It's fine. We'll get through it. Gotta keep positive.

Eleanor   You don't have to fake it with me you know.

Jack   Fake it?

Eleanor   The whole optimistic thing. It's not really my type of energy so please don't feel like you need to keep that up for me.

Jack   That's just what people expect, you know.

Eleanor   People?

Jack   People in this town. They think I'm this amazing kid. 'Jack Mills, Violet's son'. Think I don't do a thing wrong. Like I'm perfect.

Eleanor   And I'm guessing you're not? (**Jack** *smiles at this.*) Country towns, eh?

Jack   Yeh. Everyone knows your name.

Eleanor   Everyone knows everyone's name.

Jack   And your business.

Eleanor   Even before you do most of the time.

Jack   And God forbid you stuff up. That'll be the talk of the town!

Eleanor   You wouldn't stuff up that often I imagine?

Jack   You don't know.

Eleanor   What do you mean?

Jack   I'm not the perfect kid everyone thinks I am.

Eleanor   Drugs?

Jack   Huh?

Eleanor   Drugs. Are you into drugs?

Jack   No, nothing like that.

Eleanor   Well, what then?

Jack   It's just . . . I think I just feel like sometimes this town isn't the right fit for me. Too much expectation.

Eleanor   I get it.

Jack   You get it?

Eleanor   I grew up on a farm.

Jack   Really?

Eleanor   A dairy farm in the middle of nowhere. Hated it. Early mornings, lots of chores and too many cows. Country life wasn't my thing. Everyone always seemed to need to remind me that I didn't fit in, you know. I was the only redhead in the family. Stood out like a sore thumb in a family of blondes.

And I was different in every other way too. My two brothers were destined to be farmers but me . . . they used to say Ellie, Ellie, you're just not like us. You need to leave town and make something of yourself. Well, I didn't actually want to leave town at first.

Jack   You didn't?

Eleanor   I liked the safety. The comfort of knowing everyone. The community. I mean, the constant small-town gossip was annoying but it was what I was used to, you know. But everyone always said I was different. Like, I knew I didn't fit in. I didn't need to be reminded of it every day.

After a while, I started to agree with them. I'd say it before they could. Tell everyone who would listen how I was going to leave town as soon as I finished school and make something of myself in the city. That this country life thing wasn't for me. That I was somehow above it all.

I don't think I ever lost the bravado actually. Coming out here has been weird. Reminded me of so many things. Some of them good things too. You know, no matter what has happened, you've got a whole town's worth of support.

Jack   Thanks.

Eleanor   You're going to be fine. However you're feeling now, out of place or like you don't fit, it won't last forever. It gets better. You just got to ride it out for a bit.

Jack   Hey, can I ask you something?

Eleanor   You can.

Jack   If you did something that wasn't good and telling people could potentially cause an even bigger mess, would you say something?

Eleanor   I would.

Jack   That simple?

Eleanor   Not always. But sometimes it is. I tend to be very honest these days. I'd say something if I was you. For your sake as much as anyone else's. It's not easy keeping secrets. They can weigh you down.

Jack   You know, you're a lot nicer than you first seem, *Ellie*.

Eleanor   It's Eleanor, and thank you. But let's just keep that between us. Don't want to tarnish my tough boss reputation. Especially in a place like this.

Jack   You know, if you let people see this side of you, I reckon you'd feel more comfortable in this little town. You might even like it.

Eleanor   Oh, we're only here for a couple days max.

Jack   Even still. You could give it a go. Get to know some people. Relax a little. Maybe even heal some old wounds.

Eleanor   Maybe. See ya. kid. (*She goes to exit.*)

Jack   Hey. Thank you.

Eleanor *nods then exits.*

Scene Five

Mid-afternoon.

Margery   Listen up, everyone. I have news.

Everyone gathers excitedly.

Vi   Is it Izzy?

Margery   It is.

Vi   Tell me, Marge. Go on.

Margery   Well, I just spoke to my friend Sonja, who dropped off the Vinnies blankets. She said that there's talk of a girl, same age and appearance as Izzy, being found on the other side of town. It's pretty dangerous out there still and they can't get over here so she's staying with the Halliday family. But she's safe.

Vi   Thank God for that. I was so worried.

Jack *enters.*

Vi   Jack, they found Izzy. She's safe.

Jack   What?

Vi   When do they think they'll be able to get her here? Or can we get to her?

Margery   Sonja didn't say but I'm guessing we'll find out soon. Good news though.

Vi   Good news. This calls for a celebratory drink. Something strong!

Gerry (*beat*)   We have tea?

Vi   Tea it is!

Gerry   Belle! Get the woman some tea already!

Belle   Yes, boss! Follow me!

Gerry *and* **Belle** *exit with* **Vi** *and* **Jack**.

Bill   Ah, Margery?

Margery   Yes, Bill?

Bill   Good job with finding out about Izzy. Pays to chat to people I guess!

Margery   Thank you. Just the gift of the gab I guess.

Bill   You certainly do talk a lot, don't you. You could talk underwater with a mouth full of marbles I imagine!

Margery   Thanks.

Bill   No, I really like that you talk so much. All the time. To everyone. Incessantly.

Margery   Thanks, Bill.

Bill   You're welcome.

Margery   Well, I'm going to get a cup of tea now. I'll catch you later. (*She goes to exit*.)

Bill   Cards.

Margery   Sorry?

Bill   Cards. Fancy a game of cards later?

Margery   That sounds nice.

She exits to get tea with **Vi** *and* **Jack**. **Charlie**, **Gerry** *and* **Timothy** *remain and sidle up around* **Bill**.

Charlie   How's Kardla's most eligible bachelor going?

Gerry   You OK, Bill?

Timothy   Have you always had such difficulty with women?

Bill   Difficulty with women? What do you mean?

Charlie   What does he mean? He means, what the hell are you doing with Margery?

Bill   Margery is a lovely lady.

Gerry   Yes, she is but are you trying to ask her out or make her think you're a complete fruit loop?

Bill   Was it that bad?

Charlie   Take how you think it was. Then multiply that by a thousand. That's how bad it was.

Timothy   Be nice, Charlie. The man is fragile.

Bill   Well, you tell me then, Tim. Was it that bad?

Timothy   It was pretty bad.

Gerry   Very bad.

Charlie   Disastrous!

Bill   What am I going to do? I've not been in a relationship for years.

Gerry   I don't know much about relationships but I imagine they're a bit like baking. Hear me out. When I first started baking my famous lemon meringue pie, probably second only to my famous scrambled eggs, I was following the recipe book to the tee, and it turned out great. Fine. But, when I started to go off the recipe just a little and trust my instincts, add a little more sugar here or a lot more zest there, then the final taste was so much more delicious.

Bill   I'm not following.

Gerry   In relationships, throw out the recipe book, Bill. Trust your instincts. Add the lemon zest!

Bill   Right.

Charlie   Sit down, Billy boy. Listen to some advice from me. I've always found this to be spot on, no matter what situation you're in. You have to remember that women are smarter than us. Women are tougher than us. Women are braver than us. Women are more social than us. Women smell better than us. And lastly, women live longer than us.

Bill   So?

Charlie   So you've got no hope. Give up now!

Cynthia *enters, listening.*

Timothy   I think what Charlie is trying to say is that you've got to get out of your own head. Don't put all this pressure on yourself. Just keep it simple.

Gerry   You like her. You think she likes you. So go for it!

Timothy   And relax! You're both really old and in the twilight years of your life after all!

Bill   Oi!

Charlie   He's got a point, Billy Boy.

Figure 11 Timothy, Charlie and Gerry poke fun at Bill. Photo courtesy of Tyler Marsland.

Timothy   All I'm saying is that you've got nothing to lose. I've only been in town a few days but it's obvious that everyone in this town loves you, and Margery will too.

Cynthia   She could do worse. I hope you're not listening to Charlie's advice on women, Bill!

Bill   Ah these gents have had some very good points.

Cynthia   Gerry, what could you possibly know about dating women?

Gerry   Well, I know that I tend to stay well away from them!

Cynthia   Clever boy. How about you? Timothy isn't it? Timothy, have you had many relationships?

Timothy   Ah . . .

Cynthia   Yes?

Timothy   Not quite yet.

Cynthia   How many is not quite yet?

Timothy   Ah, none. But I do fancy someone at the moment.

Cynthia?   Really?

Timothy   Yes.

Cynthia   And have you been *woo-ing* her, Timothy?

Timothy   Well, I try. I've been trying to get her to like me for three years now but she doesn't even want to be friends. I figure the best thing I've got going for me is my smarts. So whenever we talk, I make sure I pass on any fascinating facts I know about the topics we're discussing. She doesn't seem very interested though.

Cynthia   I can't imagine why!

Timothy   Anyway, she's strong willed and confident and very intelligent. I am very attracted to her and very scared of her.

Cynthia   Well, us women are scary creatures. Boo! (*Startled, he jumps.*) Sounds like you may be better off as friends, Timmy boy. Goodluck, Bill. (**Cynthia** *goes to exit.*)

Bill   Ah, what is your advice, Cynthia? From a woman's perspective.

Cynthia (*clears her throat dramatically*)   Bill, it's simple: Be the brilliant Bill you were born to be! (*Chuffed with herself.*) You should put that advice on a T-shirt. While I remember, Charlie, (*batting her eyelids and adopting a baby-voice in an effort to manipulate* **Charlie**) I really have my heart set on sleeping more comfortably tonight. Have you managed to find that air mattress you were talking about earlier?

Charlie   Actually I did. It's in the kitchen waiting for you.

Cynthia   Amazing! I am due to start my twilight mantra meditation soon so would you be a doll and pump it up for me?

Charlie   That I can't do. Bad back and all. But I'll get it all laid out for you. All you'll have to do is give it a few pumps before bed and Bob's your uncle.

Cynthia   Fab! Thanks! Bye, boys, and good luck, Bill!

She exits.

Bill   Which blow-up mattress are you talking about, Charlie? Not the old blue one? That's a hundred years old!

Charlie   I know.

Gerry   And it'll never blow up. It's got a big hole in it.

Charlie   I know.

Gerry   You're a cruel man Charlie!

Charlie   I know!

Scene Six

Evening. Everyone is settling in for the night. Lights are dim and there are some lanterns being lit. Dramatically, **Cynthia** *is pumping up the air mattress.*

Gerry   Does anyone need anything before bed? If you do, give my apprentice a yell.

Belle   Thanks, boss.

Cynthia   I need someone to pump this thing up for me. Any takers?

Everyone looks at **Cynthia** *then suddenly turns away.*

Margery   I think we're all OK, Gerry. Thanks, love. I'm sure that mattress is inflating, Cynthia. Looks a bit fuller than it was an hour ago. And where did these lanterns come from? They're just beautiful. Romantic even!

Bill   Ah, I brought them in. Found them out the back.

Charlie   Of course you did.

Margery   Now, how about that game of cards, Bill?

Bill   Oh, I'd love to.

Margery   That is, if it's not past your bedtime.

Bill   I'm sure I can stay up a little bit longer.

Timothy   I'd love a game of cards too. Mind if I join?

Margery *and* **Bill** *look a little put out as* **Timothy**, *unaware, scooches between them. Meanwhile,* **Jack** *looks to* **Eleanor**. *It is clear she is encouraging him to speak to* **Vi**.

Eleanor (*to* **Jack**)   Go on.

Jack   Mum, can I speak to you about something?

Vi   Of course, darling.

Jack   It's about Izzy. There's something you don't know.

Vi   Jack, I do know.

Jack   You do?

Vi   I know that you feel guilty about the whole thing. I've seen it painted on your face. But you need to let that go. She's safe and that's the most important thing.

Jack   But, mum, there's more to it.

Vi   Darling, there isn't. She's safe and we're going to see her tomorrow and that's what counts. Now get yourself sorted for bed, love. Come on.

Bill   Got me!

Margery   Got you! I win?

Timothy   You win again.

Bill   You're not too bad at cards are you?

Margery   I guess not.

Bill   I'm normally a lot better.

Timothy   Same.

Margery   Oh? Just an off day today?

Bill   A bit distracted.

Timothy   Me too.

Margery   By what?

Bill   By you. You're very pretty, Margery. (*Beat.*) You remind me of the golden retriever I had as a boy.

Margery   I do?

Bill   Yes. Winnie was her name.

Margety   Ah, thanks, Bill.

Bill   But she died.

Margery   Right.

Timothy   I had a golden retriever too, Bill. You know, the interesting thing about dogs? Apparently they have psychic powers.

Bill (*to* **Margery**)   I think that came out wrong. What I mean is: Winnie was my favourite thing in the world. And I would have done anything for her.

Margery   Oh.

Bill   I loved her.

Margery   Well, Bill. That's very kind. That really is.

Charlie   How are you going there, Cynthia? You've still got a fair bit of blowing up to do. Better hurry up if you want to get to bed anytime soon.

Cynthia (*extremely frustrated*)   This thing will not blow up!

Charlie   I heard that it looks as though it's not doing anything and then suddenly it happens. Bit like rehearsals for one of your shows and then on open-up night, it just comes together.

Cynthia   Open-ing night.

Vi   Right, I think we're all set. Ready for bed, love?

Jack   Think so.

Vi   Good. The sleep will do you good.

(*Addressing everyone.*) Can everyone just listen up for one sec? Sorry. It's been a huge day today and, before we all go to bed, I just want to say thank you to everyone for your support. I know I've been a little highly strung. Maybe a little difficult to be around. (*Tongue-in-cheek murmurs of 'no, not at all' and 'absolutely not'.*) But I really appreciate everyone here. Even you, Charlie. And I don't know how to thank you all so you'll have to settle for a thank you, and this. (**Vi** *blows a kiss to everyone.*)

Bill   I know what you could do. To thank us all.

Vi   What's that?

Bill   Sing us something, Vi.

Cynthia   You want Violet to sing?

Bill   Come on, love. For old times' sake.

Cynthia   Not sure if she's ever worked professionally as an actress slash singer slash dancer but OK.

Charlie   Good shout, Bill. It's been years since we've heard your voice, love.

Margery   It would be lovely, Violet.

Vi   Everyone's getting ready for bed. No one wants to hear me sing.

Gerry (*pointing at* **Eleanor** *and* **Timothy**)   I bet these two would. They would have never heard you sing before, Vi. Her singing is like my scrambled eggs. Perfection.

Belle   Come on, Vi.

Timothy   We'd be keen. Wouldn't we, Eleanor.

Eleanor   I'm up for anything that'll put me to sleep.

Vi   I really don't think I could. It's getting late.

Margery   Come on, love, You'll see Izzy tomorrow. That's something to sing about. Give us a little tune before bed.

In a huff, **Cynthia** *storms off dragging the air mattress with her.*

Vi   Fine. I can do that. So, now that you've bullied me into singing something, what to sing?

Gerry   Anything by Whitney is a winner. Do you know the theme song from *The Bodyguard*?

Belle   I always thought Celine was better than Whitney.

Gerry   You're fired.

Timothy   I love opera. Can you sing some opera?

Eleanor   Or do you know 'Hammer Smashed Face' by Cannibal Corpse? They're my favourite band.

Vi   Ah, no. But I think I have one. This is a little something to bring everyone some hope tonight. This song has certainly given me some hope today. It won't be perfect so don't expect it to be.

She sings a song to lift the group's spirits, encouraging them to keep hope and maintain a smile. The lights are dimmed even further as the lanterns flicker. **Jack** *is noticeably upset.*

Margery   That was beautiful, Vi.

Bill   Just perfect.

Gerry   It was almost like Whitney was in the room.

Margery   Thank you, love.

Cynthia *storms in.*

Cynthia   Alright, who is messing with me?

Gerry   What are you talking about, Cynthia?

Cynthia   I have spent hours blowing up this stupid air mattress and it hasn't moved. Somebody help me!

Eleanor   Let me have a look.

Cynthia   Finally! Thank you, Emily!

Eleanor   It's Eleanor. Oh, there's a hole in this thing.

Cynthia   A what?

Eleanor   A hole. I can see it from here. And hear the hissing of the air escaping.

Cynthia   No wonder it hasn't blown up!

Eleanor   Something's about to blow up.

Charlie   A hole! Well, wouldn't you know!

Cynthia (*pointing vigorously*)   You!

Figure 12 Cynthia confronts Charlie. Photo courtesy of Tyler Marsland.

Charlie   Actually, now you mention it. There *is* a hole in that air mattress. I remember now. Maybe it's not worth blowing up after all.

Cynthia   You think?

Charlie   Sorry, Cynthia. Old age must be messing with my head. So forgetful.

Cynthia   You'll have more than old age messing with your head soon. Be afraid. Be very afraid, Charlie!

Charlie   And the Oscar goes to . . . Cynthia Taylor.

Cynthia   It's Te-Law! (*With another huff, she lays down dramatically.*)

Margery   On that note, I think it's time we all got some shuteye. Good night, everyone.

Charlie (*tauntingly*)   Goodnight, Cynthia!

Cynthia   Goodnight!

Vi   Goodnight, Jack.

Jack   Night, mum.

Scene Seven

Jack's dream. This optional dream scene can portray the inner workings of Jack's mind and can be conveyed through physical theatre. Through this scene, we see the guilt and desperation in Jack as we are given clues about what really happened to Izzy. Following this dream, Jack finally makes up his mind to tell Vi the truth.

Scene Eight

The next day. Early morning. Vi enters the hall, upset.

Margery (*waking*)   Vi, what is it? Vi, love, are you OK?

Vi   It wasn't her.

Margery   What?

Vi   It wasn't her. It wasn't Izzy.

Margery   What do you mean?

Vi   I went outside. To get some air before. And I saw Sonja. She said the girl that was found yesterday . . . it wasn't Izzy. It wasn't Izzy. It was some other girl from Bleach Hill.

Margery   Oh God. Did she say if they knew anything about Izzy?

Vi   No.

Margery   Where's Jack? Has anyone seen Jack?

Timothy   He was up early this morning. Said he couldn't sleep and needed to be outside.

Eleanor   He should be back soon.

Cynthia (*taking off her eye mask*)   What's going on?

Margery   It wasn't Izzy they found yesterday. It was someone else.

Vi   She's still out there!

Bill   Vi, is there anything we can do?

Margery   Can we get you anything?

Vi   No.

Margery   Do you want me to sit with you?

Vi   No.

Margery   OK.

Vi   I need to be alone.

Margery   How about we all give Vi some space? It's breakfast time anyway so I'm sure we were all about to head to the kitchen.

Cynthia   Well, I had planned to sleep in a little. (**Margery** *shoots her a look.*) But I guess I could eat. (*They leave to go to the kitchen.* **Vi** *remains.*)

Margery   I'll just be next door if you need me love.

Scene Nine

Soon after. **Jack** *is riddled with guilt and wants to speak with* **Vi**.

Jack   Mum, I really need to speak to you. About why Izzy went missing.

Vi (*in a daze*)   It wasn't Izzy.

Jack   What?

Vi   The girl they found. It wasn't Izzy. She's still missing.

Jack   What?

Vi   I can't believe it. She's still out there.

Jack   This is all my fault. This whole thing is my fault.

Vi   Jack, this is one big, awful accident. This isn't anyone's fault. This is just . . .

Jack   Mum, would you listen to me! It was! It was my fault! It was my fault!

Vi   Jack, what are you talking about?

Jack   It was me. It's my fault she disappeared. I left her.

Vi   You what?

Jack   I left her. On the side of the road. I kicked her out of the car on the way back from the shops and left her to walk home.

Vi   What?

Jack   I left her!

Vi   You said she wandered off. You said she got lost and you couldn't find her. Then this whole bushfire thing happened. And we were here and it was just awful timing. You said that. You told me that.

Jack   I lied. We had a fight and I lost my temper and . . . I didn't know there'd be these fires and that she'd go missing and . . .

Vi   So you kicked her out of the car?

Jack   Yes.

Vi   Jack, why would you?

Jack   I'm so sorry, mum. If I could take it back, I would. I'd do anything to go back.

Vi   Stop, Jack. Just stop. I need you to tell me exactly what happened. From the start.

Jack   Izzy and I went to get the drinks for lunch. And we got them. We got back in the car and she wanted to have some of her milk. I told her to wait till we got home to open the carton. I didn't want her to spill it everywhere. But she didn't listen. She opened it, then and there. Well, that really annoyed me. Why couldn't she just wait? That's what I asked her to do.

So, at the Perry and Smith Street intersection coming back, I braked hard. And she dropped the carton and the milk went everywhere. All down her front and over my leg. All on the floor. Strawberry milk everywhere. I told her. I said, 'Izzy, don't open that in here. You'll spill it'. Then I started yelling and she started yelling. And crying. And I just couldn't deal with it anymore.

I yelled at her. Screamed at her.

Vi   Jack!

Jack   I said, 'Get out of my car. You can walk home'. She wouldn't move so I lost it. I kept yelling, 'Get out. Get out. Get out'. And finally, she did. She slammed the car door and stormed off.

It was only a K or so. I didn't think anything bad would happen. I didn't know about the fires. I would have never made her get out if I'd known. (*Beat.*) Mum, say something.

Vi   I don't know what to say.

Figure 13 Jack relives his last moments with Izzy. Photo courtesy of Tyler Marsland.

Jack   I'm so sorry, mum. I am. I've been going over it since yesterday. Again and again and again. Trying to work out how it happened.

Vi   How could you not tell me this?

Jack   Well, there's been so much happening and I just . . . I tried!

Vi   Not hard enough clearly.

Jack   I didn't know how to say it! Didn't know how you'd react. What you'd think of me. Mum, please say something. Anything. Mum? Mum?

Vi   I have never been more disappointed in you.

Jack   Mum. I'm sorry. I'm so sorry.

Vi   I need you to leave. I can't see you right now, Jack. Just go.

Jack   Mum, you have to listen to me. I'm sorry. Believe me, please!

Vi   Don't raise your voice at me. You sound like him.

Jack   Like who? Like dad? (*She doesn't answer.* **Jack** *leaves.*)

Scene Ten

Later that day in the early afternoon. **Charlie** *is rolling the mattress up and putting it away.* **Jack** *is sitting to the side.* **Margery**, **Bill**, **Timothy**, **Charlie**, **Gerry** *and* **Belle** *are passing the time.* **Cynthia** *enters, clocking* **Charlie** *instantly.*

Cynthia   Rolling it up, ready for your next victim huh, Charlie?

Charlie   No. It's going in the bin.

Cynthia   Good. I'm still annoyed at you by the way.

Charlie   Look, Cynthia. I am sorry. I really am. I shouldn't have made a joke of the air mattress. That wasn't very nice.

Cynthia   You're right, it wasn't.

Charlie   Look, we've been friends for years.

Cynthia   Friends?

Charlie   Well, we've known each other for years. Let's not let this ruin it, huh? If there's anything I can do to make it up to you, just let me know. (**Charlie** *goes to exit.*)

Cynthia   There is something.

Charlie   Yes?

Cynthia   Promise me you'll say yes? You do owe me.

Charlie   Fine.

Cynthia   Well, the Kardla Dramatic Society are performing *The Boy from Oz* next year and we need a Peter Allen. I think you'd look quite fetching in a midriff tie-up top, some maracas and ruffle pants!

Charlie   Not a chance!

Cynthia   A promise is a promise.

Timothy   Everyone, there's another update. (*Reading on his phone.*) 'Incident number: N014. Greater Mordon Valley remains in an emergency zone. No loss of life reported. All properties on Pontith Street, Greater Mordon Valley have been lost however'.

Margery   Bill, that's your street! Oh my goodness. (**Margery** *hugs* **Bill**.)

Bill   It's OK, love. I figured it wasn't looking good. We can do without the material things. At least there's been no lives lost. (*To* **Timothy**.) Go on, mate.

Timothy   'Bleach Hill and Kardla, no longer in danger. Residents are urged to take precautions in returning to their residences and remain under a watch-and-act order. Weather conditions are expected to improve significantly by early afternoon. The previous notice of endangerments between Armstrong Road and Frenton Street has been removed. Residents are encouraged to return to their properties'.

Gerry   Well, that's mostly good news. Means we'll be heading home today.

Charlie   I'm sorry about your house, Bill.

Gerry   We all are.

Bill   Thanks, Charlie, Gerry. Just gotta sort out a place to stay and I'll be all fine. Could be much worse.

Charlie   If you have to, you can stay with me, Bill.

Bill (*flatly*)   OK thanks.

Margery   Or with me, Bill.

Bill (*enthusiastically*)   OK thanks!

Margery   I have a spare bed. You'd be more than welcome to stay with me for as long as you need. I have plenty of space.

Bill   Well, that might be the best offer I've ever received!

Charlie (*rolling his eyes*)   Thanks a lot!

Bill   Thank you, Margery.

Margery   You're very welcome, Bill.

Bill   Shall we go and discuss what time you like your cup of tea in the mornings?

Margery   Absolutely. Just give me a sec.

Bill *exits and* **Margery** *goes over to* **Jack** *who has started packing suddenly.*

Margery   Jack, what are you doing?

Jack   Packing.

Margery   Packing?

Jack   I need to get out of here. I'm no good to anyone just sitting around. I'm leaving to go find my sister.

Margery   Jack, it's not safe yet to do that.

Jack   I'm sorry, Mrs Mead, but I just don't care anymore.

Margery   Where's your mum?

Jack   I don't know. We had a fight a few hours ago and I haven't seen her since.

Margery   She loves you very, very much. Remember that. A mother loves her son more than he'll ever know.

Jack   Thanks, Mrs Mead. I have to go. I'll see you later. (**Jack** *goes to exit but* **Vi** *enters.*)

Vi   Jack, can we talk?

Jack   Mum, I was on my way out.

Vi   Out?

Jack   Yeh.

Vi   I really want to speak with you, Jack. (*Beat.*) I'm sorry.

Jack   You are?

Vi   Yes. For what I said and how I reacted. It was all just too much. Jack, you need to know this is not your fault. It was all just an accident.

Jack   But if I didn't . . . What kind of brother would . . .

Vi   Jack. You are a beautiful brother. You have always treated Izzy with kindness and so much patience. You've been her biggest fan since the day she was born.

Jack   So how could I . . .

Vi   You snapped for a split second, that's all.

Jack   Just like he would have.

Vi   Jack, you may have snapped but not like he used to. Not at all like he used to. Jack, your father was not a good man. You are not like him and you need to stop torturing yourself, thinking that you are.

You are gentle and you are compassionate and you are always worrying about others to the point where you worry yourself sick. You are your own person, Jack, and I know you will grow into the most wonderful man. We all make mistakes. God, I've made plenty. But we learn from them, and we keep going as best we can. Together. OK? Jack, I know Izzy is safe. I don't know how I know it but I do. It's going to be OK, you'll see. Now, come here. (*They hug.*)

Scene Eleven

Mid-afternoon. Everyone is packing up, including **Timothy**. *There is still tension in the air.* **Eleanor** *enters.*

Timothy   Hey.

Eleanor   Hi.

Timothy   So, did you hear? Bill's house was lost in the fires.

Eleanor   I know. It's terrible.

Timothy (*awkwardly*)   You know the interesting thing about fires? Apparently, a typical house fire will double in size every minute.

Eleanor   Not now, Timothy.

Timothy   Sorry. I'm just trying to get you to chat to me.

Eleanor   Well, quit trying so hard. And enough with the facts.

Timothy   You don't like my interesting facts?

Eleanor   They're just not very interesting!

Timothy   Right.

Eleanor   Right.

Timothy   You know, I was thinking, when we head back to the office, maybe we can organise a fundraiser and get some money together for Kardla. For Bill. Help him out a bit.

Eleanor   That's a really great idea.

Timothy   You think so?

Eleanor   Absolutely.

Timothy   Thanks. Maybe we can catch up and plan the whole thing out as soon as we get back. I've been doing some reading on fundraisers and, interestingly, the best fundraisers are the ones that simultaneously get people to give money whilst also getting them to . . .

Eleanor (*interrupting*)   Timothy!

Timothy   Or maybe we could just take it a step at a time.

Eleanor   Good idea.

Timothy   I'd really like to be friends, Eleanor. If you're up for it.

Eleanor   Sounds good to me.

Gerry   So, everyone, a reminder that although we're all leaving to go back home today, you are always welcome to visit 'Gerry's Place', your local friendly café. Best scrambled eggs in town!

Charlie   We'll be there, Gerry. As always. You gotta go easy on that apprentice of yours though, mate.

Gerry   Belle? Oh she loves my approach. Don't you Belle?

Belle   Yes, boss.

Gerry   She's lucky she's bloody good in the kitchen or I'd have to get strict!

Charlie   Fair enough.

Cynthia   Charlie owes me breakfast.

Charlie   Do I?

Cynthia   Yes! So we'll see you there as soon as you open again, Gerry.

Bill   Margery and I will be there too, Gerry. Absolutely.

Gerry (*to* **Eleanor** *and* **Timothy**)   What about you two? Think you can stop in for some brekky before heading back to town?

Eleanor   Actually, we're headed back to the hotel. I think we might stay around a little longer. Couple of weeks maybe. I'm sure there's a few people around here that could use a hand after all this, don't you think?

Bill   Well, you'd be very welcome to stay as long as you'd like. We're happy to have you in Kardla.

Eleanor   Thanks, Mr Hopkins. Happy to be here.

Margery (*entering, out of breath and on the phone*)   Wait, slow down. Say that again. Violet! (*She motions for* **Vi** *to come over. She continues on the phone.*) OK. I'll put her on.

(*To* **Vi**.) It's for you. (**Vi** *hesitates, unable to read if it's good or bad.*) Go on. (**Vi** *finally takes the phone.*)

Vi   Hello? Hello? Izzy? Izzy? It's you! (*To everyone.*) It's Izzy! Are you OK? Where are you? Are you safe? It's just that we didn't know if you were . . . Your brother and I have been worried sick. Everyone has been. We love you, Izzy. We love you so much. Where are you? We can come and pick you up. Right, we'll get a car sorted and be there. OK, darling. We'll see you soon. We love you. (**Vi** *hangs up.*)

(*To everyone.*) She's safe. Izzy is safe! (*Everyone cheers.*) We just have to sort a car then we can go pick her up.

Bill   Sorted! (*Jangles a bunch of keys.*) You driving or am I?

Vi   You. Definitely you. (*To* **Jack**.) Jack, it's all going to be OK. We're going to be together again!

Margery   Off you go now. Go get your girl!

Epilogue

Vi *enters.*

Vi   Kardla was ravaged by the Black Summer Fires of 2020. The record-breaking temperatures, high winds and extremely low rainfall meant the worst for our little town. For a time. But like so many places around Australia, we got through it. And we're closer for it.

As each character is mentioned, they enter.

Bill and Margery quickly became a pigeon pair. They married a few months after the fires. It was a real town celebration. Charlie was best man, only a week after his impressive performance as Peter Allen in Kardla's most successful production of *The Boy from Oz*, directed and also starring our very own Cynthia Taylor. (*She pronounces Taylor as Te-Law.*)

Eleanor and Timothy stayed for a few weeks after the bushfires then headed back to the city. They continue to raise funds for Kardla and our recovery effort. They're pretty good friends now too.

Gerry's café is busy! It really is the place to go in Kardla so pay it a visit if you're ever in town. His apprentice Belle is coming along in leaps and bounds and I've heard her scrambled eggs are even better than his. But we won't tell Gerry that!

Jack, Izzy and I are doing well. Izzy and Jack made up pretty quickly after their argument. I think they were just so happy to see each other again. I don't think we could be closer these days. I love my kids. My heart swells with pride when I think of how wonderful they are and the impact they'll have on those around them. I feel so blessed every day that they are happy and healthy and living their life so wonderfully.

Since the fires, things are different of course. They've improved now, but we are all still coming to terms with the long-term effects of what happened. So many people have lost so much. Lost their homes, their precious possessions, beloved pets, friends, family members and loved ones.

If I've learned anything from life, it's that our experiences, our memories of love and of loss and everything in between, swirl around in our chest just like embers. Embers that, at any moment, can burst into flames and remind us how much we love somebody, how much we miss those we've lost or how precious life is.

So live each day, be kind to your neighbour, hug your kids. And always search for something in each day that warms your heart, brings you joy and makes you smile.

End of show.

Ember **Discussion Questions**

1. How is the extended metaphor of the 'ember' used to explore the idea of grief in this play?

2. How is the setting of Kardla, an Australian country town, relevant to the story and how do the bushfires serve as a catalyst for character and plot development in *Ember*?

3. Hardship has a unique was of bringing people together. How is this statement true in *Ember*?

4. How is tension built and sustained throughout *Ember*?

5. How are different relationships represented in *Ember*? How do these relationships develop throughout the script and provide instances of comfort, conflict and humour for the characters involved and the audience?

6. Identify and discuss the presence of the following themes: survival, love, community, hope, grief and the strength of the human spirit. What aesthetic strategies are used to represent these themes in the play?

7. Consider the character of Jack. How might his experiences, both as a child and recently, inform his behaviour throughout *Ember*?

8. Research the Australian bushfires of 2020. How did these bushfires have immediate and lasting impacts in Australia? How were these bushfires similar to the Black Saturday bushfires of 2009 that Margery references?

Birdies

Playwright's note

'In any situation, a change of perspective can often make a birdie smile'.

I have always been fascinated by prisons. They are complex places and house a huge cross-section of individuals from different pockets of society. People from different cultures, people of different ages, people of different social standings and with different bank balances, challenges and life experiences. But people nonetheless.

Birdies explores themes of power, perspective, courage, resilience and hope. It tells the story of a group of women who find themselves in North Shores Remand Centre. For many of these individuals, a series of personal battles has led to their lock-up. But once behind bars, their battle continues. They must navigate battles of hierarchy, battles of prejudice and battles of self-discovery and acceptance. All the while, the clock is ticking on these women as they wrestle with the idea that karma might be responsible for issuing their greatest punishment. Only when they learn to shift their perspective and come together can they truly be free.

In 2020, as the COVID-19 pandemic spread across the globe, many people were forced to grapple with sudden restrictions on their freedoms, a profound sense of confinement and an overwhelming uncertainty about what the future might hold. In the midst of isolation and fear, what held us together was a shared sense of hope, the strength of our connections and the support we offered one another, powerful reminders that even in the darkest times we are not alone. Following these experiences, now more than ever, perhaps the real challenge is to focus less on what's happening around us and more on how we choose to respond to it. To shift our perspective. As Kate says in *Birdies*, 'In any situation, a change in perspective can often make a birdie smile'.

Brady Lloyd

Birdies by Brady Lloyd

Synopsis

When social worker Mackenzie is assigned to North Shores Remand Centre, she is forced to deal with corruption, greed and violence. And that's before she meets any of the prisoners. Her new boss Smiley is vindictive and power hungry and will stop at nothing to ensure his 'birdies' remain caged. As she spends more time with Jen, Shaz and the women in the unit, Mackenzie comes to realise that compassion is more powerful than cruelty and that often a change of perspective is the one thing that can set us free.

Setting

Birdies is set in the North Shores Remand Centre in 2019. Here, women are held while they await conviction and sentencing. They could be held here for a number of days, weeks and sometimes months, and will most likely go on to serve sentences in the nearby women's prison.

Characters

Nine characters (8F, 1M). Note: This play accommodates flexible and inclusive casting.
The staff:

Smiley, *36. The ruthless head of the North Shores Remand Centre.*

Mackenzie, *24. A social worker who offers compassion and support to the women.*

The prisoners:

Jen, *33. Protective and matriarchal, Jen longs to be reunited with her daughter.*

Shaz, *28. Hardened and mouthy, Shaz is an intimidating figure at North Shores.*

Tinny, *20. Tinny is Shaz's sidekick and dreams of a life of freedom on the ocean.*

Larry, *25. Book-smart, Larry inspires a more hopeful perspective in the women.*

Fog, *21. Fog is gullible and often the butt of jokes. She loves magic tricks.*

Kate, *19. Kate is new to North Shores and in the grips of a recent family trauma.*

Alice, *21. Larry's cousin. Young and hot-headed, Alice is still finding herself.*

Prologue

To a soundscape of music, each prisoner comes onto the stage and slowly removes their civilian clothing to expose their prison outfits underneath. These moments act as a symbolic re-enactment of the women's individual experiences of first losing their freedom. Jail cells are brought on and the scene is made.

Scene One

Thursday. A whistle blows and **Shaz**, **Tinny**, **Jen**, **Larry** *and* **Fog** *charge at the bars to loudly shout and terrorise the two new arrivals,* **Kate** *and* **Alice**, *who stand with* **Smiley**.

Smiley Birdies, your little cage. You'll meet this lot as soon as you've changed into something more comfortable. I'm sure they can't wait to welcome you. Down that corridor and wait at the door. (*They leave to go get changed. To the rest of the girls.*) Right, you lot. Should have these girls ready for you in no time. Remember our deal. You shake them up or you'll know about it. And girls . . . (*Like they've been instructed to do before, they make a forced smile, more like a grimace, for* **Smiley**. *He exits.*)

Jen Was that really necessary?

Shaz What?

Jen All the crashing and banging! The two things looked scared enough without you cows adding to the mix.

Shaz What did you call me?

Jen You heard me.

Shaz Say it again.

Tinny Yeh, go on.

Fog Cow, cow, cow, cow, cow!

Shaz Come over here and say it! (**Fog** *gets up to go but is stopped by* **Larry**.)

Jen Now, everyone, calm down. No need to get your knickers in a twist. (*Excitedly.*) Plus, it's about time I think! Ladies . . .

Fog Bets are open!

Jen How much?

Fog How much you got?

Jen More than you!

Larry Shaz? Tinny? You in?

Shaz Nothing else to do in this shit hole.

Tinny (*referencing* **Alice**)   My money's on the younger one. She'll crack first.

Shaz (*sarcastically*)   You think?

Larry   Girls, isn't it wrong to be betting on two innocent freshies? (*They all look at each other and then burst out laughing.* **Larry** *tries not to laugh.*) No, come on. I wonder what they'll be like. They look alright.

Jen   They do.

Tinny   It's a remand centre, not a slumber party, Larry.

Shaz   Hey, Ms goody-two-shoes, you have something on your neck. Ew, you too, Fog. Looks real gross!

Larry *sticks her finger up at them.* **Fog** *takes the bait.*

Fog   What? Where? (*She touches her neck.*)

Shaz   Oh, it's just your head! (**Shaz** *and* **Tinny** *start laughing.*)

Larry (*antagonistically*)   Tinny, don't you have some money to spend. Oh wait.

Tinny (*gets up, wanting to fight*)   Hey, shut your mouth!

Just as a fight is about to kick off, **Alice** *and* **Kate** *enter awkwardly. Everyone freezes and there is tension towards the new girls.* **Shaz**, **Tinny**, **Jen**, **Larry** *and* **Fog** *advance on the girls and surround them.*

Shaz   Well, hello, hello.

Tinny   Welcome, girls.

Shaz   You're going to love it here. It's like the Hilton Hotel. Only, it's not.

Larry (*to* **Alice**)   Well, look what the cat dragged in backwards.

Jen   You know this girl, Larry?

Alice (*confidently*)   Hey.

Larry   We're cousins.

Fog   You don't look like cousins.

Larry   Or act like it.

Shaz (*to* **Kate**)   Do you speak? (**Kate** *just looks at her, scared.*) Boo! (**Shaz** *and* **Tinny** *laugh.*)

Jen   That's about enough I think. You're OK, love. It'll all be OK. Don't worry about them.

Shaz   About who?

Jen   Who do you think, Shaz?

Tinny   We were just being friendly! (*At this,* **Kate** *moves away from the group.*)

Fog   Where you going, girl? Nowhere to go here!

Jen   Fog, just leave her.

Smiley *and* **Mackenzie** *enter, having been in* **Smiley**'s *office.*

Smiley   Right, listen up, birdies. (*The women stand in a line like they have done before.* **Kate** *and* **Alice** *follow suit. Some still make noise.*) I said listen! This is Caroline Mackenzie.

Jen   Another freshie!

Smiley   Quiet. Mackenzie's been sent here to assist with some programmes that they've decided are going to 'support' you lot. (*To* **Mackenzie**.) These are the girls of this unit. I think you'll find they'll keep you busy for as long as you can . . . well, for a while.

Mackenzie (*positively*)   Hi, ladies. It's really nice to be here. I'm really excited about the opportunity to work with you all and get to know you. I know that this place can present its own challenges but hopefully through first touching base with you . . .

Tinny   No one's touching my base thank you.

Shaz   Shut up, Tinny. Go on, Macka.

Mackenzie   Ah, hopefully by getting to know you all, I can help in some small way.

Smiley (*to* **Mackenzie**, *condescendingly*)   How inspirational. You're very enthusiastic, aren't you. We'll see how long that lasts. I'm off then. You be OK here, alone with these 'ladies'?

Mackenzie   Yes, I think so.

Larry   Hey, boss.

Smiley   What?

Larry   The table. You promised it two weeks ago. I think it would be great for the morale of the girls in the unit, you know?

Smiley   How upset would you be if the table was not here for another week?

Larry   Pretty upset. I think we all would be.

Smiley   Another week it is then. Oh I almost forgot. Smile, birdies.

They grimace. Content, **Smiley** *exits. The girls stare at* **Mackenzie**, *sizing her up.*

Mackenzie   Feel free to take a seat, ladies. (*None of them sit.*) Or not. That's OK. Standing is OK too.

Larry   You ever been away yourself?

Fog   And what's your name?

Jen   Mackenzie.

Figure 14 Larry stands up to Smiley. Photo courtesy of Cardijn College.

Mackenzie   You can call me Caroline.

Shaz (*singing*)   Sweet Caroline.

Tinny (*singing*)   Ba ba ba! (*The girls erupt into laughter.*)

Shaz   I hate that song.

Jen   Bet you've never heard that one before, hey, Macka?

Mackenzie   Well, yes, I have. But I don't mind.

Larry   You're quite upbeat, aren't ya, Macka?

Mackenzie   I guess so.

Shaz   Gross.

Mackenzie   So, girls, do you mind telling me your names?

Jen   Sure, Macka. I'm Jen. How are ya, love?

Shaz   I'm Shaz. (*Sarcastically.*) Welcome, 'love'.

Tinny   Tinny.

Larry   I'm Larry. It's nice to meet you.

Fog   Fog.

Alice   Alice.

Shaz   And you? Who the hell are you?

Kate   My name is Kate.

Scene Two

Later that day. **Smiley**'s *square office sits elevated above the communal area, giving him a clear view of the women below. He is always watching. As the scene plays out in his office, the prisoners go about their routines beneath him.*

Mackenzie   Ah, you wanted to see me?

Smiley   Yes. Just to officially welcome you to the fold.

Mackenzie   Thanks. I think it's going to be . . .

Smiley (*interrupting*)   What did you think of the girls?

Mackenzie   Well, first impressions. I think they're spirited.

Smiley   Spirited?

Mackenzie   Yes. I mean, before we were talking about . . .

Smiley (*interrupting*)   I think you'll find it's a little more difficult than you first thought with these 'spirited' girls.

Mackenzie   I assure you I don't think it'll be easy. I just . . .

Smiley (*interrupting*)   We've had a few social workers through here but never one so . . . green. I assume you have had some life experience?

Mackenzie   Yes, I have.

Smiley   I'll take your word for it. One question though. Why here?

Mackenzie   Sorry?

Smiley   Of all the places. Why choose here? North Shores Remand Centre. You look like you'd be more comfortable somewhere more . . . well, comfortable.

Mackenzie   I have my reasons.

Smiley   Mackenzie, you'll find you need to speak to the prisoners in a certain way to gain any respect.

Mackenzie   I agree. I really feel like . . .

Smiley (*interrupting*)   Please don't interrupt me when I'm speaking to you. Sometimes these girls can take advantage of certain situations and certain people if you approach with a soft touch. Now some would say that you're bound to fail or that you're inexperienced or even that, as a woman, you're probably not going to be able to have any sort of effect on these girls. I'm not saying that. I'm just encouraging you to prioritise control over kindness. You must make sure they know who is boss. And that they don't think it's them. Clear?

Mackenzie   Clear.

Smiley   Excellent. When is your first 'get-together'?

Mackenzie   Our first workshop will be tomorrow afternoon.

Smiley   And what's the plan? Braiding each other's hair?

Mackenzie   I really don't think that . . .

Smiley (*interrupting*)   I'm joking. Surely you can take a joke. You might have to learn. I look forward to hearing how it goes.

Mackenzie   Thank you. Before I go, I was wondering if you'd be able to tell me anything about the girls?

Smiley   If they've been written up, it'll be on their file.

Mackenzie   No, I don't mean that. I mean the personal stuff. Partners. Kids. Hobbies. That sort of thing.

Smiley   Why the hell would I know any of that?

Mackenzie   Oh I just thought that . . .

Smiley (*interrupting*)   They're prisoners. They've stuffed their lives up. And now they're here waiting to get what they deserve. It's called karma. That's all you need to know.

Scene Three

Friday. The women sit in a circle in what is the first group session with **Mackenzie**. *It is clear there is no camaraderie in the group as the women are defensive and uncomfortable.* **Jen** *is sitting next to* **Kate**.

Mackenzie   Thank you for being here today, ladies.

Fog   Like we had a choice.

Larry   You always have a choice, Fog.

Fog   Let's go and do a Maccas run right now then shall we?

Larry   I didn't mean that obviously.

Fog (*mocking her*)   'I didn't mean that obviously'.

Shaz   Would you two shut your faces?

Fog   Or what?

Shaz   You really want to know?

Jen   Enough. Let the woman speak. This is gonna be good.

Mackenzie   Right. I appreciate you being here. Even if you have to be. I want to spend today just getting to know a bit more about you.

Shaz   How sweet.

Mackenzie   In the hope that I can eventually offer you some support and a listening ear. I'd like you to tell me something about yourself. Something the other girls might not know. But something that's important to you. That you'd like me to know. Who would like to start?

Larry   I will. Well, my name is Larry. I've been here quite a while now. I'm not your typical prisoner I guess. I'm half way through a degree in finance.

Shaz   Majoring in stealing.

Larry (*ignoring* **Shaz** *and continuing*)   Which I hope to continue when I get out. Something interesting about me is that I have three tattoos. One on my stomach, one on my ankle and one I might show you later if you're lucky!

Shaz   Please don't.

Larry   Oh and I really want a table tennis table in here. I really think it would boost the morale. The vibe, you know. And I read about a new government initiative offering funding for prisons for health and fitness programmes in the area. So that's how we'd pay for it! And Smiley has been promising it for weeks.

Jen   You're supposed to tell us something we *don't* know about you!

Fog   Larry is always on about the bloody table tennis table.

Tinny   And balls!

Larry   Well, at my last place we had one. It's really fun. And I always say. There's no argument a game of table tennis can't fix.

Jen   She's the Oprah Winfrey of North Shores.

Shaz   You know what. She's a stuck-up princess that thinks she's better than everyone else. But she has a point. It's boring as hell in here. A table and some balls to bash around can't hurt. Macka, surely you can make that happen?

Mackenzie   Well, it's definitely something I can ask about. You said Smiley?

Larry   Yeh. That's the boss. Smith, but everyone calls him Smiley.

Mackenzie   Why?

Jen   You'll see why soon enough.

Shaz   Next! Go on, Tinny.

Tinny   OK. I'm Tinny. I don't really know anything to tell you about.

Mackenzie   There must be something.

Tinny   Nuh.

Mackenzie   Is there anything on your mind at the moment?

Tinny   Nuh.

Figure 15 Tinny and the girls share their story with Mackenzie. Photo courtesy of Cardijn College.

Shaz   That about sums Tinny up doesn't it, ladies?

Tinny   Oi.

Mackenzie   How about you explain your name. Where did Tinny come from?

Tinny   My brother. He called me Tinny first. We grew up poor but he did save up for this boat. It was only small. All I wanted to do was to get in the little tinny boat and go fishing. I'd go on and on. Tinny time. Tinny time. Tinny time. I felt so free on the ocean. It was just my brother, me and Tinny time on the water. Anyway pretty soon he started calling me Tinny and before I knew it, everyone called me Tinny. I used to hate the nickname as a teenager but one day I just decided to see it differently. I liked it.

Mackenzie   So you reclaimed the name for yourself? Took a different perspective. That's great. Do you like it now?

Tinny   Yeh. Makes me think of him. And the water. And the freedom.

Jen   You know, we also had a boat growing up.

Shaz   Congratulations, Jen. You want a medal?

Mackenzie   Thank you for sharing that, Tinny. That's great.

Shaz   So great.

Mackenzie   Shaz. I think it's probably your turn. What can you share with us about you?

Shaz   I'm not telling you anything.

Mackenzie   That's OK.

Shaz   Actually I will. Here's something for you. You can mind your own damn business and quit asking us questions and trying to get to know us. You have no idea what it's like to be away and you don't know what our life is like.

Mackenzie   With respect, how can you say that? You don't know anything about me.

Shaz   Let's keep it that way, Macka.

Mackenzie (*with some strength*)   No one is forcing you to say anything. But I will say you shouldn't make assumptions about me based on what you think my life has been like. (*Beat.*) Who hasn't gone?

Fog   Me! So hi, everyone. My name is Hannah Fogarto but everyone calls me Fog.

(*To* **Mackenzie**.) And you can too. Um, my favourite colour is blue. I absolutely love Pepsi Max. And pink marshmallows but not the white ones. My mum was a druggie and my dad was gone by the time I was two. We had a dog growing up called Leonardo Davinci and he was the cutest dog ever. But he died. And that's about it. What else you wanna know?

Shaz   When you're gonna shut the hell up.

Fog   Oh and I do magic. I was kind of famous in high school. Used to put on shows and all!

Larry   For your dog.

Jen   Probably what killed him.

Fog   No. I mostly do card tricks. I'm getting pretty good these days.

Larry   According to who? Your cell mate?

Fog   I don't have a cell mate. (**Larry** *makes a gesture and rolls her eyes.*)

Mackeznie   Thank you, Fog. Who else would like to share?

Shaz   Why don't we hear from the new girls. Who are you again?

Alice   My name is Alice. Hi, everyone.

No one replies except for **Mackenzie**.

Mackenzie   Hi, Alice.

Alice   What you need to know about me is I actually didn't do anything.

Smiley *enters, listening in the background. He is unseen by* **Mackenzie** *and the girls.*

Shaz   Oh same. We're all innocent here, right girls? (*All of the girls laugh and agree, except* **Kate**.)

Alice   No, I'm just waiting to go to court and then get out of here. My lawyers say there is no evidence so they're working to get me a court date ASAP or get me out even before that.

Larry   Lucky you.

Alice   Oh and Larry is my cousin.

Larry (*jokingly*)   Unlucky me.

Mackenzie   For the sake of this exercise, is there something you can share with the group though, Alice?

Alice   Um, I guess. Well, I got my name the same way as Tinny.

Jen   What your brother had a boat called Alice?

Alice   No. My brother and I were born in Alice Springs. We were there for dad's work.

Larry   Alice's dad is rich. (**Smiley** *clocks this, interested.*)

Alice   Shut up. Anyway, my mum and dad loved the place apparently. God knows why. It's just a big pile of dust with a rock on top. But they named me Alice so yeh.

Shaz   Well, that's not interesting.

Mackenzie   Who's next?

Shaz   How about you, freshie? You don't say much.

Jen   She doesn't have to.

Shaz   I didn't say she did. Come on, what's your name again?

Larry   It's Kate.

Shaz (*to* **Larry**)   Did I ask you? (*To* **Kate**.) Come on, Katie. You're up!

Kate   It's Kate.

Shaz   That's what I said. Your turn, Katie!

Kate (*with more strength*)   It's Kate.

Mackenzie   OK. It's OK. Kate, was there something you wanted to share with the group?

Kate   No.

Tinny   Come on, we've all done it.

Shaz   She's a bit like you, Lazza. A bit too good for us. Aren't you, Katie?

Mackenzie   Now, come on, Shaz. She's already said she goes by Kate.

Jen   Give her some time. She's only just arrived here.

Kate   I don't know what to say.

Fog   Do you have any hobbies?

Kate   No.

Figure 16 Shaz intimidates new arrival Kate. Photo courtesy of Cardijn College.

Larry   Is this your first time away?

Kate   No.

Mackenzie   What about your family? You could tell us something about them?

Kate   I'm not talking about my family. Don't ask me about them.

Tinny   Ooh, I think you've hit a nerve there, Macka!

Shaz   Haven't you just. Your family got issues, Katie? Poor Katie with her family issues!

Kate   Stop.

Shaz   What? Come on. Is that what got you in here in the first place?

Kate   Stop it!

Jen   Alright, alright. It's OK, love. It's not easy being here when things are obviously going on for you outside of this place. You're doing well, love. (**Jen** *gives* **Kate** *a smile and wink.* **Kate** *smiles back.*)

Kate   Thanks.

Jen   Right, it must be my turn to talk so listen up, ladies. (*Clears her throat dramatically.*) A few things about me. (*Playful and sarcastic.*) I love wearing the colour green. I love sharing a dunny. It's very romantic. And I love falling asleep to the sound of snoring from the cell next to mine. Fog!

Fog   Oi! It's my sinuses.

Jen   Yeh OK.

Shaz   You forgot your kid, Jen. But then again, that's not unusual, is it?

Jen   What?

Larry   Shaz, come on.

Shaz   Surprised you even remember its name! How many months has it been since you heard from it now? Does it even call you mum anymore?

Jen (*charging at* **Shaz** *and grabbing her*)   I will smash you from here to next week if you say anything about my kid again. You don't know a thing. I love that kid!

Shaz   Relax, Jen. No need to get so touchy.

Mackenzie   Please, sit. Jen, sit down now please. (**Jen** *and* **Shaz** *continue wrestling.*)

Smiley (*coming into full view now*)   She said sit! That's not a question. Sit down now. (*They sit.*) Good little birdies. Some of you need to learn when to stop chirping though. Sorry to have to interrupt, Mackenzie. How are things going in here? Your little session going well? Everyone behaving themselves I trust?

Mackenzie   Things are going well thank you. We were just in the middle of getting to know each other.

Smiley   How cute. Well, don't let me keep you. I did just want to pass on a message to the freshie. (**Alice** *stands up.*) Not you. Sit down. The other one. (**Kate** *looks.*) We've just received news this morning from St Bart's District Hospital. Your sister didn't make it.

Kate   What?

Smiley   She died last night.

Kate   Oh my God. (**Smiley** *goes to exit.*) Wait.

Smiiley   What?

Shaz   The girl's sister has just died and you walk off? Aren't you gonna tell her anything else?

Smiley   No, I'm not. (*Goes to exit again but stops.*) Actually, I will. I want to say that I feel for you. It must feel terrible to know that your family are going through hell. Through the worst time in their life. Through immeasurable pain. And you can't do anything about it because you stuffed up. Because you're a stuff-up and landed yourself here. I'm sure that must really eat you up. I know it would eat me up if I were you. But karma is a funny thing isn't it. Has a way of making everything work out exactly as it should. Mackenzie, I trust you're done here. Follow me. (*Uncomfortably, she follows him.*) Have a great rest of the day. And birdies, smile.

They grimace. **Smiley** *exits followed by* **Mackenzie**.

Scene Four

Later that day. The women sit in the communal area. **Shaz** *and* **Tinny** *sit nearby while* **Jen**, **Alice**, **Larry** *and* **Fog** *support* **Kate** *following the news of her sister.*

Jen   My God, love. I'm so sorry. Is there anything we can do?

Kate   I don't know.

Jen   It's OK. Sit down.

Larry   Was your sister sick?

Kate   No.

Fog   So you didn't expect it?

Kate   No. Well, not until . . . no.

Fog   Until what?

Jen   Fog.

Kate   I need to use the phone. How do you do that here?

Larry   You gotta wait. It's not open for another few hours. And that's if Smiley even lets us. Some days he won't if he's in a mood.

Fog   He's always in a mood.

Kate   I have to speak to mum. Find out what's going on. How has this happened?

Jen   Take some deep breaths, love. Breathe with me. (*They take a deep breath together.*) Now, talk to us. Start from the beginning.

Kate   Well, my sister. Her name is Beck. She was in an accident like two, maybe three days ago now. Someone drove straight into her car on the freeway while she was driving to work. She wasn't good. They took her straight to hospital. To intensive care.

Jen   Oh, love.

Kate   Well, I was really proud of myself because for once I was around. I wasn't drunk or locked up or passed out somewhere so I could be there. For Beck. And for mum. To help do stuff, you know. Until she was better. Anyway, I got myself to the hospital and we saw her. She looked awful, just laying there. The tubes and the blood and it just didn't look like Beck, you know. Not the sister I know.

So mum and I were sitting with Beck and the doctor comes in and tells us he has news. Well, the look on his face said it all. He just looked sad. But stony at the same time. And he was pale. He said we should prepare for the worst because Beck might not make it. Mum lost it. She just made this noise I've never heard her make. Like this shriek or cry like she'd been stabbed or something. It was too much. I couldn't be there. I had to get out and get some air. Get out of that room.

Jen   Understandable, love. That would have been terrible, seeing your mum like that.

Alice   So what happened?

Kate   So I ran. Out of the hospital. I needed a drink. I went and I nicked a couple bottles and . . . I don't remember the rest.

Larry   You don't remember?

Kate   Nothing. It's completely blank.

Fog   Geez.

Kate   It just doesn't make sense, you know. Beck is the good one.

Jen   Tell us about her. What was she like?

Kate   Beck is like no one else. Straight As in school. Great job. Great girlfriend. I reckon she was gonna propose to her soon too. And this amazing voice. Everyone always talked about Beck's singing. It was like this angel or something. The teachers always used to make her sing at assemblies. Completely on her own. She once sang 'Amazing Grace' in front of the whole school. Had all the teachers in tears. She was the best. Had everything going for her. Why would this happen?

Jen   You're still processing, love. Go easy on yourself. It's OK to feel upset.

Kate   I didn't even see her before I left. Didn't say goodbye. And now. Smiley was right, you know. I'm the stuff-up. But I'm still here and she's not. How is that fair? I gotta speak to mum. I've got to find out what happened. And I gotta be out of here to say goodbye.

Shaz (*to* **Kate**)   Oi. It's bullshit.

Kate   What?

Shaz   What he said to you. It's bullshit.

Kate   Thanks.

Larry   You going to do something about it, Shaz?

Shaz   I'm gonna speak to him. Tell him it's not right.

Jen   Well, good luck. You're gonna need it. Shaz, why you being so nice?

Shaz   None of ya business, that's why. (*Beat.*) I'm sorry about your sister.

Scene Five

Sunday. **Smiley**'s *office.*

Smiley   So it's a no.

Mackenzie   But I did some reading. Apparently there is a grant that's just been established to bolster health and fitness spaces in prisons. It's quite substantial. We could use that funding to purchase some table tennis tables. And maybe some gym equipment or . . .

Smiley (*interrupting*)   It's a no. We're not eligible for that funding. I've already looked into it.

Mackenzie   Really, because I . . .

Smiley (*interrupting*)   What are your thoughts on the two new prisoners on the unit?

Mackenzie   Thoughts?

Smiley   Yes, thoughts. Observations.

Mackenzie   Well, Kate will obviously be one to watch, with the trauma she's experienced.

Smiley   And the other one?

Mackenzie   Nothing to report really. I don't really know much about her yet.

Smiley   Apparently she comes from some family money. Have you heard anything about that?

Mackenzie   Larry did mention it before I think.

Smiley   How much money? Has she said?

Mackenzie   No. Why?

Shaz *appears at* **Smiley**'*s door.*

Shaz   Hi, boss. Macka.

Mackenzie   Hi, Shaz.

Smiley   To what do I owe this pleasure, prisoner?

Shaz   Well, I wanted to speak to you.

Smiley   I figured as much. About?

Shaz   About a few things really. I'm not happy.

Smiley   I see that. I hope you're not going to complain about anything. Because you know what happens to a birdie that complains. They get to spend some time in their own special cage. Alone.

Shaz (*deflated*)   Yeh, I know.

Smiley   Good.

Shaz   Boss, have you heard about my court date?

Smiley   Let me think. No. Was there anything else?

Shaz   Um, no. Actually yes. I wanted to ask you about the freshie and her sister.

Smiley   You know I can't tell you anything since it is actually none of your business.

Shaz   I know. I was only going to ask whether you were gonna let her go to the funeral?

Smiley   And why are you asking? Can she suddenly not talk or walk herself up here?

Shaz   She can. She's just a real mess and it'd be good if she could go. Funerals suck but they're important. Especially for a sibling.

Smiley   How unlike you. Taking time out of your busy day of throwing your weight around to think about someone else. You girls all best buddies today? How interesting. (**Mackenzie** *gives* **Shaz** *a reassuring smile.*) Mackenzie, could you give this prisoner and I a few moments? I'm sure you've got work to get on with. Thank you.

Mackenzie *exits reluctantly.*

Shaz   I didn't meant to say the wrong thing. The freshie is just upset is all.

Smiley   You know what upsets me?

Shaz   What?

Smiley   Birdies that don't know their place. That think their opinion and their thoughts and their feelings matter. That's what.

Shaz   I'm sorry, boss. Forget I said anything. (*She goes to exit.*)

Smiley   You know. I could probably make it happen.

Shaz   You could?

Smiley   But I don't know why you care so much. I thought you'd be more interested in getting yourself out of here. Maybe I do have some time to talk about the court date.

Shaz   Really?

Smiley   That's what I said.

Shaz   Have you heard something?

Smiley   Maybe. Let's just say you could be in here a whole lot longer or I could pull a few strings and move things on a little more quickly.

Shaz   You would do that?

Smiley   For a cost.

Shaz   What do you mean? You know I don't have any money.

Smiley   Something else then. I tell ya what. I'll see what I can do about your court date and your little friend's funeral excursion too. And I'll let you know about the favour you can do for me.

Shaz   I don't know.

Smiley   That'll be all. Oh and I don't imagine you'll want to tell anyone about this. Not unless you want some alone time somewhere to think about things.

Shaz   Got it.

Smiley   And, birdie. Smile. (**Shaz** *grimaces.*) That'll be all.

Shaz *exits.*

Scene Six

Later that day. The table tennis table is wheeled into the middle of the communal area.

Smiley   Birdies, behold! Look what I've managed to scrounge up!

Larry   Yes. A table! Oh my God! Finally!

Jen   Bit old-looking. Could use a facelift.

Fog   Bit like you then, Jen!

Jen   Ah shut up.

Smiley   And you can thank Shaz for her sweet talking.

Shaz   I didn't say anything about a table.

Smiley   She's being modest. She practically begged for this.

Tinny   Yes, Shaz! (*They all cheer.*)

Fog   What did you have to do to get this?

Shaz (*awkwardly*)   Just the gift of the gab I guess.

Larry   Well, thank God for Shaz. Right, who wants the first game?

Fog   I'm in. Prepare to get whipped.

Larry   Didn't take you for a chick who could play ping pong.

Fog   I'm full of surprises. Ball sports are my thing!

Smiley   Aren't you forgetting something? (**Smiley** *holds up a bucket of balls.*)

Larry (*hesitantly*)   Thanks, boss.

Smiley   It's my pleasure really. As I said, thank Shaz. It's amazing what someone will do to get what they want. (**Larry** *and* **Fog** *begin to play.*) Now, remember, girls: if there are any fights or squabbles, the table goes. (**Smiley** *moves towards* **Kate** *while she is on her own.*) Geez, why the long face?

Kate   What?

Smiley   You look like someone died. Oh wait.

Jen (*moving protectively towards* **Kate**)   All OK here, Kate?

Kate   Yeh. (*As* **Smiley** *goes to exit,* **Kate** *addresses him.*) I was just wondering when I'd be able to use the phone?

Smiley   Well, I guess we could have them available soon. Yes, I think that'll work.

Kate   It's just I really need to contact my mum to speak to her about what's happening.

Smiley   I understand. I'll do my best.

Kate   Thank you. I really appreciate it. And I was thinking that the funeral will be soon and I really need to be there so I was wondering if . . .

Smiley (*interrupting*)   Woah, birdie. Stop squawking. And remember this, prisoner. Even when things in your little life are tough, it's always important to smile. So let's see a smile.

Kate   What?

Smiley   A smile. I want to see you smile.

Jen   Do it. (**Kate** *grimaces.*)

Smiley   There's a good birdie.

He grins and goes to leave. **Mackenzie** *comes over to* **Shaz** *who seems upset.* **Smiley** *clocks this.*

Alice   What is with you and the smile thing? Her bloody sister just died!

Larry   Al, leave it.

Alice   No, he needs to quit it. Who do you think you are, you monster!

Smiley   Well, well, well. Haven't you got a lot to say for a freshie. Karma's coming for you. I think some alone time will fix you right up. We have the perfect solitary cell for a big-mouthed birdie like you. Some time to think. And maybe lose some of that attitude. Follow me. Oh and birdies, let this be a lesson to you all. You do what I say, when I say it. I say smile, you damn well smile. Now move.

Alice *exits.* **Smiley** *goes to exit too.*

Mackenzie   Hey, Shaz.

Shaz   Macka.

Mackenzie   What happened in there once I left?

Shaz   Ah, nothing. (*Becoming defensive, seeing* **Smiley** *watching them.*) Nothing. None of your business is what. Got what we wanted huh!

Mackenzie   I guess so.

Shaz (*referencing the game* **Larry** *and* **Fog** *are still playing*)   Now it's just that bloody sound that's gonna drive me nuts.

Mackenzie   I wanted to say that I think it was a really good thing you did back there, sticking up for Kate.

Shaz   Yeh. Maybe.

Scene Seven

Monday. **Kate** *waits patiently for her turn to speak to her mum.* **Smiley** *moves too close to* **Kate**, *finally allowing her access to a phone and staying close to observe her.* **Mackenzie** *and the girls are also in the communal area and listen to her phone call.*

Kate   Mum, it's me, Kate. Mum? Yeh, it's Kate. Mum, I'm so sorry. I'm so sorry about all of this.

Where? I'm in remand, mum. Yeh North Shores.

Not great. There's this guard . . . (*She sees* **Smiley** *beside her and realises she shouldn't speak.*) Anyway, it's fine.

I just lost it. I couldn't be there anymore and I left. I'm so sorry. I just went and started drinking and it all went to hell from there.

I don't remember, mum.

No, I don't remember what happened next. Just that I stole some booze and I think there was some sort of fight. And I know I got in a car but I can't even remember getting arrested. It's a blur. But they told me when I got here that it's not good. I'll probably be looking at more time. But mum that doesn't matter right now. How are you?

I'm so sorry, mum. I didn't mean to do this. I'll make it up to you. I don't know how but I will. Mum, when is the funeral?

Friday? OK.

I'm gonna do my best to be there. I have to be there. (**Smiley** *taps his watch, motioning for her to hurry up.*)

Yep. I love you too, mum.

Scene Eight

The following Thursday. The girls have their second session with **Mackenzie**, *minus* **Alice** *who is still in the solitary cell.* **Smiley** *has joined the session, standing towards the back.*

Mackenzie   Right, girls. Thank you for coming again to this session.

Larry (*puts hand up*)   Um, why isn't it just the girls today?

Mackenzie (*acknowledging* **Smiley**)   Ah, yes. It's important to . . . do some observation of practice so that we're able to ensure we are providing purposeful services for you all

Fog?   Huh?

Jen   He's here to check up on us. Now shut up and listen to Macka. Macka, go ahead!

Mackenzie   Thanks, Jen. So, I'm really aware that lots has happened since session one, especially for some of us. (**Mackenzie** *gives a nod to* **Kate**.) Something that really stood out to me from last time was how connected we either feel or want to feel to our loved ones. So this activity is going to be about that.

Fog   Is this like a *Survivor* episode when our girlfriends and boyfriends are gonna walk through the door?

Shaz (*playfully with less aggression*)   No, dumb ass.

Larry   I'm not dressed for tele if it is!

Shaz   You're really not!

Jen (*to quieten the women*)   Oi!

Mackenzie   I'd like to ask you to share something quite personal with the group. Trust me on this one, girls. I'd like you to tell the group one person you really miss. Someone you wish with all of your heart you could see more often. You can just say their name or you can tell us a bit about them. Before we start, I really want to remind us to be respectful of each other and the things we might say today.

Smiley   Good luck.

Mackenzie   Would anyone like to start?

There is an extended silence before **Shaz** *speaks.*

Shaz   Right, I'll go. A few of you know my sister. Dawn. She's visited here a few times. She's a scary cow. You think I'm tough. I got nothing on her. But she's alright. We didn't have a great time growing up and she was always there. And I miss her.

Mackenzie   Thank you, Shaz. Would you like to share what happened to Dawn?

Shaz   No.

Mackenzie   OK.

Shaz   But she died. And I was locked up when it happened. (*Directly to* **Kate**.) So I get what it's like.

Mackenzie   Thank you for sharing that, Shaz. That was really powerful. (*Looking around.*) Who would like to go next?

Fog   I miss Nutella. Can't get enough of it on buys here.

Larry   I don't think that's the point of this activity, Fog. Right, I'll go. For me, it's my brother Billy. He's the best. I don't know what I'd do without him. (**Larry** *registers* **Kate**'*s situation.*) I'm sorry, Kate.

Kate   It's OK.

Mackenzie   Tinny?

Tinny   Ah probably my brother too.

Mackenzie   Would anyone else like to share?

Jen   I will. It's hard though, you know.

Mackenzie   It's a safe space, Jen. No on will judge you. (**Mackenzie** *shoots a look at* **Shaz**.)

Jen   I miss my kid. I don't talk about her much because if I do it makes it worse. But her name is Missy and she is my world. She's the reason I want to get out of here and make something of my life.

Larry   And you will, Jen.

Jen   Thanks, Laz.

Larry   Has everyone had a go?

Jen   Just Kate to go.

Mackenzie   Kate, did you want to share?

Kate   I miss my sister obviously but I think I'm still processing that, you know. It hasn't really sunk in yet.

Mackenzie   These things take a while. Give yourself the time. Right, I want everyone to take a piece of paper and a pen and write your person a letter.

Larry   Oi, Macka, I don't know about this.

Tinny   It's like we're in bloody school again.

Jen   Come on, girls, let's give this a go.

Mackenzie *hands out equipment and the women move around the space, finding somewhere to write their letter.*

Mackenzie   It doesn't have to be huge. And you can choose to send it or keep it or whatever. I think we'll find that although we might be different women from different backgrounds, we aren't all that different when it comes to having people we love and miss. It's good to remember that.

Smiley   Mackenzie, a word?

Mackenzie   Of course.

As they talk, the girls write. **Kate** *scrunches up piece by piece and throws the paper to the floor.* **Fog** *just stares at the paper, no pen in hand.*

Smiley   You really think there is any point in doing this?

Mackeznie   I do.

Smiley   This isn't the sort of thing we normally do in here. I doubt there's legitimate benefit to an exercise this questionable. I know you probably learnt some really 'trendy' things in your degree but don't get ahead of yourself. This sort of soft, 'let's talk about our feelings' crap really just wastes everyone's time. Including mine.

Mackenzie   With respect, sir, I disagree.

Smiley   Really? How many months was it that you're on probation before you're signed off, Mackenzie?

Mackenzie   Six months.

Smiley   Interesting. And who signs you off after those six months.

Mackenzie   You do.

Smiley   I do. Might be best to remember that.

He leaves the conversation to observe the girls write their letters.

Mackenzie   Kate, how is it going?

Kate   I'm really struggling with this.

Jen   Who are you writing to, love?

Kate   I'm writing to my sister. I'm writing what I want to say at her funeral. To say goodbye.

Mackenzie   You take your time. But maybe use a pencil so we don't go through a whole pile? (*Clocking* **Fog**.) Fog, it doesn't have to be long. Just something.

Fog   I'm not doing it.

Jen   You good, girl?

Fog   Yeh, but I'm not doing this.

Mackenzie   It's OK, Fog. But can I ask why?

Fog (*shouting*)   I am not doing this! Stop asking me!

Larry   What's the matter, Fog? Just give it a go.

Fog (*shouting*)   No! I'm not doing this. I can't do this! (*Beat.*) I can't write. (*Beat.*) I never learnt.

Tinny   What? (*Looking to* **Shaz**, *ready to make a joke of* **Fog**.)

Shaz   Shut up, Tinny. (**Fog** *clocks* **Shaz**'s *defence of her.*)

Jen   I'll give you a hand.

Shaz   I can help too.

Fog   Thanks.

Smiley   Shaz, a word?

Shaz   Yep.

Smiley   I've worked out what you can do for me. You know, my favour.

Shaz   Right.

Smiley   I need you to pick an argument. I want a big fight in here, lots of fuss. A cat amongst the birdies, so to speak.

Shaz   Why?

Smiley   You don't get to ask questions. You just get to repay me. I sorted the table.

Shaz   But I didn't even ask about the table.

Smiley   I'm looking into the funeral for the freshie and most importantly for you, I'm finalising when your date is so you can get out of here. And maybe, out *out* of here. I can always scrap all of that if you like.

Shaz   No, it's fine. It's just . . .

Smiley   What?

Shaz   Well, everyone is actually starting to get along with each other.

Smiley   My heart bleeds. It's your choice, birdie. I'd choose carefully if I was you though.

He gives her a wink and leaves the conversation. The girls have been observing them speak without hearing what they're saying. They have all finished their letters by now.

Mackenzie, I need to see you in the office. (*Looking at* **Shaz**.) I'm sure the girls won't cause any *fuss* while we're gone.

Mackenzie   Sure. Ladies, let's finish up here. Larry, maybe you could collect the letters and I'll hang on to them until tomorrow?

Larry   Yep.

Mackenzie *and* **Smiley** *exit.* **Shaz** *takes a breath, reluctant.* **Larry** *goes around and collects the letters.* **Kate** *puts her letter in her pocket.* **Larry** *arrives to collect* **Shaz**'s *letter last.*

Larry   Want me to grab yours, Shaz?

Shaz   No.

Larry   Shaz, what's up?

Shaz   What's it to you?

Larry   Nothing, I was just asking.

Shaz   Well, don't just ask. You're as stupid as Fog aren't you!

Jen   Just give her your sheet, Shaz. Jeez.

Shaz   Why don't I collect them up instead? (**Shaz** *grabs the letters from* **Larry** *and starts reading one in a mocking tone.*) This one's is from . . . Jen. To my darling daughter. I love you more than life itself. What's your name again?

At this, **Jen** *lunges at* **Shaz** *and the girls start fighting. Papers fly everywhere.* **Jen** *and* **Shaz** *wrestle, screaming at one another while the girls surround them, some encouraging them and others calling for them to stop fighting. Someone throws the bucket of table tennis balls on* **Jen** *and* **Shaz** *to stop them fighting and* **Kate** *pushes the women apart. Finally,* **Smiley** *uses a whistle to get the girls' attention.*

Smiley (*smugly*)   Right, girls. Get in line. Is fighting something we do in this unit? You're behaving like animals so we'll treat you like animals. You can expect an extended period of time in your cells. I hope you enjoy it. And you should know better, Shaz. You come in asking me if there's any favours you can do to get your court date moved, saying you'll do anything I want even if it means screwing over the other little birdies, especially this one. (**Smiley** *points at* **Kate**.) Then you start a fight. That wasn't very clever was it? Shame on you.

Shaz   But you said if I . . .

Smiley (*interrupting*)   Silence!

Larry   I knew she didn't ask about the funeral.

Smiley   Enough. You should all be ashamed of yourself. A week separated should do it. Now, before I go. Smile my little birdies. (*They grimace.*) I said smile. (*They grimace harder.*) That's better. Now get out of my sight and back to your cells. (*They move back to cells off stage. To* **Kate**.) You can stay behind. I think you can have some time to think about your actions and your involvement in that fight. Maybe a few days.

Kate   But when will I be out? What about the funeral?

Smiley   Did I ask you to speak?

Kate   I have to be there!

Smiley   Keep talking and there's no way it'll be happening. While you're in here, I own you, little birdie. You'll walk if I tell you to walk. You'll speak if I tell you to speak. And you'll shut it if I tell you to shut it. Now follow me. Mackenzie, make sure they're in cells by the time I'm back.

Scene Nine

Later on Thursday. **Smiley** *escorts* **Kate** *to join* **Alice** *in the solitary cell.*

Smiley   You can sit in there with her for a bit. (*To* **Alice**.) How are you doing?

Alice   Crap.

Smiley   Good. I'll be back soon. (*He exits.*)

Alice   Hey.

Kate   Hey.

Alice   You been naughty have you? Must have been to get stuck here with me. (*Beat.*) You OK?

Kate   Not really.

Alice   Have you heard any more about your sister?

Kate   No. Smiley won't let me talk to mum again. I don't know what's happening.
I don't even know when the funeral is.

Alice   I'm really sorry about what's happening to you.

Kate   Thank you.

Alice   Life can suck.

Kate   Yep.

Alice   I wish I could think of something to make it better. To make you smile or
laugh or something.

Kate   You know, whenever I was upset, my sister always used to do this thing with
her socks. Like make these weird-looking sock puppet things. It sounds strange. Well,
I guess it was. But it was always funny.

Alice   Where are socks when you need them, hey!

Kate   Yeh.

Alice *gives* **Kate** *a friendly bump and moves closer to her.* **Smiley** *enters again.*

Smiley   Well, aren't you two getting on a treat. Move apart. (*To* **Kate**.) I have
something for you. Your mother sent this in. (**Smiley** *throws a picture on the floor.*)

Alice   Who is it?

Kate   It's Beck.

Alice   Your sister?

Kate   Yeh.

Smiley   Right. (*To* **Alice**.) You're out of here. Get up and move. Down there.

Alice   What are you doing for her?

Smiley   None of your business. Now move. (**Alice** *remains still.*) Move!
(**Alice** *moves.*)

Kate   Boss?

Smiley   What?

Kate   Have you heard anything? About my sister?

Smiley (*smirking*)   Yes. The funeral will be tomorrow. You won't be going.

Kate   Wait! Wait!

Alice   I'll tell the girls. We'll do something, I promise.

Smiley   Move! (**Alice** *exits.*) What makes you think you deserve to be there? Or that
anyone would want you there?

Kate   They're my family.

Smiley   Which makes what you did even worse.

Kate   What do you mean?

Smiley   You don't even know what you did.

Kate   I told you. I can't remember. It's gone from my memory.

Smiley   I don't believe you.

Kate   It's true!

Smiley   I don't believe you. You know what, you look innocent. Hell, you're even pretty in a strange sort of way. But God knows what is beneath the facade. To think a girl like you could do a thing like that. And to the people you 'love'. It's unfathomable. It's probably best you miss the funeral. Best for your family. Your poor, poor family. I'm going to leave you to think. Think about what you did. Let's see if it comes back.

Kate   Wait! Wait! (**Smiley** *exits. To herself.*) What did I do? What did I do?

Scene Ten

This is an optional dream sequence, where **Kate** *has flashbacks of what happened on the night of her sister's death. Through stylised physical theatre, the audience is privy to not only the events of the night but to* **Kate**'s *guilt and the feelings of her mum (played by* **Jen**) *and her sister (played by* **Alice**).

Scene Eleven

Later that day. **Smiley**'s *office. He is on the phone.*

Smiley   Yes, I know. As I said, you're going to have to get creative. It's not like we haven't done this sort of thing before. Toughen up. Play the game. Tell them what they want to hear. Hell, just grow a pair and make it happen.
Why does it always have to be me? I sorted the last one. You can sort this one.
Well, at the end of the day, money talks doesn't it? If they can make it happen, then I guess I can make it happen.
Absolutely not.
Do better than try. Otherwise, you're gonna be up the creek without a paddle. And I'll be in it too. Don't call me until you've made it happen. And remember, keep your mouth shut.

Mackenzie *has arrived and hears* **Smiley**'s *last line.*

Mackenzie   I'm not interrupting am I?

Smiley   Yes, actually.

Mackenzie   Sorry. I just wanted to speak to you about Kate.

Smiley   What about her?

Mackenzie   About her sister's funeral. Are you going to let her go?

Smiley   No.

Mackeznie   Why?

Smiley   Why are you challenging me?

Mackenzie   I just think we should be considering her wellbeing. She's extremely fragile. I know that there's been measures put in place before in these sorts of circumstances. It's not the first time.

Smiley   No. It's not happening.

Mackenzie   But why?

Smiley   Mackenzie. You are green. You're about as green as they come and there are things you just don't know. How could you? That girl was involved in some awful things. She 'doesn't remember' but the people affected certainly do. She's not going. (*Beat.*) You can leave now.

Mackenzie   At least let her out tomorrow so she can be with the other girls on the day of the funeral.

Smiley   Fine.

Mackenzie   Thank you.

Smiley   I'll allow it. But on one condition.

Mackenzie   What?

Smiley   I want you to do something for me.

Scene Twelve

Friday morning, the day of the funeral. **Kate** *walks into the communal area.*

Jen   Kate, it's good to see you.

Larry   Alice told us what happened, Kate.

Larry   He's a pig.

Alice   Such a pig.

Shaz   Did he say anything about letting you out for today?

Kate   Nah. It's not gonna happen. Girls, I really appreciate you caring but I'm just going to lay down. I just need some space.

Jen   Take your time, love. (**Kate** *exits.*) We have to do something, girls. Something to lift her spirits.

Tinny   Buys are tomorrow. We could pool our money for something for her?

Shaz   A ticket out of here maybe.

Jen   I was thinking something from the heart. Something meaningful.

Fog   I could do a magic trick?

Shaz   Real meaningful.

Fog   I could. Everyone loves magic.

Shaz   What's with your obsession with magic, Fog?

Fog   Well, when I was little, I couldn't really read or write and I was even worse at maths. I wasn't really going to school at all either but one of my mum's boyfriends bought me a pack of cards. Learnt my numbers that way. And then I got into magic.

Larry   It would probably make her laugh. What magic can you do?

Shaz   It would make *me* laugh. *At* you though, Fog.

Fog   Oi, shut up. It'd be fun. Larry, you can be my assistant. Let's grab the cards from your cell.

Jen   Well, maybe you guys could do your magic for Kate while we get set up.

Fog   Come on! We gotta practise first.

Larry *makes a face at the rest of the girls as she leaves with* **Fog**.

Tinny   Set up?

Jen   Yeh. I have an idea. We're gonna need some supplies. (*To* **Tinny** *and* **Shaz**.) And Macka.

Scene Thirteen

Friday morning. **Kate**'s *cell.* **Larry** *and* **Fog** *arrive.*

Fog   Hey.

Larry   Fog and I thought we'd swing by to make sure you're still alive.

Kate   Thanks. I'm fine.

Fog   You don't look fine.

Larry   Fog.

Fog   Sorry. I mean, you look great. It's just, you . . .

Kate   I'm fine really. I just need some time out.

Larry   We get it.

Fog   We actually thought of something to cheer you up.

Larry   Fog is very eager to show you something. Sorry in advance.

Kate   Any other day, I'd be keen. But right now, I just think I'd be a downer.

Larry (*gently*)   Oh, come on. I bet it'll make you feel better

Kate *makes a face and shrugs her shoulders. This gives the girls a green light to go ahead.*

Larry (*improvising*)   OK. Um . . . Fog, I'd love to see a magic trick if you know any?

Fog   Of course I know magic tricks. That's why we're here!

Larry (*through gritted teeth*)   I know. So how about you show me one and then Kate might like to join in afterwards?

Fog   Ohhh. (*Awkwardly, like she's reading from a script.*) Yes, excellent. What a great idea, Larry. (*She winks at* **Larry**.)

Larry   So, how about you do one then?

Fog   Oh yep. Well, all you need to do Larry is choose one card and I will tell you what it is.

Larry   How original.

Fog   Just pick one!

She holds out the cards and **Larry** *picks one.* **Fog** *places her hands at her temples and chants something while she is deciphering the card. Each time,* **Fog** *gets it wrong.* **Larry** *rolls her eyes.* **Kate** *is slightly entertained.*

Fog   You have picked a red card. Eight of hearts.

Larry   Nope.

Fog   Reveal your card!

Larry (*reveals the card*)   You suck!

Fog   No I don't. Let's go again. This has never happened to me before!

Larry   I've heard that before.

Fog   OK, OK. (*She tries again.*) A black card. Seven of clubs.

Larry   Nope.

Fog   I mean, six of diamonds.

Larry   Nope.

Fog   Four of spades?

Larry   No.

Fog   Let me see (**Larry** *reveals the card.*) Ah, exactly what I thought.

Larry   Think about this!

She whacks the card on **Fog**'s *forehead. By this time,* **Kate** *is smiling. The girls see her and sit down with her.*

Larry   We'll get you through this, Kate, you know.

Jen (*from off stage*)   We're ready, Laz.

Larry   Kate, we want to show you something.

Kate   What?

Fog (*gently bumps* **Kate**, *smiling*)   Just come with us. Promise it'll be worth it.

Kate, **Fog** *and* **Larry** *exit.*

Scene Fourteen

Friday. The communal area. **Mackenzie** *and the women prepare a makeshift memorial for* **Kate***. They hold candles, meeting each other's eyes as they light them, a symbol their connection and their shared experience.* **Kate**, **Fog** *and* **Larry** *enter.* **Kate** *is handed a candle.*

Kate   What is this?

Jen   We thought since you couldn't be with your family today, we could do something for your sister here.

Kate   This is so kind. Thank you.

Jen   Grab a seat. Come on.

Shaz (*gently*)   Kate, we thought you might like to also read out what you'd written for your sister.

Mackenzie   If you want to.

Kate   OK. (*Supported by the girls, she begins.*) I just want to say firstly thank you so much to everyone for coming today and for the support you've given to our family. We really appreciate it and I know Beck would have too. This is hard because a big part of me feels like I shouldn't have to be doing this right now. It's too soon. You were twenty. With so much ahead. But here we are. So, my sister Beck.

When I think of you, B, I think of someone who is strong. You had it all going for you. A great job that you loved and that you were good at, working with kids and making a difference. Making sure they don't end up like me. (*Beat.*) You had a partner who loved you and Mel you've become such a part of this family too. And a family who couldn't be prouder. You were the one who was supposed to do amazing things. The non-stuff-up. And you were always in a rush to get things done. To make a difference. Maybe, you knew you wouldn't have long.

Beck, you were always the kindest and the funniest in any room. And you had the voice of an angel. But one thing we all knew about you is that you sucked at replying to text messages. We couldn't shut you up in person but get you to text back more than 'yep' or 'sure'? Not happening. It was so annoying. I remember in Year 10 sending you a message after I kissed Simon Gackle for the first time. I explained the kiss to you in several paragraphs including the sloppiness factor. Every little detail. What did you text back? (*Gestures a thumbs up.*) You would always say you preferred face-to-face communication. To look into someone's eyes when you spoke to them. (*Beat.*) What I would give for that right now, B.

In the whole scheme of things, that didn't matter. We knew how you felt. We knew you loved us. Your text messages were short but your hugs were long. I'll miss so many things about you. Your weird laugh. Your sock puppet obsession. You really were twenty going on sixty five. And I'll miss giving your twenty-first speech and roasting you. Most of all, I'll miss your phone calls whenever I stuffed up. They'd pull me into line. I just wanted you to be proud. I really needed those phone calls. You were like a second mum to me. Beck, it makes me ache that you'll never get the chance to be a mum yourself. You would have been such a great mum.

I don't even know how to finish something like this. I guess I just want to say thank you for being my sister. I won't forget the lessons you taught me. I'll try to stay straight. Not mess up. Please keep looking out for me. I promise I'll make you proud.

Jen   That was beautiful, love.

Kate   Thank you.

Jen   We were going to buy you stacks of flowers and put them everywhere but flowers are expensive.

Tinny   And they make you sneeze.

Shaz   Yeh and then they die too. (*Beat.*) You know, when we lost my sister Dawn, we got all these bunches of flowers from people. They were beautiful. Expensive too. But after a week or so, they shrivelled up and went black. And started to smell. And we had to chuck 'em out. It was like another goodbye we weren't prepared for.

Fog   That sucks.

Larry   This whole thing sucks.

Shaz   It's like you're now part of a club that no one wants to be part of.

Mackenzie   We couldn't get flowers but we do have . . .

From their pockets, the women hold up their sock puppets. They have been crudely assembled, using mismatched socks.

All   Sock puppets!

Jen   They don't have eyes but you get the point!

Fog   Oi! Mine does!

The girls look at her and smirk. **Fog** *has scribbled some black marks on her puppet that look nothing like eyes.*

Kate   Thank you.

Mackenzie   We have one more surprise. This won't be as good as Beck would have done it but we'll try, huh.

The girls sing a rendition of 'Amazing Grace'. This is a beautiful moment of stillness where each of the girls reflect, especially **Kate**.

Jen   Come on, get in here

The girls hug. Suddenly, **Smiley** *enters. The girls quickly put out the candles, disassemble their sock puppets and get in line.*

Smiley   Hi, birdies. Hope I'm not interrupting. (*To* **Mackenzie**.) Mackenzie, nice to see you. I just wanted to come in as I have good news for one of you.

Tinny   What is it?

Smiley   Did I ask you to speak? (**Tinny** *withdraws.*) I have been thinking. Sometimes, it's important to make things happen. To give someone a leg up. We all go through difficult things in life. Me included. I can think of so many moments where I've really struggled. Really questioned things, you know. All I needed was for someone to give me a break. Just one damn break and I knew it would make all the difference. So, in light of that, I've pulled some strings. I've made something happen and I hope it'll make someone's life just that bit easier right now. Kate?

Kate   Yes?

Smiley   Can you come here please?

Figure 17 Smiley delivering news to Kate. Photo courtesy of Cardijn College.

Kate   Yes. (**Kate** *moves to* **Smiley**, *hopeful.*)

Smiley   I've been thinking, Kate. Doing a lot of thinking. I think helping others can sometimes make us feel better. You feel really good for doing a good deed, you know?

Kate   Yes.

Smiley   Doing things to help out another person can be so good for us. So, in light of that, can you go directly to your cell? You've got to pack.

Kate (*hopefully*)   Pack?

Smiley   Pack. (*Beat.*) Alice is getting out today. You're going to help her pack. (*To* **Alice**.) You. Move. Have a great afternoon, birdies.

There is silence as this reality sets in for **Kate**. **Alice** *is torn but moves to go to her cell. Overcome,* **Kate** *lunges at* **Smiley** *but the girls catch her.* **Kate** *falls down to the floor. The girls huddle around her. Smirking,* **Smiley** *exits.*

Shaz (*screaming after him*)   Pig!

Scene Fifteen

Saturday. **Smiley**'*s office. He is on another call.*

Smiley   No. What do you think is going to bloody happen? You've royally screwed this up, you know! I give you clear instructions. You said you understood and then this. You gotta learn to keep that trap shut. Be smarter!
What do you think will happen? You could get time for this! If they find out, it'll be a shit storm. An absolute shit storm. It can't happen. It can't.
Yes, it's serious! If they get their hands on the records, they're gonna see that the figures don't add up.

Mackenzie *enters, wanting to speak with* **Smiley**.

Smiley   If you so much as whisper my name in all this, I will make sure you go down twice as hard as me. Oh just try me. Just shut your mouth and get on with things! (**Smiley** *sees* **Mackenzie**.) What?

Mackenzie   Hello.

Smiley   You really have impeccable timing don't you?

Mackenzie   My apologies.

Smiley   Yeh whatever. What do you want?

Mackenzie   Who were you talking to?

Smiley   What?

Mackenzie   I mean, it's probably not my place to ask but . . .

Smiley (*interrupting*)   You're right, it's not.

Mackenzie   But, who were you were talking to? It didn't sound good.

Smiley   It's none of your business.

Mackenzie   Are you in some sort of trouble?

Smiley   You know something. Listening in on my conversations is a dangerous game.

Mackenzie   What do you mean?

Smiley   You don't want to find out.

Mackenzie (*with newfound strength*)   I think you have bigger things to worry about than me. I wanted to speak to you about before.

Smiley   What?

Mackenzie   About Kate. And Alice being let out.

Smiley   Oh, it's good for Alice isn't it. Good for her.

Mackenzie   Excuse me?

Smiley   What?

Mackenzie   What you did to Kate. That was not on.

Smiley   I don't know what you mean.

Mackenzie   Actually, it was cruel. How dare you set her up like that. After what she's been through. I've just come from chatting to the girls. Kate is still so upset.

Smiley   So?

Mackenzie   So, I think you should consider how you are treating these girls.

Smiley   They're crims. It's all part of punishment.

Mackenzie   They're in here. That's their punishment. It's not our jobs to do any more to make their life a misery. It's cruel.

Smiley   That's what you think is happening here?

Mackenzie   Yes.

Smiley   Those girls get what they deserve. It's called karma.

Mackenzie   Those girls deserve more than you.

Smiley   Well, hasn't the little lady found her big girl voice. Good for you. All passionate and up in arms. It's cute. Looks good on you actually. Now if the little lady wants to keep her job, she'll shut her mouth and get on with things.

Mackenzie   That's the second time you've said that today.

Smiley   I suggest you do what I say.

Mackenzie   Or what?

Smiley   Try me.

Mackenzie   Maybe I will. (*She exits.*)

Smiley   Mackenzie, wait!

Scene Sixteen

Later that day. **Shaz**, **Tinny**, **Jen**, **Fog** *and* **Larry** *are with* **Kate** *in the communal area, comforting her.*

Larry   He's the worst, Kate.

Jen   An absolute jerk.

Tinny   Where does he get off?

Fog   We're here for you though. And Macka.

Kate   Thank you.

Shaz   You know, he's always been foul. But this is too far. It's like he wants to be a pig. Just for the sake of being a pig.

Larry   I wish you actually could do magic, Fog. You could make his ugly mug disappear.

Fog   Oh me too.

Tinny (*mocking* **Smiley**)   Hello, my birdies. Goodbye, my birdies.

Kate   I hate it how he calls us that.

Jen   Same.

Shaz   Same. When he says it, I just want to tell him where to stick it!

Jen   But it's not worth messing with 'the one in charge'.

Kate   Someone like him should never be in charge of anything. Or anyone.

Larry   Hey, what if we were in charge?

Fog   What do ya mean?

Shaz   What? Like a riot? Take over?

Larry   No.

Shaz   Like jump him when he's not looking?

Larry   No. Like the reclaiming stuff Macka spoke about in one of those sessions. Like Tinny did with her name.

Shaz   Oh, come on.

Larry   No, think about it. We all think he has the power but what if we took it back?

Kate   Tell us what you mean.

Larry   Like, every time he makes us smile. He thinks he's forcing us to do something we don't want to do. We grimace and he laughs about it. Well, what if we flipped it.

Jen   What, and thought about how we'd shove a sock puppet up his clacker if we could?

Larry   No. We thought about our families or something at that very moment so our smile was genuine. And we smiled because *we* wanted to smile. That's taking the power away from him. Taking it back for us right?

Jen   Yeh. I mean, it's something.

Larry   And what about how he calls us birdies. He thinks it means that we're in some sort of cage. Like he owns us. Like we're his pets or something. What if the name birdies meant something different to us?

Tinny   Like what?

Kate   Like being free.

Jen   Like flying out of this hell hole one day.

Larry   Yeh, spreading our wings once we've done our time.

Kate   Getting a second chance.

Fog   Birds fly together too.

Jen   Yeh, in flocks.

Larry   So maybe it means that we're all together in the same flock. That we've got each other's backs.

Shaz   I like that.

Fog   Like the Mighty Ducks.

Larry   So when he calls us birdies, it doesn't matter what he thinks it means. We know what the words means to us. It's a title to be proud of. A name we want to be called. It means one day we'll fly free out of here. And wherever we are, we fly together.

Scene Seventeen

A week has passed. The girls are sitting around, chatting and playing cards. **Fog** *is trying another trick. It is clear the girls are now united.* **Mackenzie** *is with them.*

Larry   Fog, no more magic please!

Fog   Come on, this one's gonna be good.

Shaz   That's what you said yesterday.

Kate   And the day before.

Jen   And the day before that!

Fog   I've improved though haven't I?

All   No!

Fog   Well, Macka liked my magic tricks. Said so herself.

Jen   Macka likes your hair as well so she can't be trusted.

Mackenzie   Now, come on.

Shaz   You should show Smiley. Get an *honest* perspective on things.

Tinny   Where's he been anyway? I haven't seen him in like a week.

Jen   Neither.

Shaz   Hopefully he's found a cliff to fall off.

Larry   Or a road to play on.

Kate   Macka, where is he? He's still here right?

Smiley *enters with a bag. The women stand up. There is a tense silence.*

Smiley   Hello. I just wanted to come in briefly and speak to you all. It's the last you'll see of me. I've taken a job interstate. It's a promotion actually, looking after a new prison. They need some leadership, some authority. So they've asked if I'd make the move. I am really looking forward to it actually. I know we've always had a good working relationship, so I wanted to come in and tell you in person. So, all the best in your future endeavours. Try not stuff your lives up when you get out of here. Goodbye. (*He exits.*)

Jen   Well, that was weird.

Tinny   Who'd give him a promotion?

Kate   He hasn't been promoted. Something's up.

Larry   What do you mean?

Kate   I mean, there's more to it. I don't know what, but he's not telling us the whole story.

Larry   Macka, what do ya know?

Shaz   Girls, who cares! We're forgetting the most important thing! He's gone! He is gone!

Jen   There's only one thing we need to do now! (*Shouting.*) Smile, birdies! Smile, birdies!

The women shout and jump up and down, repeating the line and hugging as lights go down.

Epilogue

Four years later. One by one, the girls speak directly to the audience. After they tell their story, they gather together.

Mackenzie   It's been four years since that day. Lots has changed. I passed my probation for one thing. And I'm not so green anymore. I worked at North Shores Remand Centre for another eighteen months. I now lead a team across the state. Our programmes have been launched in four different prisons including a youth training centre. My aim is to get to these young people before they get to jail. I'm hopeful I can make some sort of difference. I still keep in touch with the girls. Especially Shaz, funnily enough.

Jen   Since that day, I spent a total of 484 days behind bars. Then I was back with my daughter Missy. That first hug outside prison walls was the single greatest moment of my life. I haven't been back inside. I won't be. Not again.

Alice   I got out which was great but have gone back in and back out and back in again. Annoying really. I hope this will be my last time inside. Gotta kick a few habits first.

Fog   I left North Shores Remand Centre after about a month and moved to the nearby women's prison. I'm still there. I will be for the next year I think. But I might be out for my twenty-fifth birthday. I dunno if that's a good thing or not. It's safe inside. I'm kind of used to it now. The outside is kind of scary.

Tinny   I also moved over to the women's prison. Actually roomed with Fog there. So guess who's been enjoying Fog's card tricks all day, every day? Yep, you're looking at her. I'm due to get out next week though. And work some of my own magic on the outside. I've already planned the day with my brother. He's going to pick me up then we're going to get the boat and head out on the ocean for some Tinny time.

Larry   I am nearly finished my Finance degree. Still inside but hoping to get out at the end of the year. Looks like that'll happen too. New life, new Larry. I'm going to move in with my brother Billy and start fresh. He has a table tennis table.

Shaz   Kate's sister dying really brought everything up for me. What it was like to lose my sister Dawn. It made me actually come to terms with it I think. Some closure. Which was good. Macka actually has really helped me. Still does. We write letters. She visits when she can. I've been out of jail for eleven months now. Got a job. A new outlook on life. I'm doing good.

Kate   I didn't get to go to Beck's funeral or even see my mum for another two weeks after that day. And that's really stayed with me. Even now. I think it's actually motivated me to stay out of trouble, stay clean and get my life back on track. And I have. And things are good with mum. They're not great yet but I hope they will be soon. Every time I have decisions to make, I just imagine what Beck would say to me. How proud she'd be when I make the right ones. And touch wood, I've been able to keep making the right ones.

Shaz   And Smiley. Well, karma caught up with him. He didn't get a promotion and wasn't moved to be in charge of another prison.

Jen   He found himself up on a number of charges and convicted of embezzlement. That's why he had to suddenly leave North Shores.

Fog   Apparently he had been stealing money for years. Ripping heaps of people off. He was not a good guy.

Alice   I'm sure he had his reasons like we all did.

Larry   But we learnt from him, even if he didn't teach us anything. We learnt to take charge of our situation. We learnt resilience and what it means to come together.

Tinny   We learnt about courage and empathy.

Kate   And we learnt that, in any situation, a change of perspective can often make a birdie smile.

Lights up on **Smiley** *in his 'office' which is now his prison cell. He is in a prison uniform behind bars.*

End of show.

***Birdies* Discussion Questions**

1. Referenced in the play's title, how is the extended metaphor of birds used to explore the idea of freedom?

2. How is the setting of North Shores Remand Centre relevant to the story and how does it serve as a catalyst for character and plot development in *Birdies*?

3. The most powerful force in the world is hope. How is this statement true in *Birdies*?

4. How is tension built and sustained throughout *Birdies*?

5. How are different relationships represented in *Birdies*? How do these relationships develop throughout the script and provide instances of comfort, conflict and humour for the characters involved and the audience?

6. Identify and discuss the presence of the following themes: perspective, power, courage, resilience, hope and relationships. What aesthetic strategies are used to represent these themes in the play?

7. Consider one of the following characters: Jen, Shaz, Tinny, Larry, Fog, Kate, Alice. How might her experiences, both outside and inside North Shores Remand Centre, inform her behaviour throughout *Birdies*?

8. Research the conditions and challenges faced in Australian remand centres and prisons. What are the immediate and lasting impacts of these conditions on prisoners and their rehabilitation prospects? How do these issues compare to those faced in earlier decades?

Encore

Playwright's note

'Always remember: you are braver than you believe, stronger than you seem, smarter than you think and more beautiful than you could ever imagine'.

Encore is where my playwriting journey began. When I first thought about the prospect of creating a story and getting it on the page, I was immediately drawn to the idea of exploring how ordinary people can do extraordinary things in the face of adversity. So, in *Encore*, and indeed all of the plays in this anthology, this theme is a constant.

Struggle can take many forms. Struggle can be represented in a fractured relationship or the heaviness felt by guilt or grief. Struggle can be characterised by the alienation of not belonging or a person enduring a crisis in identity. For many, the loudest struggle comes in the form of a mental health battle or in the grips of addiction. Someone might even be fighting for their life or be feeling immeasurable pain as a loved one armours up for the battle. We are constantly challenged in life but nearly always it is the connection we have with those around us that fill us with the bravery and hope we need to go on another day.

Encore tells the story of a family in crisis. Having endured considerable hardship before, the Rowe family learn lessons in love, honesty, hope and forgiveness as they navigate a struggle they are all too familiar with. This play is punctuated by a series of monologues delivered by Rose's loved ones. Hardship rarely affects just one person, and I chose this form as a way to highlight the ripple effect that adversity can trigger. I believe *Encore* can serve as an encouragement for us to lead with kindness, hold onto hope, offer compassion to those around us and, wherever we can, look for an opportunity to share a laugh and a loving word with the special people in our lives.

While never stated explicitly, Rose's symptoms are consistent with osteosarcoma, initially diagnosed in her thigh bone three years earlier. Now, the cancer has returned but now also with lung metastasis. All proceeds from the original production of *Encore* were donated to the Childhood Cancer Association, one of Australia's key childhood cancer support organisations providing practical, hands-on support to children with cancer and their families. I encourage future productions to consider supporting a similar organisation or cause, highlighting key messages in the play and connecting with the broader community.

Brady Lloyd

Encore by Brady Lloyd

Synopsis

Eleven-year-old Rose is sick. Again. But this time, she's not the only one in crisis. *Encore* follows the Rowe family as they navigate the fear and uncertainty of Rose's latest diagnosis, grappling with the possibility that life might be turned upside down once again. In the midst of another worrying hospital visit, a team of well-meaning staff, including effervescent Kylie-obsessed Doniella, bring hope and humour to the ward. As emotions rise and relationships are tested, the Rowe family must band together to revive the heartbeat of the family.

Setting

Encore is set primarily in a fictional Australian hospital called St Bart's, with most of the action taking place in Rosie's room, a space that becomes a meaningful hub of connection as loved ones rally around her.

Characters

Twelve characters (6F, 6M). Note: This play accommodates flexible and inclusive casting.

Rose, *11. Sweet but strong, Rose is mature beyond her years.*

Michael, *41. Struggling with fear and self-doubt, Michael yearns to be better.*

Karen, *40. A determined mother who feels the weight of responsibility.*

Felicity, *15. Felicity is a sensitive soul who finds comfort in meaningful connection.*

Ally, *17. Tough on the outside but fiercely devoted to her sister Rose.*

Andy, *32. A hospital social worker, Andy exudes enthusiasm and compassion.*

Doniella, *54. Equal parts kind and quirky, Doniella is a listening ear for Rose.*

Cheryl, *45. A steely, no-nonsense nursing unit manager.*

Doctor Standing, *40. A friendly doctor at St Bart's Hospital.*

Willy, *21. An empathetic nurse in training, still finding his feet.*

Nelson, *21. Conscientious and socially awkward, Nelson craves approval.*

Smithy, *48. A man of few words and the object of Doniella's affection.*

Prologue

In darkness, a soundscape of fragmented words and phrases offers the audience a disjointed glimpse into **Rose**'s *cancer journey so far, while simultaneously foreshadowing what lies ahead for her and the* **Rowe** *family. Included in this cacophony of sound is the pulse of a heart rate monitor.*

Scene One

The **Rowe** *household. Monday afternoon.* **Rose** *enters, nose bleeding. She is holding her nose with a tissue.*

Rose Mum, blood nose again!

Karen (*from offstage*) Grab a tissue, put pressure on the bridge of the nose and / tilt your head back.

Rose / Tilt your head back. I know, I know. You just told me you needed to know each bloody time I had one.

Karen *enters. She is getting ready, packing a bag with clothes from a basket and moving around busily.*

Karen Rose, don't swear, love.

Rose I didn't! I said bloody. I chose that word especially. (**Rose** *points to her nose.*)

Karen Context, my darling, context. (*She kisses her on the head.*) Thank goodness you're not in white. You OK?

Rose *nods.* **Karen** *continues getting organised.* **Felicity** *enters, home from school.*

Felicity Hey, mum. (*Noticing* **Karen** *packing.*) I thought we weren't leaving until the morning?

Karen (*purposefully casual*) That was the plan but I got a call a couple hours ago. They had some free space so they thought we should pop in a bit earlier.

Felicity Well, that doesn't sound good.

Karen It's fine, Flick. It's good. Better to get things checked out so we can relax this weekend. And best to leave early. It's at least a three-hour drive there, two and a half if traffic's good.

Felicity How you feeling, Rosie? Another blood nose, hey?

Rose Yeh. I'm fine though.

Rose *gets some paper out and starts making an origami crane. She is well practised and has obviously done this before.*

Felicity Leg still hurting?

Rose   Yeh.

Felicity (*referencing the crane*)   How many are we up to now?

Rose   Last count 927.

Felicity   Wow. That is impressive. Don't you think, mum?

Karen (*distracted*)   What?

Felicity   Rose has finished 927 cranes. Nearly at the 1000. (**Felicity** *starts on some origami herself, but struggles.*) You know, I bet some of those nurses will be origami experts. They might even teach you a thing or two!

Rose (*looking at* **Felicity** *struggling*)   Ha! There's one of us here that needs teaching and I don't think it's me. That looks *bloody* awful, Flick.

Karen   Rosie!

Rosie   Sorry, mum.

Felicity   Rose Hey, mum, today in school, Ms Mason gave us this assignment. We have to create something on the theme of bravery. It can be anything: an essay, a collage, a blog. I've got a really good idea I think. Can I tell you about it?

Karen (*distracted*)   Ah, can you give me a sec, love? Things are just a bit chaotic at the moment, trying to hit the road on time. Tell me on the way in? Where is your father?

Ally *enters. Headphones in and scrolling on her phone, she appears tough and guarded.*

Karen   Ally? Ally? Have you seen dad? He left to fill up the car an hour ago.

Ally   Nup.

Karen   You sure he didn't say anything on the way out?

Ally   Nup.

Karen   You going to say anything else apart from nup?

Ally   Nup.

Karen *gives* **Ally** *a loving kiss on the cheek, causing* **Ally** *to smile.* **Felicity** *notices and goes back to sitting with* **Rose***.*

Ally   How you doing, kiddo?

Rose   Good, Al. How about you?

Ally   Yeh good.

Felicity   Hi, Ally. I'm good too thanks.

Ally *shoots* **Felicity** *a look. It's clear there is tension in their relationship.*

Karen   Girls, come on. Ally, say hello to your sister.

Ally   Hello, weirdo. Oh that reminds me. Some teacher asked me to pass on a message to you.

Felicity   Well, what was it about?

Ally   No idea.

Felicity   Well, which teacher?

Ally (*pretends to think for a moment*)   No idea. But I said I'd pass it on so there you go.

Felicity (*dryly*)   Thanks. You're so helpful. What would I do without you?

Karen   Ally, do you mind grabbing Rosie's bag? It's just by her . . . (**Ally** *leaves.*) Bedroom door.

Michael *enters cautiously, playing awkwardly with his keys.*

Karen   There you are!

Michael   Hello, love. Hello, girls.

Rose   Hey, dad.

Karen   Michael, we need to be on the road in ten minutes! I said in my text that I wanted the whole family here so that we could leave with plenty of time.

Michael   I know. All good. I'm here now.

Karen   So, what did you get it for?

Michael   What?

Karen   Petrol.

Michael   Ah, it was too expensive. We can get some on the way instead. Easy done. Anything else that needs packing?

Karen   It's fine. We're nearly done.

Michael   Karen.

Karen   Just Rosie's bag I think.

Michael   I can grab it. Where is it?

Ally *enters and drops the bag on the floor while glaring at her father. Meanwhile,* **Karen** *moves towards* **Michael** *and looks at him closely. She smells alcohol on his breath. Through gritted teeth, in an effort to remain calm in front of the children, she continues.*

Karen   I'll drive. You can get the rest of this stuff in the boot.

She holds out her hand for the keys which **Michael** *gives her.* **Ally** *and* **Felicity** *watch on.*

Michael (*irritably*)   Well, you heard your mum. Don't just stand there. If we're going to go, let's go! (*He exits.*)

Ally   I still don't see why we have to go. You said everything will be fine.

Karen   And I am sure it will be. But I think it's best if we all go in together as a family. To support Rosie. So we can all be there to celebrate what I'm sure will be good news.

Ally   I hate hospitals.

Rose (*beat*)   Me too.

Felicity, **Ally** *and* **Karen** *all share a look at* **Rose**.

Scene Two

Felicity's *monologue is the first in a series of reflections that make up her school project. For each one,* **Rose** *is present, observing each loved one speak about her. This foreshadows the moment she later watches the finished video. Each speaker addresses the audience like they are speaking to a video camera.*

Felicity   'Always remember: you are braver than you believe, stronger than you seem, smarter than you think and more beautiful than you could ever imagine'.

I think it was a Persian poet, born eight hundred or so years ago, who first wrote that. But I think it's never truly suited anyone, until you. I thought it'd be a good way to start my video project. So, some context. For school we have to create something that explores the theme of bravery and Rosie, I picked you.

To me, you are bravery personified. I've thought that for a while now. I'm not sure how long. But there was one day that did it for me. 17 May 2016. My twelfth birthday party. We'd planned to go bowling and then to the movies. We'd talked all week about how we couldn't wait to see the new *Divergent* movie and how we were going to get that popcorn covered in butter. I had four friends coming, which was really big for me. Plus you and Ally and mum. We got up and got ready. You were in that fake fur coat thing you loved at the time. It was pretty hideous but it was pink so you were obsessed. It was going to be such a good day. But we never got there.

That was the day we found out. I remember when I got to the hospital and saw you laying there. You looked so small. And I was so scared. I remember the first thing you said to me when you woke up. You said sorry. You said, 'I'm sorry, Flick, for ruining your birthday party'. Your life was about to be turned upside down and the first thing you did was apologise to me, without even mentioning what had just happened to you. To me, that's brave. You're brave. And strong. And smart. And beautiful. And so, you're the chosen one for this assignment.

Scene Three

Early evening. St Bart's Hospital. **Cheryl** *is impatiently waiting,* **Nelson** *beside her.*

Cheryl   Willy! Willy! Willy!

Willy *runs in, puffed.*

Willy   Yes, here! Sorry I'm late. The traffic was so bad and the line for coffees was so long! (**Willy** *gives* **Cheryl** *her coffee. It's in her own reusable cup labelled 'BOSS LADY'.*) Anyway I'm here and ready to go.

Cheryl   Nelson was on time.

Nelson   I was on time.

Cheryl   See, he was on time. And what do I always say about being on time?

Nelson   Better to be . . .

Cheryl (*interrupting*)   Thank you, Nelson.

Nelson   You're welcome, Cheryl.

Cheryl   Better to be three hours too soon than a minute too late. Do you know who first said that?

Willy   You?

Cheryl   No, not me.

Nelson   William Shakespeare!

Cheryl   Exactly. It's really struck a chord with me. You would think that being your final placement, about to become a fully-fledged nurse, reporting to the nursing unit manager (*motions to herself dramatically*) who signs you off, you could manage to be on time. Like Nelson.

Nelson   Thank you, Cheryl.

Cheryl   You're welcome, Nelson. Right, tell me about our new patient this afternoon.

Willy   Well, I know the Rowe family are due to arrive any minute now. Patient: Rose Rowe. Remission three years. Parents concerned about a relapse. Patient experiencing pain again in the thigh region.

Cheryl   You do listen! (**Doctor Standing** *enters and walks past* **Cheryl** *who is immediately alert.*) Good afternoon, Doctor Standing.

Doctor Standing   Cheryl. Willy. And . . .

Nelson   Nelson.

Doctor Standing   Nelson, yes! How are we all today? Feeling tip top?

Cheryl   Of course, Doctor Standing. Never been better. Right, boys?

Nelson   Feeling fantastic actually, Doctor Standing. And can I just say, you're looking terrific. Have you been working out?

Doctor Standing   Well, actually, I have. I've upped my morning walk slash jog from once a week to two times a week. Making quite the difference I think.

Nelson   Absolutely, sir.

Doctor Standing   Well, I'm glad to hear things are chipper. Willy, all good?

Willy   Yes, sir.

Doctor Standing   Good to hear. I'll come past again soon. Quick loo stop first.

Nelson   Enjoy, Doctor Standing. (**Nelson** *is immediately awkward as he realises what he's just said.*)

Cheryl   Right. Before we go any further, what did we speak about yesterday, Willy?

Willy   Not being emotional in front of the families. It's just difficult because . . .

Cheryl   Good. No explanation needed. Just be sure to remember that today. I'm going to go and dive into my pile of paperwork while we wait for the family. Because, Willy, what do I always say about productivity?

Willy (*unsure*)   Productivity is . . .

Nelson   I know. Productivity doesn't . . .

Cheryl (*interrupting*)   Thank you, Nelson. Productivity doesn't happen by chance. It's the outcome of clear intention, thoughtful strategy and dedicated work. Paul Peter Potts said that. It's really struck a chord with me. Try not to stuff anything up while I'm gone, Willy. Nelson, follow me.

Cheryl *exits,* **Nelson** *following quickly after. During this time,* **Andy** *has entered and observes what's going on. He walks with a stick for support and is holding a brightly coloured clipboard.*

Andy   Willy, my man! Deep breaths, brother. You doing OK?

Willy   Just the usual. Counting down the days.

Andy   Well, I think you're a star.

Willy   You have to say that.

Andy   No I don't. I may be a beacon of positivity and light, infinitely wise and devilishly handsome. But I tell the truth. And you, my man, are doing great things so hang in there!

Willy   Thanks, Andy.

The **Rowe** *family rush in,* **Karen** *leading.*

Karen   Hello. Are we in the right place? Karen Rowe. (*Pointing out her family members.*) My husband Michael and this is Rose. And her sisters. Sorry we're a bit late. Traffic was a bloody nightmare. (**Rose** *gives her a look as she's sworn.*) Oh shush you.

Willy   No problems at all. I'm glad you made it here safely. I'm Willy, one of the nurses at St Bart's.

Andy   And I'm Andy, one of the social workers here.

Nelson (*rushing in*)   And I'm Nelson. Another nurse. So, to recap, you've got Andy, Willy and Nelson!

Ally   Wait, your name is Willy and your name is Nelson? Is that a joke? You guys into country music?

Karen (*reprimanding*)   Ally!

Ally   What? Don't you think that's funny?

Andy   I'm sure the doc and Cheryl are on their way in to have a chat with you. In the meantime, Willy, maybe we can show Rose to her room and get her settled?

Willy   Sure.

Karen   Great. Can you guys get yourself something from downstairs and pop back up soon? Stick together please. (**Ally** *takes ten dollar note from* **Karen** *and exits.*)

Felicity   Mum, I'd rather stay.

Karen   I think it'd be better if you just went with Ally.

Felicity   I can handle whatever it is that's happening. I can. I want to be here so I can help.

Karen   I know, love. And we'll let you know as soon as we know anything.

Felicity   But mum!

Michael   Felicity, just leave would you!

Karen (*warmly*)   Please, Flick. Just give us a sec, darling.

Felicity *exits as* **Doctor Standing** *and* **Cheryl** *enter.*

Doctor   Good afternoon. My name is Doctor Standing and this is Cheryl, our nursing unit manager. Please, take a seat.

Scene Four

Rose'*s hospital room. She has already placed a handful of cranes around her room.*

Andy   Rose is it? Cool name. You got a nickname?

Rose   Some people call me Rosie.

Andy   Do you mind? (**Rose** *nods.*) Right, Rosie, are you ready to undertake Andy's Amazing Quiz? Only the bravest, most brilliant kids can pass!

Willy   This'll be good!

Rose   Go on then.

Andy   Fist pump to start. (*They fist pump.*) Here we go! Name?

Rose   Rose Ann Rowe.

Andy   Good start. Favourite colour?

Rose   Pink.

Andy   Who would think it would be pink! Favourite animal?

Rose   Unicorns.

Andy   Favourite food?

Rose   Strawberry Freddo frogs.

Andy   Oh nice! Now for the most important question. Favourite social worker? (**Andy** *sticks his chest out and points to his name badge dramatically.*)

Rose   Andy Bokini!

Andy   You have passed! With flying colours! (**Andy** *and* **Willy** *cheer and clap.*) What a scholar! What a star! (**Doniella** *appears at the doorway.*) Your reward? Apart from a high five from old mate Willy here, (**Willy** *hears and gives* **Rose** *a high five.*) you win a visit from the one and only Queen of St Bart's, Doniella. Doniella is one of my favourite people at this place because she is responsible for feeding us!

Doniella (*with incredible warmth and enthusiasm*)   Hello, Andy! Hello, Willy! Hello, love! It's true. I'm kind of a big deal around here because who doesn't love eating?

Rose   So you sound like a person I should get to know!

Doniella   You bet!

Andy   This is Rosie Ann Rowe.

Doniella   Your middle name is Ann? You know who else has the middle name Ann? Kylie Minogue! (**Andy** *and* **Willy** *groan in unison.*) What?

Andy   Oh here we go.

Doniella   I just adore Kylie Minogue, Rosie. Have you ever met a singer like her? She is . . . and I just . . . you know?

Rose   Umm.

Doniella   Right. You're probably a bit young. But Kylie was the Lady Gaga (**Doniella** *pronounces 'Gaga' incorrectly, stressing the second syllable*) of our time.

Willy (*pronouncing 'Gaga' correctly*)   I think it's Lady Gaga.

Doniella   Exactly. Just great. You know, I actually owned a pair of gold hot pants just like Kylie's in my day. I used to love spinning around in them, get it? Sparkly they were and gold and itsy bitsy teeny tiny and I was quite the sight when I wore them!

Andy (*changing the topic*)   You've been here for years haven't you, Doniella.

Doniella ˙ You're right. Sixteen years this November! You'd get less for murder!

Andy   Poor old Doniella!

Doniella   Old?

Rose   Doniella? That's a nice name.

Doniella   You think? Well, aren't you a love! But yes, Doniella. The name is a bit different isn't it! Bit strange! Bit like me really, you know? Coocoo from the country they used to call me. Cause I'm a bit coocoo and I'm from the country. Originally. Anyway, named by my parents so what can you do? So close to being Dannii, isn't it! Like Kylie and Dannii, Dannii! Imagine being Kylie's sister? Now that would be amazing, you know!

Andy (*redirecting the conversation again*)   Rosie was just telling me that her favourite food is strawberry Freddo frogs!

Doniella   Really? You've got good taste. I have to say, I love a good strawberry Freddo. Just the smell gets me going. The strawberry filling is just so . . . (**Smithy** *enters.*) Delicious!

Smithy, *the cleaner at* **St Bart**'*s and* **Doniella**'*s crush, walks into* **Rose**'*s room to empty the bin. He doesn't speak, just finishes his task, nods to* **Doniella** *and leaves.* **Smithy**'*s presence renders* **Doniella** *speechless. She is completely besotted, her mouth hanging open.*

Andy   You catch any flies there, Doni?

Willy   Hello? Earth to Doniella?

Doniella   What? (*Trying to compose herself.*) Did it just get hot in here? I'm feeling all flustered. (*She fans herself with a nearby magazine.*) Andy, can you turn up the air con? Holy moly!

Andy   Rosie, in case you hadn't noticed, Doniella has a huge crush on Smithy!

Doniella   Alright. Enough of that thank you.

Andy   You're going to have to talk to him properly one of these days.

Doniella   Oh shush you!

Willy   I think he likes you. See the way he nodded right at you?

Doniella (*enthusiastically*)   You think? (*Dismissing the thought.*) Right, back to Rosie. What were we talking about? Oh, the strawberry Freddos. They always been your favourite?

Rose   Kind of. Well, when I was in hospital last, mum said I could have anything I wanted the night before I got to go home. She said it was my reward for being so brave during all the treatment and stuff. I said I wanted Freddo frogs for dinner. We had the peppermint ones and the ones with the white and milk chocolate. And strawberry ones. I'd never had the strawberry ones before. They were good. And they're pink!

Andy   Your favourite colour! Win, win!

Rose   Win, win! There was so many frogs that everyone had to help me finish them off. Even mum tucked in. Dad had chocolate all around his mouth and he couldn't stop smiling. He looked so silly. We ate so many our tummies hurt. It was the best.

Doniella   That does sound fun. I'll see if I can work some magic and rustle some up, shall I? That's if Andy doesn't eat them all in the meantime!

Andy   Oi!

Doniella   Or Willy!

Willy   Oi!

Doniella   Just kidding, boys!

Willy   As if I'd get time. I barely get a free minute without Cheryl on my back.

Doniella   Cheryl means well. She's just a little . . .

Willy   A little?

Andy   Well, it's not long to go now, brother! Then you'll be fully fledged!

Willy   I don't know. Some days I think it'll be OK, then some other days it's like I don't even want to be here. (*Realising the connotations of what he's just said.*) Ah, I meant here, in this hospital as a nurse, not . . . Sorry, I shouldn't have said anything.

Doniella   Rosie knows what you meant.

Rose   It's OK, Willy. You know what, you should have this little guy. (*She hands him a crane.*) I made it. These things always make me feel happy and like I can do anything. So maybe it'll be the same for you.

Willy   Thanks, Rosie. That's really kind of you. (*Seeing her collection.*) You've definitely got a few of them there.

Rose   Yeh, I do. I started making them last time I was in hospital. I got the idea after we read this book at school about this girl in Japan called Sadako and how she wanted to make like a thousand paper cranes. So we made heaps of them in class. I made fifty seven in the first week! Then heaps more when I was in hospital. It was actually really good because I couldn't move around much and it kept my mind from thinking about other stuff. When mum said we were going to be coming to the hospital again, I thought I'd get my origami paper out again.

Willy   That's a clever thought. So how many are you up to now?

Rose   Well that's the exciting thing. I have thirty-eight to go. According to my calculations. Got a heap more done in the car ride here. I should have one thousand done pretty soon.

Willy   That's so awesome. And that book sounds really cool too.

Rose   It is. You should read it. You can borrow my copy. I've got it here. (*She gives him the book.*) But fingers crossed I won't be here long so you'll have to read it quick. (**Andy** *and* **Doniella** *share a look and then smile at* **Rose**.)

Scene Five

Later that night. **Michael** *and* **Karen** *wait outside* **Rose**'s *room.*

Doctor Standing   So how are you both going?

Michael   Fine. Nothing a stiff drink can't fix.

Karen   Michael.

Michael   Sorry. So what's the plan, doc? Level with us. Just be completely straight. As I'm sure you can understand, we're feeling quite tense at the moment.

Doctor Standing   I understand. I'd just like to confirm Rose's medical history before we proceed. (*Reading.*) Osteosarcoma in the thigh bone. Fourteen months of treatment and it's been three years since Rose has been in remission.

Michael (*frustrated*)   Correct. But what about now? Where to from here?

Doctor Standing   Can you talk me through what's been happening lately?

Karen   Well, we're concerned that she seems to be going down a similar path to last time.

Doctor Standing   How do you mean?

Michael   Exactly what she said.

Karen   Michael!

Michael   Sorry. So, what do you think our chances are here? I mean, realistically?

Doctor Standing   Like I said, I'd like to hear a bit more about what's been going on for Rose. About your concerns.

Michael   We are concerned that she looks to be experiencing the same symptoms as last time. That we might have to be dealing with the same crap we've already dealt with. So we're here to get some help. Does that make sense, doc?

Karen   Michael, calm down.

Michael   What?

Karen   You being like that is not going to get us anywhere.

Michael   Like what?

Doctor Standing   I appreciate it's a really difficult time but if you could talk me through what you've noticed lately, we can go from there.

Karen   Well, it has been pretty similar to last time I guess. She came home from school with pain in her leg. She couldn't pinpoint where it was at first. She's started netball this term though so we thought that maybe she'd just strained a muscle. Or that she'd been burning the candle at both ends. That sort of thing. We were hoping for the best I think. After a couple days, she started to have a little trouble with movement. And the pain in her leg hadn't gone away.

Michael   We're still hoping it's just a strained muscle or something else minor but, as I'm sure you can imagine, we're a little concerned.

Cheryl   I can understand that. Once we had a patient and they were experiencing some sort of pain in their foot. Anyway, eventually, he . . .

Michael (*interrupting*)   If you don't mind nurse, I'd rather hear from the doctor. I'm sure you understand.

Karen (*embarrassed*)   Michael!

Doctor Standing   As I said, I can imagine how stressful this situation is. What we'd like to do is run some blood tests and potentially a biopsy so we know where we stand. We should have some answers soon. Might I just say, you may need to prepare yourself for the possibility of being here a little longer than just a couple of days. I'll be back to touch base just before lights out tonight.

Doctor Standing *and* **Cheryl** *exit.* **Karen** *and* **Michael** *are tense.*

Karen   Well.

Michael   Well.

Karen   You OK?

Michael   I'm fine.

Karen   Michael, you don't have to pretend to be OK. Remember, we said that if we were ever up against this again, we'd be in it together. You and me.

Michael   We are, Karen. I am with you. I just can't believe that we're here again.

Karen (*moving closer to him*)   I know.

Michael (*refusing to open up*)   Actually, I don't know about that doctor who saw us. He seemed kind of incompetent. How can we be sure he knows what he's doing? And I didn't appreciate you reprimanding me like a child while we were speaking to him.

Karen   Michael, it's just that . . .

Michael (*interrupting*)   Just that what?

Karen   Forget it. I don't want to argue with you.

Michael   You know what? Me neither. I'm going to head out for a bit.

Karen   Michael, please don't. You can't just run every time things get difficult.

Michael   I'll be back before Rose even knows I'm gone.

Karen   But what about Flick and Ally? It's not easy for them, being back here. Why don't you stay and do Flick's video project thing? You remember her telling us about it on the way here? It's a beautiful idea.

Michael   I won't be gone long.

Karen   The girls need you!

Michael   Karen, just leave it.

Karen   *I* need you! What about me then, Michael? It can't be like last time. It almost ruined us.

Michael   I won't be long. (*He exits.*)

Karen (*calling after him*)   I love you, Michael. Promise me you won't . . .

Andy *enters.*

Andy (*gently*)   Hi. I don't mean to bother you. I'm Andy, one of the social workers here. Just letting you know that we've settled Rose into her room. She's doing well.

Karen   Thank you.

Andy   How are *you* doing?

Karen   Not the best. I can't quite believe we're back in a hospital with who knows what ahead of us.

My husband. He's not a talker. He is struggling to come to terms with the fact that this is all happening again. And I get it. Because the thought of being back here is terrifying. I know Michael loves us. He does. But he is just so closed off. He can't see that we need him too. That the girls need him. He just keeps pushing us away because he's so angry.

Rosie is so quiet sometimes, but I know she's thinking. And my eldest two barely speak to each other anymore. Michael just gets frustrated at everything they do and thinks they're not helping out enough at home, and with Rosie. I've tried to get through to him and to help him, but no luck. I'm sorry, I don't even know you and I'm pouring out my heart to you.

Andy   It must be really difficult for you all at the moment. (**Karen** *nods.*) Well, you know that if you need to talk, that's my job around here. I'm happy to listen. Anytime.

Karen   Thank you, Andy.

Felicity *and* **Ally** *enter.* **Ally** *has a can of drink and* **Felicity** *has got a sandwich in a paper bag for her mum.*

Felicity   We got you something. Mum, is everything OK?

Karen   Fine, darling. Everything is fine. Thanks, Andy. And sorry. (*To the girls.*) I'll be back. I'm just going to pop to the bathroom. (*She exits.*)

Andy   Felicity and Ally right?

Ally   Who are you again?

Andy   Andy, the social worker at St Bart's.

Felicity   What was mum upset about?

Ally   I'll give you one guess.

Andy   She's just working through a few things. How are you two doing?

Ally   Fine.

Andy   It must be a mix of feelings for everyone at the moment.

Felicity   Yep. Especially mum and dad. And Rosie. I mean, she's the one going through all of this.

Andy   How about you two? How are you feeling?

Felicity   Well, I know I find it all pretty daunting. But I don't know about. . . . (**Felicity** *looks toward* **Ally**.) We don't talk all that much.

Ally   At all.

Andy   Maybe you should. (*Beat.*) Just a thought. I'm going to take off but my office is the first one on the right after the lift.

He leaves. There is awkwardness between the two sisters.

Felicity   What do you think?

Ally   About what?

Felicity   About what Andy said. (**Ally** *shrugs.*) He might have a point. (*Beat.*) Do you think mum is coping?

Ally   No idea.

Felicity   Because I'm worried about her. And dad. And things had been going well with them lately. (*Beat.*) Are you OK?

Ally   Fine. Why do you care anyway?

Felicity   What do you mean? Of course I care.

Ally   It's not like we talk. It's not like we have anything in common. We're not friends.

Felicity   We could be. (**Ally** *rolls her eyes.*) Why couldn't we be?

Ally   Look at you. Look at me. We couldn't be more different. (**Ally** *goes to put her headphones back in.*)

Felicity   We both have the same last name. And we both hate the colour pink. And we both don't have many friends at school. (**Ally** *glares at* **Felicity**.) It's true. And both of us are here dealing with this crap again. And we're sisters. That's got to mean something. Anyway, I'm here for you if things aren't going well underneath that resting bitch face. (**Ally** *looks at* **Felicity** *again, this time with less venom.*) And Ally eye roll. (**Ally** *rolls her eyes, smirking.*) Maybe we should stick together in all of this.

Ally   Maybe. You want to go see Rosie together?

Felicity   Yeh. And, hey, could I ask you a favour?

Ally   What?

Felicity   Could you please . . .

Ally (*like she's been asked before*)   No! Look, you're my sister. And I'm glad I'm not the only one dealing with crap this again. But I'm not doing your stupid video!

Scene Six

Ally's video message to **Rose**.

So, I'm doing Flick's stupid video. It won't be perfect and I'll probably stuff it. I'm no good with words the way Flick is.

Anyway, Rosie. You know I never wanted another little sister. When mum and dad told me, apparently I threw myself down on the floor in aisle six of Woolies and screamed the place down. They had to leave then and there, dragging me to the car kicking and screaming. Mum was preggers and all. Anyway, it turned out OK. Most people think little sisters are just plain annoying. But, I don't know. I've always thought you were alright.

School sucks right. Hate it. Kids are weird and they think I'm even weirder. But I remember on my first day of high school, I got dressed and was ready to go. I felt so nervous I nearly vommed. But you walked into my room. And you said you thought I looked beautiful. It was really nice.

This video is supposed to be on bravery and how you're brave and all. But that day, you made *me* feel brave. So I think that counts. So don't go anywhere, Rosie.

Scene Seven

Rose's *hospital room, after visiting hours. In the room is* **Rose**, **Karen**, **Felicity** *(sitting on a chair with her bag and jumper on the chair next to her)*, **Doctor Standing**, **Willy**, **Nelson**, **Andy** *and* **Doniella**. **Doniella** *is giving out hot drinks and biscuits.*

Doctor Standing   So, you're all settled in and ready for tomorrow. Rose, we plan to run some tests so we can get a better picture of things then we'll plan our next step.

Rose   Yep, I remember how it goes. Like last time.

Doctor Standing   Good. Well, I will see you tomorrow morning. Get a good night's rest.

Karen   Thank you.

Doctor Standing   Cheryl, can I catch you about a couple of things?

Cheryl   Of course. (**Doctor Standing** *exits.* **Nelson** *goes to leave with* **Cheryl** *but she stops him before she leaves.*) Nelson, why don't you stay and get to know Rosie and the family a bit more.

Nelson   Sure thing.

Karen   So, darling, how are you feeling about tomorrow?

Ally *enters.* **Felicity** *moves her stuff and* **Ally** *takes the now vacant seat next to her. They both clock this as a moment of connection.*

Rose   Good.

Karen   Good.

Nelson (*awkwardly*)   So, Rose. How are you feeling?

Rose   I'm OK.

Ally   She just said that.

Karen   Ally!

Doniella   Now, who had the peppermint tea?

Karen   That was for Ally.

Ally   Thanks.

Nelson (*earnestly trying again*)   Because I know that if I were having a biopsy, I might be feeling really nervous. I mean, not nervous because of anything bad that might happen. More nervous because I'm quite a nervous person. Just naturally, quite nervous. I mean, growing up I used to get the shakes whenever I had to meet new people or whenever I was stuck in social situations that I felt awkward in. (*Beat.*)

But, anyway, back to you. If you are nervous, then I've read that it's good to speak about our nerves to make us ultimately less nervous. I've also heard Chinese food is good for the nerves. But whatever works for you. I'm not a fan of Chinese food myself. But anyway, if you're feeling nervous, then don't worry. Being nervous is perfectly normal.

Ally   Geez, if she wasn't nervous before!

Karen   Ally! Thank you, Nelson. We appreciate that. I think we're all good for now.

Nelson   No problems at all. You're very welcome. Happy to help. Both Willy and I are happy to help.

Willy (*slightly embarrassed*)   Absolutely.

Andy   You know what I think would help? (**Andy** *motions to* **Doniella** *who pulls out a strawberry Freddo frog and hands it to* **Rose**.)

Doniella   Ta-da!

Rose   Thanks, Doni!

Karen   Well, this is a blast from the past! How did you know?

Rose   Doni's the best in the business, mum! And she reckons I have great taste!

Michael *enters*.

Michael (*slurring his words slightly*)   Right. I'm here. You OK, Rose?

Rose   Yep.

Michael   Where's the doctor gone? We pay all this money for a doctor to look after our little girl and he's not even here!

Andy   Doctor Standing just popped in just to check that everything was all set for tomorrow.

Willy   He's left for the day now.

Michael   Righto then.

Karen   Michael, how about you take a seat?

Michael   I don't need to sit. I'm perfectly happy here.

Felicity   Dad, you're slurring your words.

Michael   No, I'm not. I'm fine.

Felicity   Dad, you're not. Have you been drinking?

Michael   What?

Ally (*under her breath*)   Here we go again.

Felicity   You said you wouldn't.

Michael   I don't think anyone asked you to say anything. Did anyone ask Felicity for her opinion? Does anyone ever ask Felicity for her opinion?

Felicity   Dad!

Ally   Don't talk to her like that!

Michael   She speaks!

Karen   Michael!

Michael   What?

Karen   Please!

Rose   Dad, are you OK?

Michael   Sweetheart, I am fine. And I know everything is going to be fine.

Andy   Michael, can I get you some water, mate? Or perhaps we head out for some fresh air?

Michael   No thanks, little man. Lightning doesn't strike twice. Rosie, you're going to be fine. The doctors will do what they do. And we'll be done with hospitals. And appointments. And scans. And waiting. All of the waiting.

Karen (*with more force*)   Michael, I really think you should sit.

Michael   I don't want to sit.

Karen   You need to sit down!

Michael   No I don't.

Karen   Michael, sit!

Michael   I need to stand next to my daughter while I still can! (*Beat.*)

Karen   They've made up the room next door for you. It's time you went to bed.

Michael *exits.*

Doniella   That might be our cue, everyone.

All leave except **Karen** *and* **Rose**. **Doniella** *slips a packet of strawberry Freddo frogs in* **Rose**'s *lap with a wink and exits.*

Scene Eight

Rose's *hospital room. Later that night.* **Karen** *sits by* **Rose**'s *bedside.* **Rose** *is trying to teach* **Karen** *how to fold origami again.*

Rose   And then you fold this edge like this. And then take this side and fold it this way.

Karen   Gosh, I don't know how many times you have showed me this. I can never remember!

Rose   You're doing well. (**Karen** *holds up her origami creation to prove her wrong.*) Well, you're doing your best.

Karen   That's all we can do in life isn't it! I don't think I'll be winning any awards anytime soon!

Rose   Are you doing alright, mum?

Karen   Yes, of course, darling. (*Redirecting the conversation.*) Now aren't the staff here just lovely!

Rose   They are.

Karen   And you got some strawberry Freddos too!

Rose   Yeh.

Karen   Well, keep them away from me!

Rose   Yep. (*Beat.*) Mum?

Karen   Yes, love?

Rose   I'm sorry.

Karen   Sorry?

Rose   Yeh.

Karen   Why are you sorry? You have nothing to be sorry about.

Rose   I do. I know that it's hard for you too, mum. Me, being sick, and us being here again. I know that it makes you sad.

Karen   Now, come on.

Rose   And I'm sorry that you and dad fight when I'm sick.

Karen   Now, listen to me. That is just not true. We both love you so much. And we are so proud of you.

Rose   I know. But you have to admit, dad was really weird before

Karen   He doesn't mean to be like that, darling. He's just got a lot going on inside his head I think.

Rose   Why doesn't he talk about it then?

Karen   You know, I think the same thing. Look, your dad just deals with things a bit differently.

Rose   But I just don't get why he acts like that.

Karen (*trying her best to explain*)   You know how you love origami?

Rose   Yeh.

Karen   Well, think of us all as origami creations. Every design is different. Some origami designs have only a few instructions and you can see all the folds clearly. They look beautiful almost straight away.

Other origami patterns are different. They take a lot longer to understand and they might have lots of layers and steps and folds that you can't see from the outside, almost like secrets. They're still wonderful, just more complex and maybe not as easy to comprehend.

It's the same with people, I guess. Some people are relatively simple. Others can be made up of lots of folds which are not always visible from the outside. You have to be patient and take time to learn each intricate layer. It doesn't make the product any less beautiful at the end. It just takes a bit longer to understand because they're a bit more complicated. Your dad is like that.

Rose   Mum, you know that whatever happens, it'll be OK right?

Karen   Rose, what do you mean darling?

Rose   Well, if the tests show that things are bad, I'm ready.

Karen   Ready?

Rose   Ready. (*She goes to say something else but stops, choosing instead to say what she feels* **Karen** *needs to hear.*) Ready to fight so things can go back to normal for all of us. (**Karen** *kisses* **Rose** *on the head and gives her a squeeze.*)

Scene Nine

Cheryl, **Willy** *and* **Nelson***'s video message to* **Rose**.

Cheryl   Hello, Rose. Is this thing on?

Nelson   Yes, it is. *Nǐ hǎo,* Rose!

Cheryl   Willy, say something.

Willy   Hi, Rosie!

Cheryl   Rose, your sister Felicity has asked us to speak into the camera and say something about you and about bravery. Go on, Nelson.

Nelson (*reading from cue cards. Heavily scripted and obviously written by* **Cheryl**)   We thought it best to tell you our favourite quote about bravery and the strength of the human spirit. (*Clears throat.*) 'I believe in one thing only. The power of human will'. I wonder who said that? Cheryl, do you know?

Cheryl   Why yes I do. It was a gentleman named Anonymous. (**Cheryl** *pronounces 'Anonymous' incorrectly, saying the final syllable like 'mouse'.*)

Nelson   Yes, Anonymous. Wow. That quote is so great. In fact, you could say that it's really struck a chord with me.

Cheryl   And me!

Nelson   And as it turns out, Anonymous has written several inspirational quotes.

Cheryl   He's all over the internet.

Nelson   So I hope you like that quote, Rose.

Willy (*pronouncing Anonymous correctly now*)   Anonymous? You do know what anonymous means right?

Cheryl   Shh, Willy. Nelson, keep going.

Willy   And I think I've heard that quote before. It was by someone well known.

Cheryl   Be quiet, Willy! Go on, Nelson!

Nelson   Well, that's all from us. Goodbye, Rose. Say goodbye, everybody.

Cheryl   Goodbye, Rose!

Willy   I remember now. 'I believe in one thing only. The power of human will'. I'm pretty sure Joseph Stalin said that.

Cheryl   Who?

Nelson   Oh really?

Cheryl   Is he related to Anonymous?

Willy   Oh my goodness.

Cheryl   Well, who cares. It's an inspirational quote and I'm sure this Joseph man was inspirational too. So I hope you are inspired, Rose! Finish it off, Nelson.

Nelson   Goodbye from us all!

Cheryl   Bye, Rose! Willy, say goodbye.

Willy   Bye, Rosie!

Cheryl   You could have said a bit more, Willy.

She turns off the camera awkwardly as she and **Nelson** *exit. After a moment,* **Willy** *turns the camera back on.*

Willy   Me again. I wanted to just say something to you without the other two. (*Holding up the book.*) I've been reading the book you lent me, *Sadako and the Thousand Paper Cranes*. It makes sense now. Thanks for the tip. And thanks for this. (**Willy** *holds up the paper crane* **Rose** *gave him.*) I'm going to hang on to this as a reminder. To be brave. Just like Sadako. And just like you.

Scene Ten

Rose*'s hospital room. The next morning and day of the biopsy.* **Rose**, **Ally**, **Felicity** *and* **Andy** *are munching on strawberry Freddos.* **Doniella** *has put on some music and flicks through a magazine.* **Rose***'s room has been completely made over. There is a new pink bedspread on the bed, a pink sparkly pillow and fairy lights and origami cranes strung up. Another Freddo frog packet is being passed around.*

Felicity   So you've seen Kylie Minogue how many times?

Doniella   Ah, love, probably more times than you've had birthdays.

Felicity   Why do you love her so much?

Doniella   Oh it's just the way she struts around that stage. And her songs. And the girl just does not age! It is scientifically unbelievable.

Felicity   You know, I heard that she wrote *I Should Be So Lucky* in forty minutes.

Andy   Oh please don't encourage her.

Figure 18 Rose settles into her new room with Doniella, Felicity, Ally and Andy.
Photo courtesy of Cardijn College.

Doniella   Amazing!

Rose   What are some of her other songs, Doni?

Doniella   I'm glad you asked! We'll make a Kylie fan out of you in no time! Well, there's *Locomotion* and *Better the Devil You Know* and . . .

Ally (*by now, she has the packet of Freddo frogs*)   You know, I've always thought her music was a bit average. (**Doniella** *reacts dramatically.*)

Andy   Oh no you didn't!

Doniella (*smiling*)   Well, no more Freddo frogs for you my girl! (*She takes the packet from her.*)

Andy   You've got to be very careful when you talk about Queen Kylie in front of Doni! She's Kylie crazy! She's Minogue mad!

Felicity   Ally's more of a death metal kind of girl. The real screamo stuff.

Ally   Oi! (*Beat.*) Nah, she's right. I had this boyfriend in Year 9 who said that girls shouldn't listen to death metal. I've been hooked ever since.

Smithy *enters to collect the bins. It's as though time has frozen.* **Doniella** *tries desperately to play it cool.*

Smithy   Hey.

After replacing the bin bag, **Smithy** *nods in* **Doniella**'s *direction then exits.* **Doniella** *mumbles word vomit, practically hyperventilating.* **Karen** *enters. She enjoys the mood of the room.*

Karen   Hi, everyone. All good in here?

Felicity   All good! How's dad?

Karen   I was just chatting to him before. He'll be in shortly.

Ally (*looking at* **Doniella**)   Do you need to tell us something, Doniella?

Doniella   I don't know what you're talking about.

Felicity   Who was that man?

Doniella   Which man?

Rose   The man that was just in this room!

Doniella   Oh that man! His name is Smithy, I think.

Andy (*enjoying the teasing*)   You think?

Felicity   Are you sure you're OK? You've gone very red!

Doniella   Yes, it's just the smell of . . . chocolate in the air.

Andy   You mean the smell of love!

Doniella   Stop it! (*Changing the topic, addressing* **Karen**.) How are you, Karen?

Karen   Good. Things are good. (*To* **Rose**.) How are you? Give me an update.

Rose (*excitedly*)   Well, Doni is in love with the cleaner, Smithy. He likes her too because every time she is in my room, the bins suddenly need emptying. And that one was empty!

She begins to laugh but grabs her chest and starts to wheeze. Both sisters jump to comfort her as **Rose** *steadies her breathing again.*

Felicity   Just breathe. That's it.

Ally   You're doing great.

Doniella   Rosie has told me that you girls have been a great support for her over the last years. I see what she means.

Ally   I don't know about that.

Felicity   A bit I guess.

Rose   It's true, Doni. They are the best.

Both sisters brush off the praise, embarrassed. **Michael** *enters sheepishly. He stands away from* **Rose** *and just observes. The others notice him but carry on.* **Doniella** *turns the music down.*

Andy   Rosie, what is it that makes them such good sisters?

Rose   Well, Flick always hangs out with me. (*To* **Felicity**.) Even though you've got heaps on with all your study and your tutoring. And I love how you write little notes for me and put them in my lunch box. And sometimes they're jokes and they're really funny.

And Ally. Well, you always check on me before bed to make sure I'm warm enough. She thinks I'm asleep but I'm not most of the time. And you always let me watch you put make-up on in the morning and get ready for school. And I know you hate hospitals but you still come when I'm sick because you know it helps mum to have us all together.

Andy   That's really nice.

Rose   Whatever happens today, if the cancer has come back . . .

Felicity   You don't have to worry about any of that now.

Ally   Flick's right. You got this, kiddo.

Doctor Standing, **Cheryl**, **Nelson** *and* **Willy** *enter.*

Doctor Standing   Hello, kiddo! (**Ally** *rolls her eyes at him.*) I see you've got plenty of company here. And some 'sick beats' playing too! Anyway, I thought I'd just pop in to say hello and go over the plan for today.

Rose   OK.

Doctor Standing   So basically, we are going to do what's called a biopsy. We're going to take a really small part of bone tissue from your leg so we can do some tests and confirm a few things.

Rose   Will it hurt?

Doctor Standing   We're going to give you some laughing gas to make you nice and sleepy so you won't feel a thing.

Rose   OK.

Doctor Standing   So we'll be seeing you soon.

Karen   Thank you. I appreciate you coming in.

Doctor Standing   No problems at all.

Doctor Standing *and* **Nelson** *exit and* **Cheryl** *follows but pauses to hear the conversation between* **Willy** *and* **Rose**.

Rose   Willy, is he telling the truth? Will this biopsy hurt? Tell me, honest.

Willy   Maybe a bit. It might be uncomfortable afterwards too. But nothing to worry about. You got this. Piece of cake.

Rose   Thanks, Willy.

Cheryl *exits.*

Michael   Can I just chat to my family for a minute?

Andy   Of course.

Willy   We'll see you soon, Rosie.

Doniella   See ya, love.

Andy, **Willy** *and* **Doniella** *exit.*

Felicity   Dad, can I speak to you about this video project I'm doing?

Michael   Flick, your mum already did. I'll see. Just leave it for now. (*To everyone.*) So, I just wanted to say that things got a bit out of hand last night for a few reasons. But let's focus on what we have to focus on today. And that's this scan.

Ally   So you're not going to apologise? Typical.

Michael   Ally, I don't think this is the time or place for another argument.

Ally   I'm surprised you can remember all of the arguments we've had!

Karen   Ally!

Michael   How dare you speak to me like that. I came in here this morning to patch things up. And all you've done is . . .

Ally   What?

Karen   That's enough, everyone! This stops now.

Ally   Fine by me.

She exits. **Felicity** *looks at her dad and follows* **Ally.**

Michael   Rosie, I'm sorry that happened. I didn't mean for it to go that way.

Rose   I know, dad.

Michael   And you know I love you girls?

Rose   Yeh.

Michael   Good.

Rose   But I don't think Flick and Ally know.

Scene Eleven

Michael*'s video message to* **Rose**. **Karen** *stands in the background to support him.*

Michael   Hi, Rosie. Your mum has asked me to do a video for you. Well for Felicity. For her project thing. But about you. I don't really know what to say to be honest. Something about bravery and about you.

He is lost for words, too caught up in the situation and his own anger. The pace of his breathing increases and he becomes agitated and overwhelmed.

You know what? Maybe I need to do this another time. I just can't do this right now.

Scene Twelve

Later that morning. The biopsy.

Doctor Standing   Hello, Rose. It's good to see you again. Now, I want you to take a deep breath. (*She does.*) Good. Now, we're now going to make you nice and sleepy. Just relax and don't worry about a thing.

Rose   OK.

Doctor Standing   You'll start to feel drowsy in three, two, one.

Under anaesthesia, **Rose** *drifts off and has a vivid dream. This optional dream scene can be a representation through physical theatre of the inner workings of* **Rose**'s *mind, her fears around the unknown landscape of her future and the guilt she feels for being sick again and putting her family through stress.*

Scene Thirteen

Later that morning. **Michael** *waits outside* **Rose**'s *room as the biopsy occurs. He is frustrated and impatient.*

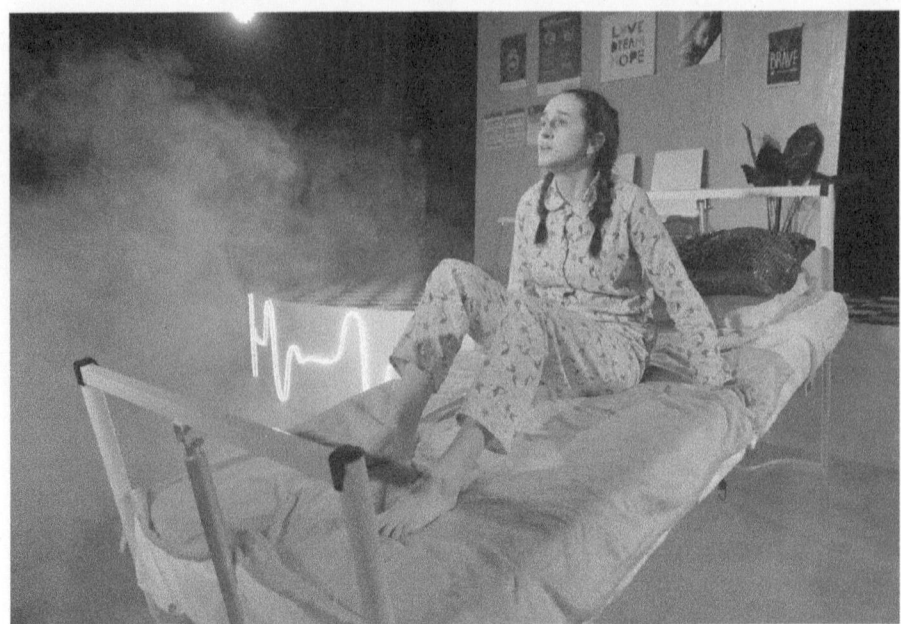

Figure 19 Rose is troubled by a vivid dream. Photo courtesy of Cardijn College.

Andy   Hi, Michael.

Michael   Hi.

Andy   How you travelling?

Michael   Fine.

Andy   You sure?

Michael   What does it look like? I was actually going to take off for a bit. Get some air.

Andy   I was just speaking with Karen.

Michael   Oh really? How'd that go?

Andy   Good.

Michael   So that's why you're here? To have a crack at me? Fire away.

Andy   That's not why I'm here.

Michael   Fine.

Andy   Your family needs you, Michael.

Michael   My family don't want me here. And I don't need the drama.

Andy   I disagree.

Michael   Oh do you? You trying to tell me what I need?

Andy   Not at all. I'm just trying to help.

Michael   Well, piss off. That'd help.

Andy   Michael.

Michael   I need a drink. That's what I need.

Andy   Come on, Michael!

Michael   Excuse me?

Andy   I said come on! Wake up! What are you doing? Look, I get it. Life is seriously hard for you at the moment. But that doesn't give you a free pass to be a jerk. Open your eyes! Hell, everyone is battling something.

Michael   How dare you talk to me like that!

Andy   Well, someone has to. Your wife walks on eggshells around you. And your kids? They love you but, from what I've seen, you just push them away. If you're not careful, you're going to wake up one day and . . .

Michael   And what? Lose them? Guess what, mate. You don't get to make comments about my family. You don't get to give me advice. You know nothing. You're a counsellor, right? You think you have all the answers? You think you're so high and mighty that you can tell me what to do?

Andy   I'm not saying that.

Michael   Well, I'll tell you right now. I don't need your advice. I don't need you butting in. We're not some Brady Bunch family with a perfect picket fence out front. But we're fine. We've been getting through this hell just fine.

Andy   I don't think you have been.

Michael   What do you know? You don't even know me. You have no idea what I've been going through.

Andy   Talk to me then.

Michael   I don't want to talk to some nobody counsellor! Don't you get it?

Andy   Well, you're going to have to talk to someone. Because, in case you haven't noticed, things are not fine. You are not fine. The way you're treating your family is not fine.

Michael   You should leave or I'm going to do something I might regret.

Andy   Talk to me.

Michael   Leave!

Andy   Talk to me!

Michael   Leave!

Andy   Talk to me!

Michael   I don't want to! What's the point? What is the point of talking about how I feel sick to the stomach every time I walk into another damn hospital room and smell that smell. Or that I don't have the energy to be upbeat and positive anymore when we keep getting kicked down time and time again. What possible good is going to come from me talking to some counsellor about how I'm failing at life. As a husband, and a dad.

There is nothing I can do to protect her. She has laid in too many hospital beds, her tiny little arms and legs hooked up to tubes and machines, and what can we do? Nothing! Talking is not going to change anything. And it's not going to change the fact that my little girl is sick. She's really, really sick. And she might not get better!

So don't lecture me about talking to you. I don't want to even think about my life right now, let alone talk to some stranger who has no idea about what it means to struggle.

There is a considerable silence before **Andy** *responds.*

Andy   I haven't always walked with this stick. When I was nineteen, I was in an accident. Completely totalled the car. A Torana it was. My very first car. It was late one night and I'd been out since the afternoon. I'd started the day counting drinks but things got out of hand.

When I went to leave, I didn't even think about it. I stumbled out to my car, got in and turned on the ignition. I couldn't even see in front of me. Whether that was the booze

Figure 20 Michael listens to Andy. Photo courtesy of Cardijn College.

or the fact that the street wasn't really lit up, I don't know. But I drove home. I remember wanting to get home fast and putting my foot down. And there being a corner and the car spinning and . . .

What was almost worse than the accident was the rehab. And all the other crap that came after. It was like I'd had this accident and lived. But the anger I felt was the thing that was killing me. From the inside out. Like I was drowning and pulling everyone I knew under with me. The only thing that saved me was talking. Talking about how I felt. Letting those feelings of anger and guilt go. It was hard. But it was my way out. And it could be yours too.

Michael   I just think it's all gone too far. I want to fix it. I just don't know how.

Andy   Speak to Karen. Speak to your girls. Tell them how you're feeling. This whole thing is not easy, but it'll be a damn sight easier if you go through it together.

Scene Fourteen

Karen's *video message to* **Rose**.

Karen   Hello, darling girl. Flick's asked me to say something about you. What to say?

Let's see. You are the girl that licks the bowl when I'm making chocolate brownies. You are the girl that I can rely on to start everyone off singing 'Happy Birthday' whenever we have a family do. You are the girl that is brave and brilliant no matter what is going on in your life.

I remember when you first got sick. People kept saying you looked fine and that it was all in your head. In my head too. But we knew something was wrong. I kept taking you to doctors and specialists over and over again. To try to get to the bottom of things. Through it all, you stayed positive. That kept me going. Kept us all going. I remember one particularly bad day. It was after another specialist visit who said it was just 'growing pains'. You looked at me with your beautiful brown eyes. You said to me, 'Mummy, you are the only person in the world who truly believes me and how much pain I'm in'.

I will always remember that moment. And I will always be here for every difficult moment in your life, my darling. We all will. You are brave. You are bloody brave. And I love you.

Scene Fifteen

Rose's *hospital room. Early afternoon.* **Rose**, **Felicity**, **Ally** *and* **Doniella** *are doing a magazine quiz.* **Rose** *is groggy and resting.*

Felicity   Next question. (*Reading.*) Which is the largest Spanish-speaking country in the world?

Doniella   Barcelona.

Felicity   The answer is the name of a *country*.

Doniella   I don't know the name of any countries in Spain. (*Beat.*) Oh.

Ally   Let me read one. (*Reading.*) Name an animal found in the marsupial family that can often be confused for a wild cat or a giant rat.

Doniella   Tiger.

Ally   No.

Doniella   Ferret.

Ally   No!

Doniella   Donkey!

Felicity/Ally   No!

Doniella   What was it then?

Ally   A quokka.

Doniella   A what?

Rose *shifts in her bed.*

Felicity   Hey, girl.

Ally   How you feeling?

Rose   You guys stop worrying. I'm fine.

Felicity   You know, I just think you're amazing how you're handling all of this. I don't think I could do it.

Ally   Or me.

Felicity   We're really proud of you for being so strong.

Ally   It's true kiddo.

Felicity   And we're sorry that you had to see that argument with dad last night.

Rose   I think you should talk to dad.

Ally   Maybe.

Rose   At least hear him out. Promise me you will?

Ally   Promise.

Felicity (*standing and gesturing to* **Ally** *that they need to go*)   Listen, we have to catch Andy about something. Doni, I'll fill you in later alright?

Doniella   No worries.

Ally (*to* **Rose**)   You sure you don't need your big sisters to stay and annoy you?

Rose   No, you guys go. Doni's here.

Felicity *and* **Ally** *hug* **Rose** *and exit.*

Doniella   You comfortable enough, love?

Rose   Yeh.

Doniella   So, how are you really feeling? (**Doniella** *offers* **Rose** *another Freddo frog but* **Rose** *refuses.* **Doniella** *unwraps one and starts eating it herself.*)

Rose   I'm OK.

Doniella   Only OK?

Rose   I guess I haven't had much time to think about everything you know? (*There is a pause.* **Doniella** *just waits until* **Rose** *goes on, listening.*) It's weird being back in hospital after everything that happened last time.

Doniella   I bet it is, love.

Rose   The doctor said that we have to wait for the biopsy results to know exactly what's happening. But I know they don't do all these tests unless they are pretty sure what it is. I know it doesn't look good. I just feel . . . I don't know.

Doniella   You can talk to me, love. I'm all ears.

Rose   I feel bad.

Doniella   Bad?

Rose   Guilty. Last time this happened, my mum and dad were fighting all the time. And dad pretty much stopped talking to Flick and Ally altogether. And now we're here again. Because of me. And I'm worried it's going to be worse. And I can't talk to them about it because it just makes them more worried. Which causes more fights.

Doniella   Rosie, love. This is not your fault. Whatever happens, happens. Unfortunately being sick is just one of those things we can't control. And your mum and dad and your sisters understand. They love you a lot and they're just worried about you.

Rose   I know.

Doniella   I'm very proud of you, you know. For thinking of your family when you must be feeling a lot of things yourself. You're very brave.

Rose   But I'm not. Everyone keeps saying I'm brave but I don't feel brave.

Doniella   How do you feel?

Rose   I'm angry.

Doniella   Angry?

Rose   Yeh. I mean, why is this happening to me again? To my family. I just want everything to be normal. I want to have normal friends And go to school, not to hospital. And whinge about homework, not chemo. I've already been sick. I already had cancer. I got better. I don't know if I can do it all over again.

After some time, **Doniella** *speaks.*

Doniella   One day, you will see Kylie Minogue in concert. Won't you?

Rose   Umm.

Doniella   Won't you?

Rose   Yes, I will. Yes.

Doniella   Good. When you do, you'll notice the costumes and the dancers and the music. But you'll also notice that she will perform non-stop for two, maybe three hours. She'll sing heaps of her songs and dance around the stage. Then, at the end of the concert, the lights will go down. The crowd will be clapping and cheering and yelling out her name, begging her to come back, to sing again. And so, after a little while, she'll come back on stage. She'll do an encore. Have you heard that word before?

Rose   No.

Doniella   An encore is like an extra performance that sometimes happens at the very end of a concert, after everyone thinks the show is over. Kylie has to do one every time she performs even though she's tired and exhausted and she's given her everything. Maybe you should think of this as your encore. You've given an amazing first performance, kicking cancer the first time. But you have to come out on stage again. For a bit longer. To beat it again. You've got to give an encore. And you, my dear, will give the best bloody encore the world has ever seen. You will be as magnificent as the great Kylie Minogue. I'm sure of it.

Rose *and* **Doniella** *hug.* **Andy** *enters.*

Andy   Doni, could I catch you for a sec? (*In a whisper, trying to be secretive.*) It's about the video.

Rose   What video?

Doniella   Oh nothing at all! (*Kissing* **Rose** *on the head.*) You get some rest, love. Chat soon.

Scene Sixteen

Later that day. **Willy** *and* **Nelson** *awkwardly wait for* **Cheryl** *near the nurses' station.*

Willy   So . . .

Nelson   So . . .

Willy   You up to much this weekend?

Nelson   No.

Willy   Cool. (*Beat.*) Seen any good movies lately?

Nelson   No.

Wlly   Right.

Nelson   I don't have time for movies.

Willy   Oh. Nah. Me either. (*Beat.*) You think you'll hang around this hospital after placement?

Nelson   Sorry?

Willy   You think you'll try and get a job here?

Nelson (*says it like a rehearsed speech*)   Yes. I think Cheryl is a fabulous mentor and I'd be lucky to learn from her.

Willy   She's not around you know.

Nelson   I know. (*He looks around to make sure.*)

Willy   Right. Well, for what it's worth, I reckon you'd get a job here easy. Cheryl loves you. You've got it made. Me, she's not so keen on. (**Cheryl** *enters, out of sight of* **Willy**.) She hates me. (*Imitating her.*) 'Umm, Willy. Umm, blah, blah, blah. You know who said that? Oh, it's really struck a chord with me you know!' Yeh,

I'm getting used to the old battleaxe bossing everyone around and storming around like she owns the bloody hospital.

Cheryl   Good afternoon, boys!

Willy   Cheryl. Hi. I was just . . .

Cheryl   Oh, I'm aware. Quite good hearing you know. For an old battleaxe. Anyway, what are you two doing, standing there like stunned porcupines?

Nelson   Waiting for you and the results, Cheryl.

Willy   Please tell me it's good news. I don't know what I'll do if it isn't.

Cheryl   Well, that's just the thing.

Willy   What?

Cheryl   It's not great.

Willy   What?

Cheryl   It's not great. And I think you should be the one to talk to Rose about it, Willy.

Willy   Me? I can't.

Cheryl (*softening*)   Willy, you know this is all part of the job too.

Willy   I know.

Nelson   I know too. (**Cheryl** *nods at* **Nelson**.)

Willy   But I just don't think I can be the kind of nurse that can tell people this sort of news. Life is so unfair sometimes. Maybe it just hits harder when things happen to kids. I mean, how can cancer happen to Rosie once, let alone . . .

Cheryl   Willy.

Willy   Yes?

Cheryl   I know you love it when I reel off an inspirational quote.

Nelson   I love it too, Cheryl.

Cheryl   I know you do, Nelson. But Willy, I heard something recently that really struck a chord with me.

Willy   Oh yeh?

Cheryl   And I'm going to repeat it to you now. 'You got this. Piece of cake'. You know who said that? (**Willy** *shakes his head*.) You did.

Willy   Oh.

Cheryl   You are much better at this nursing thing than you think you are. And much better than I probably give you credit for to be honest. But you'll have to learn that difficult news is an important part of our job, Willy.

Willy   Can we at least wait and tell them after the thing for Rosie?

Cheryl   The what?

Willy   The thing we're planning. For Rosie. It's happening later today. To cheer her up. You guys should get involved!

Nelson   I hardly think we have time to get involved in activities beyond our regular nursing duties.

Cheryl   I'll give it a go.

Nelson   OK, I'm in too.

Scene Seventeen

Andy *and* **Doniella**'s *video message to* **Rose**.

Doniella (*speaking too loudly*)   Hello, Rosie!

Andy   Hi, Rosie.

Doniella   It's us, Andy and Doniella.

Andy   She knows, you know.

Doniella   Just making sure.

Figure 21 Doniella and Andy record their video message to Rose. Photo courtesy of Cardijn College.

Andy   We wanted to do our video to you in song.

Doniella   Inspired by the Queen herself!

Andy   Who else?! Rose, this song reminds us of you because you are truly golden!

Doniella   We've got another surprise for you too, but you'll get that one later in person. Here we go.

She does a quick comical vocal warm-up. She and **Andy** *then sing a heartfelt song for* **Rose***, a tribute to her bravery and the love they have for her.*

Doniella (*as* **Andy** *switches off the camera*)   I thought that went well!

Scene Eighteen

Later that day. **Rose***'s hospital room.* **Karen***,* **Felicity** *and* **Ally** *sit around* **Rose***'s bed as she sleeps.* **Ally** *and* **Karen** *are making origami cranes.* **Felicity** *works on her computer, checking her watch regularly.*

Karen   Darling, how many more do you think we need to make?

Ally   Well, on Rosie's tally, she's got eight more to go. If we all make a few each, then she can make the last one to get to her one thousand.

Felicity   Nearly done here then I can help.

Ally   You're all good. We've got this, don't we, mum.

Karen   I'm not sure mine actually pass as cranes. I mean, this one looks more like a grumpy sausage dog but still. It's the thought that counts right?

Ally   It'll count.

Felicity   Hey, mum.

Karen   Yes, darling?

Felicity   Where's dad?

Michael *enters.*

Michael   Here I am. How is everyone?

Karen   We're good. How are you?

Michael   I'm better. I'm a lot better actually. Look, I need to apologise properly to all of you. I'm going to be really honest and say upfront that I've found this really difficult. Being back in a hospital. The possibility that things could go awry again. And just seeing Rosie dealing with all this, I was struggling to deal with it. And I took it out on you, Karen, and you, Flick, and you, Ally. And that is completely unfair. And I see that now. And it's going to stop today. I know that I haven't been the best dad in the last couple of weeks and I wasn't the best dad when we were going through this stuff the first time. I can't take back what has happened but I can work on things moving forward. I love you all dearly and I'm really, really sorry.

Karen (*walks over to* **Michael**)   It took a lot of courage to do that.

Karen *kisses* **Michael** *on the cheek. After this,* **Michael** *looks to the girls. They get up and give him a hug.*

Michael   And Flick, I've had a think about what I want to say for your video and I'm ready to go when you are.

Karen   Maybe you guys could get it done now?

Felicity   I think we should hang around here for a bit. (**Rose** *begins to wake up.*)

Ally   Yeh, we need to stay in the room for another few minutes at least.

Karen   Why?

Felicity   No reason.

Michael   Have you guys planned something?

Ally   Not us exactly but you could say that.

Felicity   We should actually probably wake Rosie up. (**Rose** *awakens.*)

Ally   Speak of the devil!

Karen   How are you feeling, love? Do you need to keep sleeping?

Rose   Nah, I've had enough sleep. (*Cheekily.*) Plus isn't there something I need to wake up for?

Ally   I think you should definitely stay up for a bit.

Felicity   Do you hear something, Ally?

Ally   I think I do, Flick!

Doniella (*from off-stage.*)   Sometimes there are little girls that need cheering up! Sometimes there are hospital staff that need to perform! So, since you, Rosie Rowe, haven't seen a Kylie concert. We thought we'd bring a Kylie concert to you! Starring the one and only me!

The big performance. **Doniella** *comes out and lip syncs to a medley of upbeat songs. Eventually,* **Andy, Cheryl, Nelson, Doctor Standing** *and* **Willy** *join her as backing dancers in hot pink feather boas. They all wear eighties workout wear. As the performance ends, everyone applauds.* **Doniella** *is in a dramatic finale pose as* **Smithy** *walks in, also applauding.*

Doniella   Smithy!

Smithy   Hello! That was amazing.

Doniella   Oh really? Well, thank you. Just something I threw together you know. Standard weekday, really.

Michael   So *that's* Smithy!

Karen   Shhh.

Smithy   You seem very talented! And very flexible.

Doniella   Thank you.

Smithy   And I like your outfit. You look just like Kylie herself.

Doniella (*overwhelmed by the compliment*)   Thank you! (*Scrambling for something to say.*) So, do you come here often?

Smithy   Yep. Every day. To collect the bin.

Doniella   Of course. Silly me.

Smithy   So I'll just . . . do that now.

He goes to collect the bin, empties it and ties a new bag. All the while, **Doniella** *is frozen with excitement. Everyone in the room encourages* **Doniella** *to say something to* **Smithy**.

Michael   Say, I reckon it must be pretty tiring being a cleaner of such a big hospital. That right, Smithy?

Smithy   Yep.

Michael   You must get pretty hungry on the job, huh? If only there was someone around here that was responsible for feeding everyone.

Doniella (*realising*)   Oh, me! Hello! (*She rummages in her apron and finds a pack of strawberry Freddo frogs.*) Would you like one of these?

Smithy   I'd love one. Thanks!

Doniella   You're welcome.

Smithy   I don't think this will do the trick though.

Doniella   Oh.

Smithy   But dinner tomorrow night would. Would you let me cook you dinner?

Doniella   I'll bring dessert.

Everyone cheers. **Doniella** *gives everyone a big grin and thumbs up and leaves with* **Smithy**.

Doctor   Well, that's us done, I think! Shall we?

Cheryl   We'll see you soon, Rose. Come on, boys. Nelson, did you want to give me back your feather boa?

Nelson   No, I might hang on to this one. Quite enjoying it to be fair. (*He flicks the boa around his neck.*)

Andy   We'll catch you first thing tomorrow, Rosie.

Willy See you, Rosie. Save me a Freddo alright?

Rose Deal.

Doctor Standing, **Cheryl**, **Andy**, **Will** *and* **Nelson** *exit.*

Rose (*to* **Michael**) Dad, it's good to have you here.

Michael It's good to be here. Plus, not sure I'd ever forgive myself if I missed that!

Rose You know Kylie beat cancer? (*There is tension when 'cancer' is mentioned.*)

Ally Did she?

Rose Yep. Pretty cool. So I'm guessing they'll tell us how the biopsy went tomorrow.

Karen Right, darling.

Michael Remember, whatever happens, we're a family and we can get through it. All of us together.

Rose I know. And I know that if it is cancer again, it will be OK.

Ally You don't have to be thinking about that just yet.

Rose But I do.

Felicity You don't, Rosie. There's no point worrying about something that might not even happen.

Rose I know that no one likes to talk about cancer or even say the word itself. But I find it's less scary if I do. If we do. Then it's not like a yucky secret we can't say out loud. It's just something that's happening right now. Something we're dealing with together.

Ally Fair enough, kiddo.

Karen You are so brave, darling. I know you say you're not. But I am so proud of you.

Rose Thanks, mum.

Michael We all are.

Ally Speaking of brave, Flick you should show Rosie your thing?

Felicity Now?

Rose Show me what?

Felicity Nothing.

Rose Is it the video?

Felicity What?

Rose You know, the one that you're making for me for the school project?

Felicity How did you know about that? (**Rose** *smiles and shrugs her shoulders.*) Well, it's not quite done yet.

Michael I've still got my video to do, love.

Karen But we could watch what you've got so far?

Ally Yeh, come on, Flick.

Felicity Well, if you want.

Rose I'd love to see it!

Michael We all would.

Felicity Really? OK.

Karen Right, everyone squish in. All together. Nice and close. Is everyone comfy? (*Everyone murmurs a yes or nods.*) Good.

Felicity Here we go . . .

She presses play. We hear the words of the first video as the family embrace, united.

'Always remember: you are braver than you believe, stronger than you seem, smarter than you think and more beautiful than you could ever imagine'.

End of show.

Encore **Discussion Questions**

1. In what ways are the origami crane and the idea of an encore used as metaphors to communicate complex ideas in the play?

2. How does Rose's latest health concern bring characters together in unexpected ways and serve as a catalyst for character and plot development in *Encore*?

3. Through immense struggle, it is almost always our relationships that give us the motivation we need to face another day. How is this statement true in *Encore*?

4. How is tension built and sustained throughout *Encore*?

5. How are different relationships represented in *Encore*? How do these relationships develop throughout the script and provide instances of comfort, conflict and humour for the characters involved and the audience?

6. Identify and discuss the presence of the following themes: bravery, hope, family, overcoming struggle, isolation and forgiveness. What aesthetic strategies are used to represent these themes in the play?

7. Consider the character of Rose. How might her experiences inform her behaviour throughout *Encore*?

8. Research the significant issue of childhood cancer across Australia and the world. How does childhood cancer affect individuals and their families? What support services are available for impacted families?